NAPOLEON
SOLDIER AND EMPEROR

BY OCTAVE AUBRY

NAPOLEON
SOLDIER AND EMPEROR

ST. HELENA

THE KING OF ROME
NAPOLEON II, L'AIGLON

EUGÉNIE
EMPRESS OF THE FRENCH

NAPOLEON, ON HIS RETURN FROM ELBA
From the Portrait by Prud'hon

NAPOLEON
SOLDIER AND EMPEROR

BY

OCTAVE AUBRY

AUTHORIZED TRANSLATION
BY
ARTHUR LIVINGSTON

WITH 25 ILLUSTRATIONS
IN DOUBLETONE

PHILADELPHIA   NEW YORK
J. B. LIPPINCOTT COMPANY
LONDON   TORONTO
1938

CONTENTS

Contents

ILLUSTRATIONS

NAPOLEON
SOLDIER AND EMPEROR

CHAPTER I

The Eaglet Tries His Wings

IT WAS SEPTEMBER 17, 1793. CARTEAUX'S ARMY WAS BE-
fore Toulon, which the Federalists had handed over to
the English. A short, slender young man, hollow-cheeked,
carelessly dressed, uncouth perhaps, appeared at Headquarters. He said he was a Corsican. There was, in fact,
a greenish cast to his olive complexion, and he showed a
trace of Italian accent in his speech. His name was
Napoleone da Buonaparte. But those were revolutionary
times: Napoleon Buonaparte, therefore—Captain Napoleon Buonaparte.

He had been on a trip through the Rhone valley, looking for munitions. At Marseilles he ran across a friend of
his, another Corsican. Saliceti, however, had gotten somewhere in the world. The Convention had sent him as its
Commissioner to watch Carteaux. The man in charge
of the artillery at Toulon had been wounded. Couldn't
Buonaparte take his place? Napoleon was delighted. He
accepted at once and hurried off to Toulon.

The thing struck him as no less than a windfall.
Twenty-four and still nobody, with everything still to
come from determination, hard work, luck!

11

He had passed a rough and rustic childhood back in Ajaccio, his native town in Corsica, where he had been born on the 15th of August, 1769. That was shortly after the Annexation. His father, Charles de Buonaparte, had been a friend and henchman of Pasquale Paoli, the Corsican dictator. When the cause of the island's independence seemed lost, Charles had gone over to the party of the conquerors.

From those days Napoleon remembered especially the sting of the ferule which his mother, Letizia, née Ramolino, had wielded with the severe straightforwardness of one of Plutarch's Roman matrons. Napoleon was a tough, quarrelsome boy—always in a fight with the rogue next door, stealing figs in the orchards outside the town, tearing his clothes on the sharp rocks that bristled with cactuses along the shore. At nine he went to a rather anemic school kept by some Jesuits. There he showed some talent for arithmetic, but he did not learn to read well or to write a decent hand, and he came away still talking nothing but the native dialect. Suddenly they tore him up, as it were, by the roots, and tossed him ashore in the land of the conquerors. At Autun he found himself talking French very soon, but he had hardly had time to settle down when they swept him along to the military school at Brienne, telling him that he had to study hard if he wanted to be an officer in the army of the king of France. He was to be there six years, without seeing a soul from home except his father—once.

Those were hard days. The boys at Brienne did not like the gloomy little foreigner at first. He was just a Corsican! Then suddenly he began to win them, and the teachers too. He had no particular gift for anything literary. His marks in Latin and German were very low. But there were few to match him in mathematics, and he had poise, too, and under pressure a way of standing his ground. The winter of 1783 was a long hard winter. In a snowball fight he led an attack on a fort and carried it. When he gave an order, it was an order, and he seemed to have a gift for putting spirit into a charge. So the days of sulking and aloofness ended. He had gotten used to the place! Still he was not of it. His heart was back at home with the familiar faces, images, landscape. He made only one friend—young Bourrienne. They had scientific tastes in common.

What arm of the service was he headed for—navy, artillery? Napoleon did not have the slightest idea. M. de Keralio, inspector of the king's schools and examiner, picked him for the fleet. "That boy has the makings of a fine sailor," he noted in his report. "He is good material for the school in Paris."

But Mme. Letizia did not like that and tried to dissuade the boy from such a choice. She had a feeling that nothing good would come of the sea. Chance was to decide that issue, as it was to decide many others in the course of that incredible life. Inspector Keralio was replaced by another examiner, Reynaud de Monts. De Monts classified Buonaparte for the artillery. After the final examinations in 1784 he was appointed to that branch as "gentleman-cadet" in the Military School in Paris.

That was a change of worlds indeed, as compared with life in the little rural town in the Champagne. The academy at the Champ de Mars was a palace and the cadets were housed, fed and served with a luxury and an elegance that no academy for army officers would dream of today. Young Buonaparte was there a year, working hard, but still in the old ruts. High marks in mathematics, in fact, brilliant! But he wrote an illegible hand, spelled like an illiterate, and one would not have suspected that he had ever opened a Latin grammar. "He's just half-witted!" pronounced Bauer, the German teacher.

But other instructors had been impressed by his personality, his dignified demeanor, his strong keen face, a way his eye had of taking you in from head to foot. Domairon, the teacher in French literature, remarked of the strange, fiery style in which the youth expressed himself: "It's granite, heated red-hot in a volcano!" He made one more friend—Des Mazis, and one enemy—Phélippeaux. He was to run across Phélippeaux again, later on, at the siege of Saint John of Acre. Family worries, too! Charles Buonaparte was having trouble with his stomach. He went to Montpellier to consult a specialist and died there—pyloric cancer. But the death of a father was not the worst of it. Joseph, the eldest son, was a good fellow, perhaps—people liked him and all that. But he never got anywhere with anything. What would become of the family in such hands? Young Napoleon began thinking of himself as head of the family then and there, and for a long time he was to have but one concern—to rescue the Buonaparte clan from the predicament in which his father's bad management and death had placed it.

He left the Military School at sixteen, going as a second lieutenant to the La Fère Regiment, which was in garrison at Valence. He was to spend a year there, com-

pleting his training as a soldier and an officer and making some few agreeable acquaintances. But he was beginning to feel the shortcomings in his education, so he
shut himself up in his room in the intervals between
drills and struggled to improve his mind, or rather to
build it over again from the rudiments up. Pen in hand
he read ancient and modern history slowly, attentively,
taking fulsome notes on Machiavelli, Buffon, Mon-
tesquieu, Volney, Mably, Raynal, Voltaire. On one
writer, however, he gorged and drank to the point of
intoxication—Jean Jacques Rousseau, the romantic, sentimental Rousseau of the *New Éloise* and the *Confessions,* the philosophic Rousseau of the *Social Contract*
and *Émile,* the tormented and maligned Rousseau who
had declared openly for Corsican independence and had
aspired to become Corsica's law-giver.

Working on the outlines of a history of Corsica Napoleon tried to imitate Rousseau's style and wrote out long
naïve declamations in the Rousseau manner. As the
young author conceived it, his history of Corsica was to
be a fierce attack on French rule. An officer of Louis XVI,
Buonaparte was still a Corsican first of all and ambition
was nudging him less toward a general's rank in the royal
army than towards the rôle of a new and luckier Paoli.
His mission in life seemed to be cut out for him. He
was to redeem his little island country from slavery to
the foreigner!

The attempt to write a history was the birth of Napoleon as a statesman and a publicist. All his life long he
was to write with a fertility that would never languish.
A great captain and a born executive, Napoleon was
always to be the publicist at heart. In days when he could

ask no more of glory he would still be sending anonymous articles to the *Moniteur*. At St. Helena he was always brewing a pamphlet in between dictations for his memoirs.

Buonaparte left France for Ajaccio in September, 1786, on a six months' furlough. He had not seen his native town for eight years. He was to stay a long time, obtaining successive extensions of his leave from the Ministry of War. It is not commonly realized that between 1785, when he graduated from military school, and 1793, when he appeared at the siege of Toulon, Buonaparte passed exactly sixty-three months in Corsica. That means somewhat more than five years. He spent them getting hold of family affairs, gathering the little clan of the Buonapartes about him, winning the attention of Paoli and so laying the foundations of a local influence from which he expected ease for the members of his family and a good position in life for himself.

During occasional visits to the mainland—to Auxonne, to Valence, to Paris—he saw the great storm of the Revolution gather on the horizon, gradually cover the sky and finally burst.

In the perspective of a century and a half one can look back upon those days with a certain dispassionateness. On the one hand one may regret the fall of a monarchy which had given France her unity, which beyond any doubt had many grievous defects but which was sound in many other respects and might have been overhauled and adapted to changed conditions without any root-and-branch destroying. On the other hand, one must not be unjust towards one of the greatest movements in human history. As cannot be too often repeated, the

Revolution was the work of young people, who made their mistakes and often went to the most reprehensible extremes. But the severity of modern judgments on them must be tempered by the fact that they never for one moment lost sight of the greatness of their nation.

Napoleon was one of those young people and he shared their mystical faith; but from the very outset he was a thoroughgoing realist and therefore did not follow his comrades in their aberrations. He was not for the Revolution of the speculators and the "stocking-knitters," for the Revolution of the *noyades* and the guillotinings, for the Revolution of Marat and Saint-Just, for the Revolution of assassination and plunder. With all his earnest fiery heart he was for the Revolution of liberty and justice, for the Revolution of national honor. Our day, alas, bears many resemblances to the day he knew, a day when beliefs were crumbling one after the other, when self-respect and respect for one's fellow man were declining along with all the civic virtues. In our day many Frenchmen would still stand with Napoleon for the Revolution of which he approved.

The Revolution, at any rate, enlisted him in its ranks and made him a soldier under its banners. Those banners he was to carry to Italy and Egypt and gloriously display, riddled with bullet holes from victory after victory. But when the Revolution became a sewer of anarchy, a dung-hill of ferocious demagoguery, abject and shorn of all greatness, he reared against it, brushed it aside with the flat of his sword, bent over a France that lay prostrate in the gutter, lifted her to her feet and held her there with arms that had suddenly grown strong enough and proud enough to support his country.

Buonaparte declared for the Revolution at the very first and in outspoken terms. Hurrying home to Corsica he got himself named a lieutenant-colonel in the National Guard. That meant a break, requiring no little courage, with the party of Paoli, the veteran of Corsican independence, whom he had so greatly admired, whom he had aspired to serve, and whom he was to respect, at the bottom of his heart, down to the last moments of his life. Paoli's policy was to take advantage of the troubles in France and invite the English into the island. A bitter struggle therefore developed between Paolists and Loyalists. Napoleon tried to seize the citadel at Ajaccio in the interests of the Loyalists. He failed. There was talk of arresting him and the enemy in fact raided the Buonaparte mansion, pillaged it and set it on fire, Mme. Letizia fleeing with the young children to a little farm she owned at Milleli. The young officer made an effort to secure a foothold on the coast; but it was soon apparent to him that the policy he had tried to support and lead in Corsica had failed. Reluctantly he decided to leave the island with his family. He put them aboard an open fishing smack (June 11, 1793) and set out by sail and oar for Toulon.

Such the beginnings of Bonaparte.[1] He was a Corsican educated in France. Restive to French influences at first, he found that they had soaked into his being quite in spite of himself. Who, in fact, could have resisted them? The soil of France has such a powerful and such a pervasive charm that few can live upon it without coming

---

[1] [Napoleon was known as "Bonaparte" in France from this point on. He still called himself Buonaparte, however, dropping the "u," for the first time in a written document, at Nice in 1796. See below, p. 34.—A. L.]

to love it. Had Paoli chanced to look with favor upon Bonaparte's local ambitions, the future emperor might have remained content to stick to the independence movement and acquire a certain local dominion along the lines of the petty princelings or town-dictators of Italy during the period of the Renaissance. Repudiated, instead, stripped of his property, proscribed, fuming at his country's mistreatment, he turned towards the welcoming arms of France and threw himself into them. The stuffy, small-sized quibblings and squabblings through which he had lived had opened his eyes to the greatness of a country which had proclaimed freedom in the face of the world, which had fallen into disorganization and anarchy but which still proudly faced a Europe in arms with unshakeable faith in victory. It was of that country that he would ask a future. Chance, instinct, ambition, a strange mixture of forces, all had their part in his choice. He had resolved to become a Frenchman, was one already. Toulon was to give him his naturalization papers and countersign them in letters of fire.

CHAPTER II

Toulon

GENERAL CARTEAUX, A MAN PAST MIDDLE AGE, HAD BEEN
an artist, or rather a dabbler in painting, in his private
life. The prodigious wastage of men which the Revolution confronted had raised him to the command of an
army.

Twirling his mustaches in good-natured condescen-
sion, he surveyed the young Corsican critically. Finally
he said:

"There was really no need of your coming. We are
all set to take the town tomorrow. However—there is
room for everybody. Come along! Perhaps we can let
you burn a house or two! Meantime—won't you stay to
dinner?"

Carteaux was an idiot pure and simple. Everything
was chaos in the republican army. Bonaparte had seen
at a glance that to take the Needle (*L'Éguillette*), a fort
that commanded the narrows at the mouth of the harbor at Toulon, was to take Toulon. Carteaux ridiculed
the suggestion:

"Get more tan on your nose and you'll know something about geography!"

Weeks, rather than days, went by. With nothing to do,

Bonaparte began to sour and then to intrigue. He managed, through Saliceti, to get his plans before Gasparin, the other Commissioner from the Convention. Saliceti and Gasparin both grasped the idea. When Carteaux still held stubborn, they persuaded the Committee of Public Safety to relieve him of his command in favor of Dugommier. The latter adopted the plan of the young Corsican, promoting him meantime to major in charge of a battalion.

Dugommier, among other things, began to set some order to the confusion that had reigned in the army under Carteaux. He asked for reinforcements in men and munitions and got them. Bonaparte also was coming into his own. Marvelously active, he was to be seen everywhere. One morning he was working on a redoubt under fire from the English. Calling for an orderly to dictate a command, he found before him a young Burgundian sergeant, Junot. As he stood writing, a cannonball struck at Junot's feet, spattering his uniform and the piece of paper with earth.

"Good!" commented Junot, laughing. "We won't need any sand to blot it with!"

Bonaparte was delighted at such coolness and asked to have the man appointed as his personal aide. Junot was to go far in the trail of the conqueror and eventually to win a general's epaulettes, which, however, he never developed the brains or the character to wear with distinction.

Never leaving his men, sharing their dangers, sleeping among his guns, wounded a first time and then a second, Bonaparte seemed to have become the soul of the siege. General O'Hara tried a sortie, was repulsed and made prisoner. Bonaparte was credited with a large share in the victory and the Commissioners (by now Fréron and the younger Robespierre), named him adjutant-general, subject to the approval of the Convention.

However the enemy still held out in a formidable net of earthworks that had come to be called "Little Gibraltar." Bonaparte beat the place with all his guns for three consecutive days. Standing on the central parapet of the "Battery of the Fearless" he directed the rain of bombs and solid shot. At Bonaparte's urging Dugommier ordered an assault in force. A furious hand-to-hand battle took place in the dark. "Little Gibraltar" fell.

"You can go to bed and sleep tonight!" said Bonaparte to his general. "We have taken Toulon."

In fact the English made haste to evacuate the town that very night and the army of the Convention entered the following morning without resistance. In recognition of that day the Commissioners made Bonaparte a brigadier-general.

So at Toulon Napoleon made his real debut. Las Cases was later to write: "History picked him up in her arms just there and was never to drop him again. Toulon was the beginning of his immortality."

Bonaparte did not lose his head at so much glory. With a shrewdness surprising in a man so young, he declined command of the Army of Paris, which had been suggested by Augustin Robespierre, brother of the Incorruptible. Bonaparte was a Jacobin but he disliked extremist enthusiasms. He disavowed and despised the Terror. He did accept a much more obscure post as a coast inspector. He thought that a job of that sort would permit him to gather his family about him and enable him to look after the interests of his brothers and get them started in life.

Bonaparte's relatives were to be one of his chief concerns all through his career and he was always to share his successes with them. At the moment the family was in a very bad way. The mother and the girls were living in a barracks that had been assigned to refugees on the outskirts of Marseilles. On taking his new post, which carried a fair salary, Bonaparte set them up in a house in town. His younger brother, Louis, he had already supported in the academy at Auxonne, paying his board, tutoring him in his studies, dividing his meager resources with him and giving him much of his spare time. He now made the lad his aide de camp. Joseph, his elder brother, had grown up to be a young man of attractive personality and distinguished manners. He had just married Julie Clary, daughter of a rich businessman at Marseilles. Napoleon found a place for him in the commissary. Lucien was a youth of great talent, but erratic and hot-headed. Impulsive escapades on his part had been largely responsible for the break with Paoli in Corsica.[1] Napoleon procured his appointment as keeper of stores at Saint Maximin, a post near Toulon.

[1] [The allusion is to the kidnaping (1791) of Morati, leader of a Corsican party that supported Paoli. Pozzo di Borgo was a member of the Morati party. Hence his lifelong feud with the Bonapartes; for Pozzo, too, was to get somewhere in the world.—A. L.]

CHAPTER III

The 13th of Vendémiaire

GOING OVER HIS LIFE AT ST. HELENA NAPOLEON WAS to remark with rare modesty that no man ever owed more to fortunate circumstances, to downright luck, than he. At just this moment, nevertheless, the "breaks" went against him. Dumerbion, commander of the republican armies in Italy, was hard-pressed for an artillery expert. Bonaparte was transferred to his staff and was to serve for two months along the Riviera. But this was a dangerous period in Bonaparte's life. Robespierre had fallen, the Thermidorists were cleaning up, and the friends that Bonaparte had had in the government had either died on the guillotine or were seeking safety in exile. Bonaparte was arrested near Antibes on suspicion of spying and spent two weeks in confinement in the Square Fort, so-called, near that place. He managed to clear his traces and returned to service, figuring materially in Schérer's victory at Dego (September 21, 1794). In the spring of 1795 he was ordered to transfer to the infantry and proceed to the Vendée. This seemed to be a disciplinary measure aimed at officers who had taken part in an unsuccessful venture against Corsica. Bonaparte alleged ill-health, and after a time set out for Paris

24

in order to look into the transfer. At the capital he found himself a marked person, suspected of Jacobinism at the War Office and frankly disliked by the Minister of War, General Aubry.

Aubry was one of the many mushrooms of the revolutionary committees. His outstanding exploit so far had been to promote himself from captain to general with one stroke of his own pen. He insisted on Bonaparte's transfer to the infantry and also on the assignment to the Vendée. Bonaparte refused:

"Why can't I stay with the artillery in Italy?"

"You are too young for that!"

"One ages rapidly on the battlefield. That's where I come from!"

The thrust touched Aubry in a sore spot and won Bonaparte a place on the reserve list without pay. At the moment he had no money and was even without clean linen. He walked the streets of Paris for some weeks in acute distress, looking for political wires that might be pulled in the direction of winning a new commission in the army. He spent many a day without eating at all, but then again he was often asked to dinner at Bourrienne's or at Madame Permon's—Madame Permon was an acquaintance from the old days in Corsica. Junot had been Bonaparte's inseparable companion since Toulon. The two men were always together during these painful weeks in Paris.

In his quest for influence Bonaparte had found encouragement in two men who had seen him at work in the south. One was Fréron, the other Barras. Barras had become virtually omnipotent in the Assembly since the fall of Robespierre, as was clearly indicated by the fact that as the "Sections of the 12th of Vendémiaire" began to gather, the Assembly entrusted him with its defense against the threatening insurrection by the Royalists and other factions of the Right.

That was a most disconcerting responsibility for Barras, who felt miserably out of his element in military affairs. He did have the inspired idea—and from the very first, it seems—that everything would depend on artillery. He was in fact looking about for an officer of that arm to help him. Suddenly he thought of the little artilleryman of Toulon who had been hounding him for a job and had actually sent in his card again that very morning. Bonaparte had spent the evening of the 12th at the Feydeau theater. By a fortunate chance he happened to be loafing about the corridors at the Tuileries, whither he had gone on seeing that trouble was brewing. An orderly recognized him and led him at once to the office of the Committees of the Convention—a room that had formerly been the bedroom of Marie Antoinette.

Barras, Fréron and Carnot were there. In a few words Barras laid the situation before Bonaparte. The idea was to put him in command of the Army of the Interior.

A decisive moment in a great life! A decisive moment in the whole future of Europe! That moment, moreover, was to call Bonaparte's whole character into action. Placed by events in the face of an agonizing situation, he was to deal with it as a man, as a soldier, and especially as a Frenchman. He had come with the notion, or indeed with the hope, that his opinion might be desired on some point or other. He had never remotely dreamed of any such proposition as Barras made to him.

The minister's words took him quite aback. He blushed scarlet, then threw a hand to his throat as though he were stifling. Finally he stammered a request that he be given a little time to consider. Barras frowned:

"I give you three minutes!"

And he took out his watch.

No one spoke in the dimly lighted room. Bonaparte stood with his eyes closed. He was thinking hard. He had, in fact, plenty to think about. A few moments earlier, on leaving the theater, he had seen Menou's troops retiring in disorder down the rue Vivienne, and he had remarked to Junot, who was walking at his side:

"If the Sections would put me in charge, I would guarantee to put them in the Tuileries inside of two hours and make an end of those bums in the Convention."

He was a Jacobin, to be sure. But he hated terrorism and he despised intriguing politicians. Could he now enter the service of those same politicians and help suppress the revolt in the capital? Would that not be dangerous for his future? Paris meant France, for the nation always followed Paris. Would Paris ever forgive a man for spilling the blood of her citizens? Victory over Frenchmen would never have the luster of victory. Defeat would mean death.

His teeth pressed deep into his lower lip. His hands twitched nervously. His impulse was to refuse. But he checked himself. The Convention was not the only thing! There was France too! Success for the Sections, the fall of the Assembly, would leave the country defenseless and hand it over to the enemy. The frontiers were threatened. Fifty thousand Austrians were advancing on Alsace. Two English fleets were cruising off Brest. There stood Europe in arms! Rearing stiff and stern on her last legs, heroic, inhuman, pike in hand, France had held them off. Let her show signs of faltering and they would rush upon her and tear her to shreds! . . . At that moment Bonaparte was making a spiritual adoption of his greater country. The Corsica that he had loved was melting into a larger entity. France only counted. To her he owed everything. From her he hoped everything.

A sort of shiver ran over him. Rising like a soldier of old in defense of the state, he felt ready to sacrifice everything, his life, his ambition, his dreams. Confident of his strength and ability, he banished all scruples, all fears. They were consumed as in a fire that flamed deep down in his spirit. He raised a hand and brushed back his hair. He was ready for action:

"General, I accept. But I warn you: Having once drawn the sword, I shall not sheathe it till order is restored."

His voice deep, earnest, peremptory, Bonaparte laid before the Commissioners his ideas as to the best manner of stifling the revolt. In that atmosphere of all-pervading panic he alone saw clearly and thought coldly. Where were the cannon? There were none! Well, get some—at the camp at Sablons! Murat, the commander of the cavalry, was despatched at breakneck speed to procure them. He came back, after a bold and hazardous ride, with forty.

Bonaparte deployed them in such a way as to protect the palace from the expected onslaught of the Sections. Before long, besides, reinforcements of troops arrived. In the course of that night the Royalist mobs could have taken the Tuileries almost without firing a shot. By the

28

time they made up their minds it was too late. They advanced on the Convention in two columns. One came down the rue Saint-Honoré upon the Tuileries. It was stopped in front of the church of Saint-Roch, Bonaparte sweeping the street clean with salvos of grape. The second, aiming at the Palais Royal, was repulsed on the quai Voltaire by Verdière. Barras himself dispersed the mobs in the rue Richelieu. By ten o'clock on the evening of the 13th (October 5, 1795) Paris was quiet again. During the forenoon of the 14th the rebellious quarters of the capital were all in the hands of the government.

The Convention did not slaughter the vanquished. It did not have the strength to do so. It merely recompensed the conquerors. Barras was named Director. Bonaparte was introduced before the Assembly by Fréron as "the man who had smitten the Royalist hydra." He was named commander-in-chief of the Army of the Interior—in other words, he became military master of Paris.

Young as he was he acquitted himself marvelously of these important duties. He proceeded to disarm the Sections family by family. He reorganized the National Guard and formed two new corps—the Guard of the Directory and the Guard of the Legislative Body. At once he made himself abidingly popular in those organizations. The shortage of food was acute and he was commissioned by the government to superintend the distribution of supplies. Eager to win back the people of Paris he rode with an escort of officers through the poorer districts and about the markets. One day bread failed at the bakeries. A threatening mob gathered clamoring about him, and a fat housewife called:

"All these gold-braiders make fools of us! As long as

29

they can eat and grow fat, what do they care about us poor folks?"

Bonaparte singled her out with his raised arm:

"Look me over carefully, mother! Well—who is fatter, you or I?"

Bonaparte established headquarters in the Seventeenth Division building, assuming from the outset the demeanor and the habits of a leader. He wore authority easily. Command came natural to him. His unkempt hair dropped in "dog's ears" about the collar of his uniform, but a strange prestige emanated from his personality. He was attractive and yet, somehow, disquieting. There was nothing French about him physically. He was a Mediterranean type, a mixture of the Florentine and the Greek. Though at first glance he seemed to be far from handsome his individual features were singularly pure. Most remarkable was the expression of his eyes. Whenever he looked up two glittering spots seemed to rest upon one. Of a grayish blue ordinarily, they changed color with passing impressions, often seeming almost black. Most people found them hard, but they softened as he smiled and the smile seemed to lend his face a sort of ingenuousness, yet an almost unhuman nobility. His gait was not imposing—he cantered. His gestures were spasmodic, jerky. He talked concisely, dryly. Then again, in moments of relaxation and expansiveness, when he chatted of his childhood days or of his dreams, his words would take on an unexpected eloquence that was warm with color and imagery—poetic. No one dared to interrupt him at such times. For that matter, people could sit for hours listening to him.

CHAPTER IV

Josephine

Shortly before the 13th of Vendémiaire, at a party given by Mme. Tallien, "Our Lady of Thermidor," mistress to Barras, Bonaparte had met a charming woman from the French colonies in the West Indies—Josephine Tascher de la Pagerie, widow of General Beauharnais, sometime president of the Constituent Assembly and for a moment commander-in-chief of the Army of the Rhine. Beauharnais had been guillotined under the Terror.

Bonaparte did not see the Beauharnais woman for what she really was—a frivolous creature who had dropped Hoche for Barras and had got along in life from hand-to-mouth by petty traffickings in influence which she was able to conduct through the occasional favors allowed her by powerful paramours. Bonaparte knew nothing of society and his heart was still unspoiled. He mistook Josephine de Beauharnais for a great lady of the old court circle who had somehow strayed as a lost soul into the hit-and-miss society that had been born of the revolutionary turmoils. Flattered by the deference she paid him, he formed an attachment for her and was soon thinking of marrying her. Josephine already had two grown children—Eugene and Hortense. She was six

31

years older than Bonaparte, though he did not know it.
She was penniless, and that too he did not know. What
he did know was that she was sweet, attractive, gay,
stylish. She delighted him immeasurably. They were
homebuilders, those Corsicans. Joseph Bonaparte had already set an example for his younger brothers. Why
should Napoleon not marry too? To tell the truth, the
match seemed rather shabby to Citizeness Beauharnais.
Barras undertook to persuade her:

"He is going far, that little sawed-off!"

Barras had good reasons for saying that. He was in
power in France and he had made up his mind to provide the bridegroom with a fine command. Bonaparte
had always favored attacking Austria through Italy and
had long amused himself by drawing up plans for a campaign on that front. The Directory was considering giving him a chance to execute them.

Not a few historians have alleged, with no specific
proof, that the command in Italy was given to Bonaparte by Barras as a dowry to Josephine, whom the dashing Director was beginning to find a nuisance. There can
be no doubt that there was an understanding, and almost a bargain, between Barras and the Citizeness Beauharnais. But Bonaparte had no part whatever in an intrigue which he would have spurned out of pride, quite
apart from any scruple. He was counting strictly on his
military skill and on the logic of events to sweep him
to the front of the stage in France. He got wind of grum-
blings among the generals at his rapid advancement
through wire-pulling, and commented:

"Do they think I need influence to get somewhere?
Well, soon they'll be only too glad to pull wires for my

JOSEPHINE
From the Portrait by Appiani

influence. My sword hangs at my belt. With it I am going to go far."

It seems certain, in fact, that Bonaparte would have been appointed to the Italian command regardless of any marriage with Mme. de Beauharnais. Men were scarce. Schérer had been put in charge in Italy and had demonstrated his incompetence. It was Carnot and not Barras who suggested that the Directory replace Schérer with the "artilleryman of Vendémiaire." Barras, of course, seconded the motion, but he was now associated closely with the Corsican and was counting on him as a prop for the future. He could only have voted as Carnot voted.

Bonaparte was appointed commander-in-chief of the Army of Italy on the 2nd of March, 1796. A week later, in the mayor's office in the 2nd ward in Paris, Josephine de Beauharnais became the Citizeness Bonaparte. It was a hasty, irregular business. In the marriage document Josephine lied egregiously about her age and Bonaparte made himself a year and a half older than he was. Curiously enough, were his false affidavit to be taken as true, he would have been, at the time, not a citizen of France but a subject of Genoa.

On the exchange of certificates the young general hurried with his wife to the mansion she occupied on the rue Chantereine. All the following day he spent with his officers going over maps of northern Italy. There was not a moment to lose. The Austrians and the Piedmontese were about to cross the southeastern frontier of France. On the morning of the 11th, Bonaparte tore himself from Josephine's arms, leapt into a carriage and was off at a gallop—towards Headquarters, towards Italy, towards glory, a more sudden and more dazzling glory than had ever crowned a captain twenty-seven years of age.

He stopped at Marseilles to call on his mother and sisters. He assumed his command at Nice. The military leaders whom he found in charge and who were about to become his subordinates were not very glad to see him. With them he had no great prestige. In the eyes of the army proper he was just a "riot general" whose gold braid had been polished up by wire-pulling and intrigue. Masséna, Augereau, Joubert, Berthier, Sérurier, Dommartin, were generals who had far more imposing records. But he "squashed" them at the first encounter (the word is Augereau's). As for the rank and file, he electrified them. In a proclamation (which for the first time he signed with the single word "Bonaparte," written without the Italian "u"), he declaimed:

"Your patience under privation, your bravery in the face of danger, have aroused the admiration of France. Her eyes are upon you in your sufferings. You have no shoes, no clothes, no shirts. You have almost no bread and the stores are empty, while those of the enemy overflow with everything. It is for you to win those things for yourselves. You can. You are going to. Let us be off!"

Berthier, Bonaparte's chief of staff, has left a detailed inventory of that army. Sixty thousand men on paper, it counted barely forty-five in the fact. Jacobin rancors had disorganized it. There were no supplies, no clothes, and worst of all no discipline. The soldiers were living as ruffians on the country. There was no money in the army chest—Bonaparte left Paris with 24,000 francs.

Equipment was wretched. There were thirty cannon, but of 3000 horses barely a half were fit for work.

While waiting for a chance to improve conditions of living for his soldiers, the general began working at their morale. He forbade foraging on pain of death and established regular, frequent drills and rigid inspections. "I will reduce these brigands to order or give up the job," he wrote to the Directory. "I have been bending every effort here to restoring service. Victory will do the rest."

Of victory, an immediate victory, so necessary to France, to the army, to himself, he had not the slightest doubt. He was sure of it. He had it inside him. The time had come at last when he could apply principles which he had formulated from a study more remotely of the military science of the great Frederick but more immediately of the strategists of the Revolution. Two years earlier he had written to Augustin Robespierre:

"It is the same with open fighting as it is with sieges of fortresses: you must concentrate your fire all on one point. With a fortress, once the breach is opened, the balance is upset and the rest of it does not count—it is taken. You must not scatter your attacks. . . . You separate to live, you concentrate to fight. . . . Unified command is necessary for success." [1]

---

[1] [There was nothing strictly new in these principles. They had been formulated by Bourcet and Guibert, among other theorists of military strategy under the Revolution. Bonaparte's genius lay not so much in his concepts of tactic as in his grasp of the situation at the opening of a campaign or on a battlefield, in his capacity for lightninglike action and above all in the confidence and enthusiasm he never once failed to inspire in his men.—A. L.]

CHAPTER V

Italy

THE ITALIAN CAMPAIGN WAS A THUNDER-BOLT.

The Austrian and Piedmontese armies together counted 70,000 men. Crossing the frontier Bonaparte slipped between them. He beat the Austrian army at Montenotte on the 12th of April, 1796, and the Piedmontese at Millesimo on the 13th. The Austrians were beaten again at Dego on the 14th and retreated towards the east. Bonaparte turned west in pursuit of the Piedmontese and defeated them for the second time at Mondovì (April 22). Entirely cut off from his allies, the King of Sardinia was forced to sign an armistice at Cherasco (April 27).

Bonaparte talked down as lord and master to the Piedmontese envoys who were disposed to haggle over terms. Taking out his watch he said:

"Gentlemen, I advise you that our general attack is set for two o'clock. Unless I am certain that Coni is in my hands by nightfall the attack will not be postponed for an instant. I may some day happen to lose a battle, but you will never find me losing a minute on anybody's word or by laziness on my own part."

The Sardinians were struck speechless and yielded.

Nice and Savoy were ceded to France. The Directory
had forbidden Bonaparte to discuss settlements without
orders from Paris. The young general did not have time
to obey, nor the inclination either. Stepping easily into
his rôle as a diplomat he wrote briefly to his government:

"I trust that my conduct falls in with your views."

From that moment on, the statesman and the captain
went hand in hand in him. His ideas were definite, sound,
far-seeing. Dealing energetically with the present he
never lost sight of the future. Intelligence, energy, a
sense of realities—he had them all. He was a true child
of that other Italian, Machiavelli. He showed himself a
born manipulator, a master in diplomacy, from those
very first negotiations. Whence such precocious mature-
ness of judgment? It came, one may suspect, from his
severe self-disciplining. The fact that he had known
suffering may also have figured in it. At any rate, in the
flush of success he showed the greatest consideration for
the vanquished.

Thenceforward Bonaparte was to win battles and make
treaties simultaneously and more or less as he saw fit.
Professing a necessary regard for the sensibilities of the
Directors he was to go over their heads indifferently in
his proclamations and bulletins. In speaking to his troops
he addressed the whole people of France and from the
very first. At Cherasco he said:

"Soldiers: You have won six times in two weeks . . .
but we have done nothing since we still have much to
do. . . . Your country is expecting great things of you.
. . . Is there one among you whose courage is quail-
ing? No, for we are all bent on humbling the proud

kings who have set out to put us in chains. When we go back to our homes we all want to be able to say with pride: 'I was with the Army in Italy.' "

A vibrant style, flowery, pompous, and at the same time terse and forceful! It was the style of a born leader of men. A great image-finder Bonaparte aimed at the imagination and knew the art of touching it. His sentences were ready-made for legend, just as they were ready-made for the inscriptions on his future statues.

Bound to Italy so closely by birth he may have been thinking already of sowing the seeds of a personal fortune in that country, for in an "Address to the Italians" he strove to exalt their hearts and give them his liberating sword for a battle standard:

"Peoples of Italy: The French army has come to break your chains. The French people is the friend of all other peoples. Meet it half way in all confidence! Your property, your religion, your customs, will be respected. We are generous enemies in war. We hate only the tyrants who are enslaving you. . . ."

The Austrians retreated beyond the Adda. He broke their line again at the bridge at Lodi (May 10) and drove them from Lombardy.

Just then a strange message came from Paris. Alarmed at the independence Bonaparte was developing, the Directory ordered him to give half his army to Kellermann, leaving the latter in charge of the province of Milan while he, Bonaparte, marched on central Italy in order to "tap the huge treasure that had been accumulating there for fifteen centuries."

Bonaparte reared and offered his resignation:

"If you break up unity of military policy in Italy, you

PASSAGE DU PONT DE LODI LE 21 FLOREAL AN 4.

Commandé par le Général Bonaparte en chef.

THE PASSAGE OF THE BRIDGE OF LODI

will, I am sorry to say, be losing your fairest opportunity
for forcing your will upon that country. I can render
essential services to the nation only in case I am entirely
and absolutely invested with your confidence. . . . Kellermann will do as well as I, for nobody is more convinced than I am that victories are due to the courage
and boldness of the army; but I cannot willingly serve
with a man who thinks himself the first general in Europe. . . . I refuse to brook any interference."

He felt himself strong enough already to talk in that
tone of voice! One of his aides expressed a fear that
the Directors might accept the resignation. He replied:

"If they dared do that they would have the whole
of France upon their backs."

Without giving his men a chance to catch their breath
he raced for Milan. He arrived there at Pentecost and
made formal entry, like a Roman emperor, into the
Lombard metropolis. It was a bright sunny day. A column of prisoners led the march, which passed under
a triumphal arch of green. While flowers rained from
balconies, the streets were lined with shouting mobs who
cheered and cheered with joy as at the breaking of a new
day. Never was Bonaparte, never was Napoleon, to know
a more thrilling triumph. Riding at the head of his
ragged but haughty soldiers with his horse at a walk, the
young man seemed suddenly to have been lifted to an
heroic greatness. He sat pensive in the saddle, with his
eyes half closed. He sketched a smile now and then at
some salvo of vivas. Of the entry into Milan he was to
say later, at St. Helena:

"I suppose the happiest moment of my life was in
Milan after my first victories in Italy. What enthusiasm!

39

What shouts! . . . I could see the world whirling under me as though I were being carried along through the air."

He was already quite definitely conscious of his future and of all that he might become, for he said to Marmont that evening as he was getting ready for bed:

"Well, what do you think they are saying of us in Paris?"

"Enthusiasm must be wild. . . ."

"They haven't seen anything yet! The future holds much greater successes for us than we have had so far. Fortune has not smiled on me in this way just for me to spurn her favors. Fortune is a woman. The more she does for me, the more I shall ask of her. In our day people haven't seen anything great. I am going to show them something."

He had sent for his wife to come to him in Italy just after Cherasco. Josephine refused, finding the pleasures of Paris more to her liking. Before long Bonaparte could have had no doubt that she was betraying him. Hurt, deeply hurt, he squared his shoulders and went on in silence, his duty as a leader mastering his feelings as a man. Activity, activity on a grand scale, was not exactly to console him for his wounded love—it was to distract him.

Setting himself up in princely style in the Serbelloni palace, he was already a ruler, creating the organization of a future state and receiving ambassadors. They came from the Pope, from the Duke of Parma, from the Duke of Modena, and of them he demanded millions, and along with the millions, rare manuscripts, rare pictures, priceless marbles. He rushed the booty on to Paris.

Starving, greedy, Paris was, as Bonaparte shrewdly guessed, just a Cerberus which would close its triple gullet only if he stuffed it with chunks of gold. Each of his letters announced a new despatch of treasure: On June 1: "Two millions in gold left for Paris today by special wagon." On June 8: "A million has started by way of Basel. You have eight millions on deposit at Genoa. You can draw upon them." The Directors, as he had calculated, looked upon all that treasure as the price of his glory. Their tone changed. Kellermann stayed at Chambéry and the question of dividing the command was dropped.

"You have the confidence of the Directory," Paris wrote. "The very considerable sums which the Republic owes to your victories prove that you are as attentive to the interest as to the glory of our country."

Meantime all eyes in France were upon him. Citizeness Bonaparte could not appear in public without being hailed as "Our Lady of Victory."

But after a first glow of enthusiasm the Italians began to resent the French occupation, finding that liberation was coming at too high a price. Lombardy was a fat country, where people lived comfortably on money which they had earned by honest toil. Provisions and supplies went into hiding. The masses began to grumble, the nobility to intrigue, the clergy to agitate. Stray soldiers were murdered in the rural hamlets. There were riots at Pavia and in Milan itself.

Bonaparte waved a strong hand and proclaimed:

"The French army will deal in a spirit of paternal gentleness with peaceful, law-abiding citizens. It will fall like fire from heaven upon rebels and upon towns that shelter them."

To point an example he had the municipal officers of Pavia shot by a firing squad and allowed his soldiers to plunder that city.

However, he was holding a foreign country by main force and he had to fight on. He fought on and won.

General Beaulieu rallied the Austrian forces and sought revenge for Lodi at Borghetto (May 30). He was beaten. Half his army took refuge in the fortress at Mantua (a great stronghold that controlled both the valley of the Po and the passes across the Alps). The other half retreated upgrade into the Tyrol. Bonaparte sent Augereau to invest Mantua. Masséna entered Verona while he himself occupied Bologna and then hurried on to Livorno—a shrewd move that eventually was to lead to the recovery of Corsica. The King of Naples thereupon sued for peace. Venice, frightened, crawled into her shell in the lagoons, while the Grand Duke of Tuscany, brother to the Austrian emperor, Francis, welcomed "the illustrious general" as a "guest" into Florence (and the republican conqueror deigned to play the little comedy with him).

Austria, meantime, did not despair of rewinning Italy. One after the other she sent four armies, commanded by her most illustrious captains, across the Alps to relieve Mantua. That was the critical moment in the Italian campaign and it forced Bonaparte to display all his resources in energy, versatility and military genius. In a magnificent turning movement along the south shore of the lake of Garda he beat Würmser at Castiglione (August 5) and again at Bassano (September 8), cutting the

Austrian's line of retreat. Würmser too was obliged to shut himself up in beleaguered Mantua.

The French troops were tired and many were sick with fever. They were short in guns and ammunition and their numbers had dropped to 36,000 men. In November 60,000 Austrians, commanded by the aged Alvinzi, appeared in Italy. Bonaparte defeated them on the causeway at Arcole (November 17), leading the charge in person, carrying a flag, and almost losing his life in a marsh. Alvinzi retreated but then, having received heavy reinforcements, he advanced again to try his luck on the plateau at Rivoli. He was badly beaten for a second time (January 14), and Würmser, short of provisions and munitions, saw himself forced to capitulate at Mantua (February 2). Bonaparte granted him the honors of war and allowed him to march his army home to Austria.

The Pope had been figuring on an Austrian victory and so had broken the truce of Bologna. Bonaparte now turned on him—for a military promenade rather than a campaign. The pontifical army everywhere gave ground before the French, and the Holy See, after five days of parleying, signed a peace at Tolentino (February 19, 1797). On that day Bonaparte addressed a deferential letter to Pius VII, which illustrates his farsightedness:

"All Europe is aware of the pacific inclinations and the conciliatory virtues of Your Holiness. I am sending my aide de camp to express the wholehearted esteem and veneration that I have for your person . . ."

To be sure, the Pope had paid for that by ceding Avignon and the Marches, Romagna and Ancona, by paying a thirty million indemnity and by handing over precious works of art. But the moderate language that Bonaparte used towards the Holy See surprised and irritated the Directory, which was a group of fanatical atheists tempered by one theophilanthropist, La Revellière-Lepeaux. However, it did not dare to disavow Bonaparte and, in fact, on his repeated demand, it went so far as to send him 20,000 men from the Army of the Rhine.

They were commanded by Bernadotte, and they arrived in the nick of time. A last Austrian army was coming down from the Tyrol under Austria's best general, the Archduke Charles. Well seconded by Masséna and Joubert, Bonaparte marched into the province of Friuli, beat the Archduke in four battles—on the Piave, on the Tagliamento, and in the passes at Tarvis and Neumarkt. The Archduke retreated along the Vienna road. Bonaparte was at Klagenfurt on March 21. Thence he addressed the Archduke with a dignified letter in which he did not disdain to offer peace:

"I would consider myself more honored by the civic crown that I might feel I had deserved than by the melancholy glory which may still come from further military successes." [1]

The Archduke hesitated. The Austrian cabinet was never able to think very quickly and was disposed to argue. Bonaparte pressed on. By April 7 he was at Leoben, hardly more than seventy miles from Vienna. The Emperor was now anxious to halt him at any cost and

[1] [In these advances Bonaparte was trying to checkmate Hoche and the Directory, who had the Austrians in a bad way on the northern front. His unauthorized signing of the armistice at Leoben robbed the government of a crushing victory over Werneck on the Nidda. The drive into Corinthia and the Carniola was aimed as much at Paris as at Vienna.—A. L.]

sent emissaries to sue for peace. An armistice was signed some days later, the 18th.

The Leoben agreement gave France the left bank of the Rhine and Belgium. Lombardy was organized as the Cisalpine Republic. To punish Venice for her dubious attitude her mainland possessions were handed over to Austria. The Directory would have been more than willing to continue so profitable a war, but it was in no position to repudiate Bonaparte, whose prestige had come to overshadow all others in France. Besides, it was too greatly in need of him. Over-riding Carnot, who would not consent to the annihilation of Venice, it gave Bonaparte full powers to conclude a peace. Five months were required to obtain Austria's final signature.

During that time, the conqueror occupied the castle of Mombello, near Milan, surrounded by his family. Josephine finally yielded to his imperious entreaties and joined him there. Representatives from the Emperor, the Pope, the kings of Sardinia and Naples, nobles from the Lombard aristocracy, the generals of his staff, made up what was virtually a sovereign's court. While negotiating with Austria, Germany and Switzerland, Bonaparte governed northern Italy as an absolute dictator. Venice revolted at the confiscation of her territories and French soldiers were killed at Verona. Bonaparte therefore occupied the proud city on the lagoons and raised the tricolor on the campanile of St. Mark. Accepted as arbiter by the Grisons and the inhabitants of the Valtelline, he annexed the latter to the Cisalpine Republic. The island possessions of Venice in the Ionian Sea were taken over by France.

While its young general was thus assuming the man-

ners and the realities of an all-powerful pro-consul, the
Directory had been now winning, now losing, in Germany with Jourdan, Moreau and Hoche. Its position
was growing more and more difficult. The elections of
the Year V gave the Royalists a majority in the Councils
and France seemed to be headed for anarchy once more.
The government therefore appealed to Bonaparte, who
sent Augereau, the most brutal of his generals, to Paris.
With that strong-armed support Barras was in a position to stage the coup of the 18th of Fructidor, by which
Carnot and Barthélemy, some fifty deputies and a hundred newspapermen were banished from France and a
Jacobin dictatorship re-established (September 4, 1797).[1]

Bonaparte approved of all that—he was still a republican; but besides, just at that moment, he was working
overtime in trying to conclude the Treaty of Campo-
Formio. Austria still seemed disposed to bicker and haggle. Finally he overawed Cobenzl, the Emperor's negotiator, by dashing a precious coffee service to the floor:
"I will smash your empire into as many pieces as those
cups before snow flies," he threatened. And he ordered
the resumption of hostilities.

Cobenzl yielded at once, and, for that matter, the
terms of Campo-Formio were more favorable to Austria
than those of Leoben had been,[2] for she got the city of
Venice as well as all Venetian territory on the main-

[1] [The basic element in the disturbances of September was the failure
of the Directory to pay interest on debt bonds, thus angering many holders
of small savings.—A. L.]

[2] [Cobenzl was not thinking altogether of the broken crockery. He was
playing Bonaparte against the Directory, which was trying to force harsh
terms in order to outplay Bonaparte before French opinion. The important
thing with Bonaparte was to have the victory his.—A. L.]

land. So, after ten centuries of glory, the republic of the doges became a thing of the past.

Bonaparte had grown attached to Mombello, to Milan, to the Italy which in the course of one short year had raised him to a point where he had no equal in France and where no one could recognize him as his old self. He departed with regret for the conference at Rastatt which the German states had called together in order to ratify the stipulations that concerned the Holy Roman Empire. For five days at Rastatt he was courted by a groveling throng of Rhineland princelings. But he was eagerly looking forward to Paris and made for that goal at the earliest possible moment. He reached the waiting capital on the 5th of December, 1797.

CHAPTER VI

Egypt

THE DIRECTORY WAS NOT ANXIOUS TO INCREASE A REPU-
tation that was already damaging its own prestige, but
yielding to the pressure of public opinion it decided
to celebrate the delivery of the Treaty of Campo-Formio
by offering Bonaparte the most spectacular public reception that had been witnessed during the period of
the Revolution. The Altar of the Nation stood in the
great court of the Luxembourg. About it, awaiting the
conqueror of Italy, gathered the five Directors in costumes of silk and gold that had been designed by David. Ministers, ambassadors, Ancients, Five Hundreds,
packed temporary stands that had been erected to form
an amphitheater in front of the altar. Scores of conquered flags had been worked into trophies and their
silken folds glistened under a bright December sun
and fluttered in a cold wind. While cannon thundered
the victor of Lodi advanced towards the altar in step
with a hymn composed for the occasion by Méhul.

For a time there was no applause, not even a whisper
—just a dense silence. Then suddenly came one mighty
roar, a sort of hoarse cry from a thousand throats: *Vive
Bonaparte!* It drowned out the cannon and the music

48

from the bands. He came on, wearing his ordinary field uniform. Its faded colors offered a fascinating contrast with the gay and glittering display about him. His face was pale from the same emotion that gave a twitch to his fingers. Whether through timidity or modesty he kept his eyes to the ground.

Talleyrand, the Minister of Foreign Relations, presented him to the Directors in a carefully worded speech. Bonaparte responded briefly, to the point: He was glad that peace had come to bring prosperity to the Republic. But he added a sentence that suggested different horizons:

"When the happiness of the French people shall have been grounded on a better organic law, all Europe will be free again. . . ."

Followed by an enthusiastic, shouting mob Bonaparte made his way back to the rue Chantereine (which was to be renamed in his honor as the rue de la Victoire), and re-entered the mansion that Josephine had rented from Julie Talma.

The crowd had surged in front of his door all day long for day after day during those two weeks. He had avoided the public eye as much as possible, making a few calls, and receiving at home only members of his family and a few friends. "What a change!" That was the most frequent comment. Less than two years before he had been a party general, a debated favorite, an adventurer crowding ahead among hosts of other adventurers. Now his name was in every thought. Milan had treated him as a prince. In Paris he was just a citizen returned from abroad. But it was Paris that gave him the real sense of his greatness.

And he took fright. Would not such frenzied popularity alarm and perhaps anger men from whom he still had much to expect or even to fear? The general saw that he had to escape from it as a danger to the success of his plans. Factions began to play for him in all directions, eager to make him their standard bearer. Patriots, Jacobins, Royalists—all were bidding for his patronage.

However, he refused to become the tool of any party. He was determined to hold himself in reserve as the leader predestined to save France, whenever—the next day, perhaps—she might weary of the demagogues and appeal to the sword. What could he do just then? Upset those mediocrities, those thieves, those "rotters" (*pourris*), and strip them of a power that he knew they were unworthy of? No, the time had not come for that. His glory had not weathered yet—there was too good a chance of his failing. "Had he tried to seize power at that time," Marmont writes, "nine-tenths of the country would have withdrawn their support from him."

The Directory, moreover, had smoothed out its differences with the two Councils and had recovered some of its prestige. Bonaparte was not yet mature enough to become a dictator. Framed by such colleagues, just one of their clique, he could only lose through contact with their mediocrity. As regards the army he indeed had no rival now that Hoche was dead. But Moreau's star was gradually rising, and Moreau did not like him. Following its general's lead, the Army of the Rhine was jealous of the Army of Italy. Not only that! Could Bonaparte trust his own subordinates? Bernadotte was a cautious intriguer, Augereau an impulsive brute.

Either of them might desert him. There was no understanding the impenetrable Joubert. In the direction of
the army, therefore, as well as in the direction of the
public, the watchword had to be "Wait!" Very well!
He would wait! He could afford to wait, since some
day his hour was sure to come!

In order to quiet all mistrust, he kept very much to
himself, spending most of his time at home with his
wife, working over his maps and charts. When he chanced
to go out it was in citizen's clothes—a gray afternoon
coat—and without a bodyguard. He held strictly aloof
from official society and saw very few people at home—
a few generals, mostly those belonging to his staff, and
two or three statesmen, Cambacérès, Talleyrand, Barras,
men who might be of use to him in the future, when he
would need shrewd, discerning minds for the task of
splicing the new day to whatever he would choose to
save of an older France. In this sense he was even more
attentive to Talleyrand than he was to Barras.

The society which he really sought and cultivated
was that of scholars, artists and writers. Arnault and
Talma had been friends of his penniless days. To his
table they now brought David, Méhul, Legouvé and Bernardin de Saint Pierre. He gained the esteem of the Institute and accepted a seat in the branch of the Sciences
that it offered him. He attended meetings regularly and
read papers, discussing metaphysics with Siéyès, astron-
omy with Lagrange and Laplace, poetry with Marie
Joseph Chénier, law-making with Daunou. His marvelous memory was enriched by these contacts. On the
other hand he rebuffed anyone who tried to get a hold on

him. Rudely he discarded Mme. de Staël, who had thought of becoming his Egeria:

"Of what sort of woman do you most approve, General?" she asked of him one day, coyly.

"Of the one who has the most children!" he retorted.

Her feelings were hurt and she was never to forgive him.

Inactivity weighed heavily upon Bonaparte's restless, over-active mind.

"My glory is wearing out here," he remarked one evening as he sat alone with Bourrienne and Josephine. "Nothing is ever remembered in Paris. If I stay here much longer without doing anything, I am lost."

That was exaggerating. His popularity was not on the wane. Actually he was fretting under the pin pricks of the article-writers and parlor wits. The Directory, for its part, could not conceal its uneasiness. "What a nuisance an unemployed conqueror can be!" remarked Thibaudeau. To be rid of him while at the same time appearing to satisfy him, they offered him command of the "Army of England." That mythical force was a body of coast guards scattered along the Channel from Brest to Antwerp.

Bonaparte set out to inspect the defenses on the north shore and for the first time confronted in cold reality one of the controlling ambitions of his life: the conquest of England. Returning to a language he had learned at school, he thought of France as a new Rome threatened by a modern Carthage. Not that he hated England. He had respected and admired that country from his very boyhood. But, he thought, England was the inveterate, the instinctive enemy of France, an enemy that had all but absorbed her during the Hundred Years' War and then, within a mere half century, had robbed her of Canada and banished her from the Cape and from India. Now there she was again! Refusing to accept the Revolution of 1789, the British oligarchy had blockaded the French coasts, destroyed French foreign commerce and marshaled all the soldiers available in Europe on the frontier of the Alps and along the Rhine. The republic had managed to repel the invasion and punish its aggressors. England alone stood haughty, secure, erect upon the seas. If England were not crushed she would organize new coalitions and these might one day have better luck. Before she could hope for a secure peace and real power as a nation, France would have to make one last effort and floor her rival. The only blow that could count would be a blow at the heart. Where was the heart of that empire that sat sprawling over two hemispheres? London, obviously! The problem, therefore, must be to land a well-equipped army on those chalky cliffs that could be discerned from Boulogne. Would such a thing be possible?

With a little black notebook in hand, Bonaparte visited the arsenals, the stores, noting the resources of each harbor and questioning sailors, outfitters, even smugglers. Completing his tour of inspection at Antwerp he concluded that the enterprise was too hazardous. "I would not play the whole fortune of France on one card," he said. There were few ships and no siege material. Munitions were scarce for such few batteries as actually existed. Everything was old, worn out—at any rate unfit for service. Two years' time, a hundred millions in money and full powers would be required to put the navy in condition.

But agile, resourceful, he kept pondering the problem. England could be attacked, but not directly in Europe. There the frightened English were lining their shores with forts. He would have to attack them at some other point. Where? On the road to India! Egypt was England's weak spot. The idea had been in his mind for a long time.[1] Two years earlier he had actually written: "The way really to destroy England is to get possession of Egypt." But at this moment the idea returned to him with enthralling persuasiveness. The East, the native land of glory! Everything there was vast, brilliant—horizons, shores, the names of the cities, the languages of the peoples! The East was the land where the names of great men were wrought in gold, where mortals became divinities!

"Europe is a rat-hole," he had remarked in Italy. "Nothing really great can be tried there. Only in the East, with its six hundred millions of people, can great civic and religious revolutions be made." Alexander, the besetting example, won crowns from the priests of Ammon and the magi of Babylon—but in the East. It was in the East that Caesar, a nearer, more present example, stifled the last cries of Roman liberty. Belisarius, Mahomet, Tamberlaine, rose as great specters over their tombs and seemed to be beckoning to him with outstretched arms to follow them.

With Egypt conquered and out of the way, should he

1 [In November, 1797, he had sent a personal agent to Malta to purchase a surrender of the Knights in case he should ever appear at Malta on the way to Egypt.—A. L.]

push on, following the trail of the Macedonian to the Euphrates and the Indus? What could he not do on those shifting soils where a victory won not a province or a river passage but boundless realms, prostrate peoples, empires? . . . He could not make up his mind just then. Perhaps he might forget Europe and finish his days as a modern Genghis Khan, basking in the solar splendor of an Indian or Chinese throne. On the other hand he was child and product of the Latin world. Would he not miss it? France, for instance? Could he ever give up France—so rich, especially in possibilities, and so beautiful? With such a nation in one's hands, reformed, remodeled, one could rule the world! One thing was certain: If ever he came back from the East, it would be to seize France, take her in his slender hands, mold her, knead her, refashion her to be the wonder of the universe! The conqueror of Italy was too much of a mushroom, too much of a novelty. But the conqueror of Egypt would have an irresistible prestige. The sewage that was ruling the Republic would dissolve of its own accord, without resistance, without fuss. Alexander? Caesar? Well, the course of events would again decide which!

He broached his plan to Barras the moment he returned from Antwerp. Had the Director, Barras, taken life a little more seriously he might have been a fairly good statesman. He did not like the idea. Forty thousand men away off to the Nile! Could the army stand it? Freed of the nightmare of an invasion from across the Channel England would turn Europe topsy-turvy in her scramble for allies. Then again Egypt belonged to the Turks, allies of France since the day of Francis I! Why break just those ties—the only ones that had survived the Revolution? But under the cover of those very creditable considerations Bonaparte could see others that the Director was not emphasizing. Barras was really thinking of keeping Bonaparte handy in Paris for use in case of political need. The general answered all the arguments just as disingenuously as regarded his own intentions. Even reduced by 40,000 men the French army would be more than adequate for any attack from abroad, granted that such an attack was possible. Europe was war-weary and in no condition to start another conflict. England, meantime, would be too busy on the road to the East to do anything on the Continent. As for Turkey, her interest in Egypt was purely nominal—Egypt was really a Mameluke despotism.

Barras was silenced but not persuaded. However, Bonaparte won the support of Talleyrand, and the Directory, after a long discussion, authorized him to begin preparations.

They were fantastically comprehensive, the thirty million that Brune had squeezed out of Switzerland covering the first outlays. Bonaparte was considering not a military raid but a permanent occupation. He besieged the Luxembourg and the War Ministry night and day, pressing through by main force the decrees and orders that he thought necessary and supervising their execution in person. His couriers burned all highways from the Atlantic to the Tiber, stirring up the arsenals, the navy yards, the army's encampments. And all that in the greatest secrecy! Europe and France were to be left in the dark as to the real design down to the very last moment. Imagining that the attack was being leveled against her coasts, England continued fortifying. The statesmen of Austria were looking for an early return of Bonaparte to Rastatt.

On the 14th of Floréal Bonaparte dined with Barras and then appeared with him at the Théâtre de la Nation where Talma was doing *Macbeth*. Thence he set out for Toulon accompanied by Josephine. On the 29th he set sail on the *Orient,* the flagship of a fleet comprising 13 ships of the line, 14 frigates and 300 transports. The roadstead at Toulon was alive with shipping. While the cannon aboard replied to salutes from the cannon ashore, the regimental bands on the transports played the "Song of the Girondins." The waterfront was packed with milling crowds. Every face was pale. It seemed that with Bonaparte and his army the genius of France was putting to sea (May 19, 1798).

By some miracle the huge fleet escaped English observation. Nelson had been keeping close watch over the coast of Provence, but exceedingly heavy weather had obliged him to take refuge under the south shore of Sardinia. The sea therefore was free. The fleet arrived at Malta on the 10th of June, seized that island, then sailed on to Crete and thence made in a straight course for Egypt.

Bonaparte spent most of his time aboard the *Orient* lying flat on his back either on deck or in his cabin. He was afraid of seasickness. Bourrienne read to him aloud —travel books, the Koran, Plutarch on Alexander the Great. Oftentimes, after luncheon, the general assembled what he called his "Institute" for long discussions. He had brought with him a whole regiment of scholars, scientists, historians, artists, writers, surveyors: Monge,

Laplace, Berthollet, Geoffroy Saint-Hilaire, Denon, Arnault. His staff comprised the best generals the Republic could boast: Kléber, Berthier, Davout, Murat, Desaix, Lannes, Duroc, most of them comrades of his debut in Italy. Bonaparte had long talks with Admiral Brueys on naval maneuvers—and, by the way, where was Nelson? He was expected to heave into view at almost any moment from the mists along the horizon. But Bonaparte had faith in his star. Standing at the rail each evening with his head resting on his elbows, he could see that star rising and rising in a bluer and bluer sky. Now it was almost at the zenith.

Nelson was surely out of luck. Sailing this way and that over the Mediterranean not once did he catch a glimpse of the French squadron.[1] By incredible good fortune it reached the offings of Egypt without incident.

Bonaparte effected a landing in a heavy sea on July 1st and at once advanced upon Alexandria, which fell at the first assault. The general made haste to reassure everybody:

"Peoples of Egypt: You will be told that I come to destroy your religion. Do not believe that. Answer rather that I come to restore your rights, to punish usurpers. Answer that my respect for Allah, for his prophet and for the Koran is greater than my respect for the Mamelukes."

Bonaparte left a small garrison at Alexandria, sent a naval expedition to take Rosetta and then ascend the Nile to rejoin the main army, and he himself started for Cairo on a trying march across the desert. The extreme

---

[1] [The main British fleet was concentrated at Gibraltar, in fear that the French expedition might be heading for the Atlantic.—A. L.]

heat, thirst, scanty provisions, dysentery, were a greater
torment to the soldiers than the skirmishing with the
enemy. A first brush at Kebris raised spirits somewhat.
Then at Embaleh, under the Pyramids, Bonaparte met
Mourad-bey in force. At that point the Mameluke chieftain had concentrated all his forces to block the road to
Cairo.

At dawn on July 21st Bonaparte galloped along the
front of his troops and he is said to have shouted, point-
ing to the first streamers of daylight: "Remember, soldiers: Forty centuries are watching you from the tips of
these pyramids." He disposed his army in hollow squares
"with donkeys and scholars in the middle." Dashing
cavalrymen, the Mamelukes charged the squares full-tilt
but without bending them. Meantime their own lines
thinned out under musket fire, while the solid shot tore
great gaps in them. Finally their desperate valor quailed.
When three-fourths of his men had fallen or else been
drowned in trying to escape across the Nile, Mourad
fled, abandoning his camp, which overflowed with booty
—horses, fine harnesses, silken garments, rugs, jeweled
weapons. The French had not lost a hundred men between killed and wounded.

Bonaparte halted at Gizeh and then entered Cairo on
the 25th. Thence he completed the conquest of Egypt
by pursuing Ibrahim-bey, the commander-in-chief of the
Mamelukes, to Salieh, where he crushed him completely,
the bey taking flight to Syria.

The day of this last victory also brought news of a
great disaster. Nelson finally discovered the whereabouts
of the French fleet and on August 1st he took it by surprise in the harbor at Aboukir. Admiral Brueys was

wounded but refused to quit his post: "A commander
must die giving orders." He was finally killed by a cannonball, his ship blowing up a few moments later. Six
thousand Frenchmen were either killed, wounded, or
taken prisoner in that great sea battle which left the army
of the East entirely cut off from France and Bonaparte
the captive of his conquest.

"Well," he reflected. "All we can do is die here, or
else go home as great as any of the ancients!"

The army seemed to be depressed for a moment by the
disaster at Aboukir. Bonaparte kept the men busy, however, with fortifications, formal reviews, minor expedi-
tions. Gradually enthusiasms returned. Meantime he was
planning nothing less than to organize the country as a
self-sustaining power capable of existing and defending
itself with its own resources. "We must learn to get along
by ourselves," he said.

Egypt was a rich country. The only problem was to
utilize her wealth. She had once been a powerful kingdom. Why could she not become even more powerful
when reorganized by modern knowledge, modern science,
modern art and industry? Bubbling over with energy,
indefatigable, Bonaparte proceeded to sow the ancient
soil of the Pharaohs with a seed of ideas, inventions, public works, that was to blossom and bear fruit in very
short season. Never had Bonaparte felt so free. "In
Egypt," he said, "I found myself released from the tram-
mels of an embarrassing civilization. I could dream anything and I had the means of realizing anything I
dreamed. I was creating a new religion. I could see myself riding out on the road to Asia on an elephant's back,

with a turban on my head, and in my hand a new Koran that I could write in any way I chose."

Passionately creative, scrupulous in all details, his activity embraced every field. While Desaix was ascending the Nile to conquer Upper Egypt, he was busy organizing a police force and a system of courts, and opening powder factories, foundries, arsenals, grain mills, bakeries, and even a printing plant that issued a newspaper. His engineers, especially Lepère, began to hunt down the courses of the old canals, while he went in person to Suez to study the project of cutting that isthmus. "Traces of the old canal are plainly visible," he reported. "There is no doubt in my mind that some day boats will be carrying goods from Alexandria to the Red Sea."

The "Institute of Egypt" had Monge for its president. It was divided into four branches—mathematics, physics, political economy, literature and the arts. Bonaparte's scholars were busy delving into the history, geography and monuments of the country, while his scientists studied its fauna, flora and mineral resources. Work was begun on an Arabic grammar and dictionary. At Rosetta Commander Broussard discovered the famous Rosetta stone, an epigraph in Greek and Egyptian which made it possible to decipher Egyptian hieroglyphics. "Everything is running along smoothly," Bonaparte wrote to the Directory. "The country is orderly and is beginning to get used to us. There is wheat, rice, hemp, sugar, cotton, indigo and coffee in abundance. The climate is very salubrious. Never has a colony offered such rich advantages." Towards the natives he followed the policy which he had promised on his arrival, trying to gain their friendship in every way. Indifferent at heart to all

61

religions, he manifested a profound deference for the Prophet and for Mussulman beliefs. In an order to his soldiers he wrote:

"You will treat mosques and the ceremonies prescribed by the Koran with the same respect that you would have for convents and synagogues, for the religions of Moses and Jesus. The Roman legions protected all religions. You will meet here customs that are different from those of Europe. You must get used to them."

He himself began a serious study of Arab rites and ceremonies. He gave orders for purchases to caravans setting out for Mecca, and conversed with the imans. He sought to revive local institutions that had all but lapsed under the despotic rule of the Mamelukes. He visited the sheiks and strove to awaken patriotic sentiments in them. He made overtures to the Copts, promising to ameliorate their lot. He instituted divans of notables in the provinces and organized tax-collecting on fair bases. His courts were managed by cadis. During his residence in Cairo the time for the annual inundation ceremony came, and he presided over the festival of the Nile with a pasha at his side, himself giving the signal for the cutting of the dike that liberated the fertilizing waters. Meantime he was inviting sheiks to celebrations of republican holidays and entertaining them in all honor at his table. Pacific conquest, in a word, after military conquest! The policy astonished and attracted the Egyptians. It was to linger long in their memories. France was popular in Egypt.

Trouble did not begin till news of a declaration of war by Turkey arrived. Under pressure from England and Russia the Sultan called all Mussulmans to arms against Bonaparte. An insurrection broke out in Cairo on October 21st, three hundred French officers and soldiers being massacred by mobs of fanatics.

Retribution was immediate and severe. Bonaparte turned his cannon on the mosque of Al-Ahzar. His columns swept the provinces back and forth. The rebellion was cowed and Egypt again submitted. Meantime the Turks were advancing on Egypt by way of Syria. Bonaparte decided to deal with them en route, for the conquest of India had not yet faded from his mind. He courted an alliance with the cherif at Mecca and sent an emissary to Tippoo-Sahib. However, the Ganges was too far away. The immediate task was to cover Egypt.

Bonaparte set out, February 10, 1799, with 13,000 men and three generals, Lannes, Kléber and Murat. After taking Al Arich the army occupied Gaza and arrived before Joppa on March 3. The town, badly defended, was stormed in one attack and put to sack. Two thousand Turkish soldiers were killed in battle and three thousand prisoners were coldly massacred for lack of supplies to feed them.

Coming to Saint John of Acre, Bonaparte found the place defended by an old schoolmate of his, Phélippeaux. He invested it, only to find that it was being victualed from the sea by English vessels under Sir Sydney Smith. It held out against all attacks. The French clung to the siege for two months, but in vain. Meantime Murat and Kléber were in contact with the Turks in the neighborhood of Nazareth. Bonaparte hurried to their aid and won a brilliant victory at Mount Tabor, April 16, 1799.

Returning to Saint John of Acre, he stubbornly resumed the siege. Had that town fallen, the East would have been his. He remarked to Bourrienne: "I will go on and rouse all Syria to arms. Then I will take Constantinople, overthrow the Turkish empire and found a new one of my own which will fix my place in history. Perhaps we shall go back to Paris by way of Vienna, annihilating the house of Austria on the way! . . ."

Dreams! Saint John of Acre did not fall. Weary of their futile efforts, the soldiers began to lose heart. The plague had broken out among them. Furious with chagrin Bonaparte finally decided to raise the siege and retreat upon Egypt. It was his first set-back, and the one perhaps that was to be of greatest weight in his destiny. "A grain of sand stopped me," he was to reflect later at St. Helena. "Had Saint John of Acre fallen, I would have changed the face of the world."

It was a long and desperate march across trackless, waterless deserts. At Joppa Bonaparte visited the sick in the French hospitals. He could not think of abandoning them to the cruelty of the Turks and suggested that incurables be put out of the way with a dosage of opium. Desgenettes, the surgeon-general, refused. "My business," he said, "is to cure human beings, not to kill them." Bonaparte moved on. The growing number of litters that carried the sick and wounded slowed up the march, which was a terrible ordeal under those blazing suns. But at last the agony was over. A mere remnant of the army arrived at Cairo, where Bonaparte was welcomed by the natives with the title of "Sultan Kebir," Great Sultan.

He had come back just in time to face a new and terrible danger. A Turkish army had gathered at Rhodes, off Alexandria, under the protection of an English fleet.

Bonaparte marched to the sea, and on July 24, 1799, completely destroyed the Turks at Aboukir, so burying the memory of the naval disaster under a victory on the same spot.

Kléber arrived on the field to take part in the action. Throwing his arms about Bonaparte's neck, he cried:

"Let me embrace you, General. You are as great as the world!"

That was the last feat of Bonaparte in Egypt. For some time he had been thinking of getting back to France. His failure in Syria had turned his eyes westward again. He had no news of Europe. The English blockade had been intercepting all his despatches to the Directory. He was so anxious to learn the situation in France that he opened negotiations with the English Admiral, Sir Sydney Smith, under pretext of arranging an exchange of prisoners. The admiral gave him a bundle of newspapers, which, for that matter, were long out of date. As the Englishman had foreseen, they overwhelmed Bonaparte. Jourdan driven back across the Rhine! Schérer beaten! Italy lost—Italy, the dearest of his conquests!

"The wretches!" he cried. "All our victories wasted! I must get home again!"

He confided his decision to Marmont:

"The situation in Europe obliges me to take this great step. . . . With me absent everything had to go wrong. . . . My return will rouse enthusiasms, give the army back a confidence that it has lost and fill all good citizens with hope in a better future."

He laid his plans in deepest secrecy. Making a fictitious appointment with Kléber, he left for him a sealed letter which named him commander of the Army of the East.

He himself, with a few intimates, went to a deserted beach near Alexandria on the night of August 22, 1799. There the party slipped aboard two little frigates and set sail for France.[1]

How did they get through the English blockade? There is no explanation. It was the same mad luck that had enabled Bonaparte to reach Egypt in the first place. Five weeks later his ships sighted the cliffs of Corsica and were soon at anchor in the bay of Ajaccio. The general stopped for seven days in his native island—the last he was ever to spend there—in order to wait for a storm to pass. Then his ships sailed on. The English were still patrolling the coast off Toulon. To avoid them Bonaparte ordered a landing at Fréjus. His feet touched French soil again on the 9th of October.

[1] [Kléber was murdered by a Mohammedan fanatic a year later, June 14, 1800. Menou, Kléber's successor in the Egyptian command, was beaten at Alexandria by Abercromby, March 21, 1801. He surrendered in August of that same year, the surviving French troops receiving the honors of war and free transport to France.—A. L.]

CHAPTER VII

The 18th of Brumaire

IT WAS A TERRIBLE SPLASH IN THE SMOOTH POND OF THE Directory. There were men, like Talleyrand, who had foreseen and desired Bonaparte's return, or who, like Fouché, were waiting for a chance to hitch their wagons to his star. But for most of them—Directors, ministers, politicians, generals—his home-coming was a great annoyance. Had it not been for Bonaparte everything would have been running smoothly in the best of all possible republics. Luck had been changing for the better during the months just past. At home the Chouans were surrendering, the Royalists in the south had been crushed, banditry was on the wane. Abroad, the Anglo-Russians had been beaten by Brune in Holland and Masséna was chasing Suvorov across the Alps. Europe would probably hole in again with thoughts of peace.

But with Bonaparte in Paris the situation of a reviving Directory became precarious. How could he be satisfied? What, for that matter, would he want? He seemed quite able to ask for anything. However exorbitant his demands might be, the nation would rally en masse to support him. The country had missed him during the year and a half that he had been tramping the sands of

Africa. There were other generals, to be sure—Masséna, Bernadotte, Moreau. But instinctively, not to say audibly, everyone thought of Bonaparte as chief of them all. Things had turned out exactly as he had foreseen. Absence, distance, exile, had removed him from the public view but only to clothe him with a luminous prestige. He was older, taller, from having won on historic soils where only the mightiest could triumph over the silence of the ages. Above his head now hovered the halo of the East. Oh, if only he would return! Then one could forget all the hardships, all the mourning. Only because of his absence had the greatness of France been shaken. Had he been present, there would have been no disasters. He would not have lost Italy (for Italy had not been recovered). He would not have allowed Europe to camp insolently along the frontiers of France. With him in command there would have been nothing but successes. His name was synonymous with victory. He was the living incarnation of a triumphant republic.

A new era was opening in public feeling in France. There had been ten years of revolutions and costly wars. The country, bled white, had lost much of its passion for liberty. It wanted peace, quiet, public order. Bonaparte seemed to be the only one capable of providing those things. He was not just a soldier skillful at feats of arms. As Italy and Egypt had both shown, he was an organizer, a diplomat, a statesman, and never had France felt such need of just those talents. There she was, the proudest nation in a world that trembled at her name, but governed worse than a little dog-kennel of the Italian Renaissance—discord, intrigue, thieving, hesitation, spinelessness! From the very depths of the country's

BERNADOTTE

heart sprang a yearning and a resolve to live again in might and in honor.

Bonaparte reached Paris at daybreak on October 24. Berthier, Monge, Berthollet and Eugene de Beauharnais rode in his carriage with him. Waiting to welcome him at home he found his mother, his brothers and sisters and—not his wife! Josephine had thought of going to meet him and she had taken the wrong road. While she drove south through Burgundy he was coming north by way of the Bourdonnais. She did not learn of her mistake till she got to Lyons.

Her brothers-in-law had been making life miserable for her in Paris. In Egypt Junot had recounted to Bonaparte all the gossip about her pre-marital escapades. Now his brothers made haste to inform him that she had been scandalously betraying him during his absence overseas. Hurt in his pride, furious, Bonaparte resolved to throw her out of doors. And yet a few days later, on her return, he succumbed at once to her charms and her tears and readily forgave her. In the brief weeks that were to intervene before Brumaire, Josephine was to be constantly at his side, suggesting, advising, expertly seconding him with her knowledge of people and of public affairs.

At the moment of Bonaparte's arrival the Directory was made up of Gohier, Barras, Siéyès, Roger-Ducos and General Moulins. In spite of its uneasiness the government decided to ignore Bonaparte's unauthorized desertion of his army and even his flouting of customs and sanitary regulations at the port of entry. The Directors were obliged to overlook such technical irregularities if they wanted to avoid an uprising in public opinion. To be rid of him again they offered him the command in

Italy. Bonaparte refused, alleging poor health and his need of a rest. In fact he kept to his house for some weeks following.

But day after day, at the mansion in the rue de la Victoire, there was just one procession of deputies, ministers, public officials, academicians, newspaper writers, military men, old comrades of the campaign in Italy. Each obtained a few minutes' conversation in the drawing-room or in the tiny work-den that opened off it. There were protestations of devotion, offers of service. Bonaparte did not refuse. Prudent, gracious, friendly, intimate, he accepted everything, but always with strings and provisos. His simplicity charmed. He sat before an open fire with a gray cape thrown over his shoulders and a house cap on his head. He had never liked to shake hands. Now he was doing little else.

He seemed natural, easy, altogether superior to any personal ambition. What interested him was the situation in France. The government had brought the nation to the brink of ruin. He spoke bitterly of the Directory as a system, but flatteringly of the individuals who composed it. Cordial towards Barras, he was deference itself towards Gohier, and all admiration for Siéyès as a constitutional expert. His attitude seemed to be that so many and such great talents needed better organization. All those scattered forces should be better co-ordinated. There was general agreement that another sort of government was called for. With a little good will on all sides all Frenchmen, however great their differences in opinion, could be brought together and made to work together. France had once been and could again be one great family, a real family, in which each individual would find his place and in which fraternal affections would prevail.

As had been his policy on his return from Italy, Bonaparte declined group invitations, public receptions. He went regularly to the Institute and supped with the disabled veterans at the Invalides. He spent one day at Malmaison, a pretty château near Paris which Josephine had bought but of which he had had a mere glimpse before leaving for Egypt. He went to see a performance of *Ariodant* at the Favart theater. He sat in a barred box that had been curtained off, but when the spectators learned that he was present, they surged upon him cheering. He managed to get away in time.

Coaxed cautiously along in this way his popularity grew and grew. Paris was already his. Let him venture out of doors and crowds gathered about him. He therefore made all his trips by carriage—a very modest carriage. His mails were stuffed with cards and notes written in a language fit to induce dizziness in a soul less balanced than his. They seemed to have no effect on him. He saw the situation clearly, weighed all pros and cons, never underestimated dangers. The political situation was becoming more and more involved each day. Cliques, combinations, deals seethed on every hand at every moment. Paris was one great stew-pot of conspiracies, each having its favorite, each its plan. Everyone agreed that a coup d'état was inevitable. But would it be Bonaparte? Would it be Siéyès? Would it be Barras? Those were the only questions, except the question as to the when and the how. Would Bonaparte back Barras, or Siéyès, or would he go it alone?

He could not make up his own mind. He had given up

71

a first idea of working into the Directory and boring from within. He had concluded that the Constitution of the Year III was out of date. Something better, something sounder, was called for. The two Councils were packed with idiots who thought that the country could be saved by voting ten different bills a day for 365 days! All that had to be swept clean and a new France built, a France big enough to make room for all Frenchmen!

And yet a resort to brute force involved too many risks. If he failed, he would be left just a mutinous and untrustworthy general. He ought to manage somehow to get into power by ostensibly legal means, and in order to do that he had to have the support of one or more of the Directors.

Should it be Barras? For a moment Bonaparte thought of that alliance, but Barras dilly-dallied. Why? Was he awaiting the outcome of negotiations that he had secretly opened with the Bourbons? Was he afraid that sooner or later Bonaparte would discard him and seize power to his own profit? One thing is certain: Barras could have had no perception of the power that lay in the rising tide of revolution. He destroyed himself by failing to make his choice. Though Bonaparte did not give up all hope in Barras's direction, he turned to Siéyès. Talleyrand, Roederer, Lucien Bonaparte, all advised that change in tactic.

Siéyès, for his part, was frankly hostile at first, but he became more pliable as the danger of a Jacobin uprising grew. Bonaparte finally called on him.

The Director was haughty, gruff, sour, Bonaparte jovial, good-natured. He compared their misunderstanding to the rivalry of two duchesses for the purchase of a

tea-stand at an auction, admired Washington and en-
vied the lot of that disinterested servant of a country.
The general's manner gradually drove the frown from
the Director's face. Siéyès opened up. Yes—he was ready
to co-operate, but he wanted to make sure that republican liberties were guaranteed. On Bonaparte's promise
that Siéyès would have an eminent position in the future
government, whatever it might be, Siéyès revealed his
famous plan, a plan that everybody was talking about,
that nobody had seen, but which, he declared, would
establish the happiness of the nation on unshakeable
foundations.

Siéyès had patiently been waiting for his hour and he
thought that it had struck. The sometime priest who had
become a regicide hated the nobles and despised the
common people. He dreamed of making France a
strongly organized but good-natured state over which
he would rule as dictator, but at a long and safe range.
The "mole of the Revolution" shunned the light of day,
preferring the cabinet conference to the forum debate,
government by influence to leadership by prestige. He
was unfortunately cursed with a faded, funereal complexion. His reticent ways, his inconclusive gestures, his
inflexible positiveness and dogmatism alienated sympathies. Well educated, even a man of letters, he was intelligent, methodical, willful. He often betrayed a pride
of which he was unaware. Among the older generation
of revolutionaries, who had calmed down and were living on their pasts, he had a great reputation for his
knowledge of the science of government, for "construc-
tive" talents. Of Siéyès Mirabeau had said: "His silence
is a public calamity." That exaggerated tribute had made

73

the man and he had improved his position by continuing to talk no more than necessary. While others were wearing themselves out in public clamor, he nursed his reputation by reticence.

On making the Directory, Siéyès thought that he was at last in a position to begin positive work on the constitutional edifice which he had been designing for ten years. "I am looking for a sword," he kept repeating. He first thought he had found one in Joubert, but Joubert was killed at Novi. Then he turned to Moreau. Just as Moreau was backing out Bonaparte suddenly sprang from the ground in Egypt. Siéyès did not like the fellow. He suspected that the general's overpowering reputation would prove to be too great a nuisance. However, with the edges smoothed away by the first contacts, Siéyès stood ready to admit that Bonaparte was the one man who could save France (and Siéyès along with France) from slavery to new demagogues, or from another danger that could be seen skulking around in the shadow of Barras—a return of the Bourbons.

Bonaparte and Siéyès met at Lucien Bonaparte's on the night of the 10th of Brumaire (November 1). They sealed their alliance and determined the form that the coup d'état was to take. Siéyès controlled the Ancients, a large following among the Five Hundred, Roger-Ducos among the Directors and several heads of departments in the bureaucracy, among them Cambacérès. Bonaparte could contribute his name, his ascendancy over the army, the cash that would be required. As president of the Five Hundred his brother Lucien would hold that body in check. With those elements in hand, the Constitution could be used to destroy itself. The Ancients would pass a bill transferring the Councils to Saint-Cloud on a pretext of protecting them from an imminent anarchist outbreak. Command of the troops would be entrusted to Bonaparte. Those developments would create a great stir among the politicians. In the hubbub it would be easy to persuade the Legislative Bodies to vote a changed system of government, which would be proclaimed to the public by notices secretly printed in advance.

What would the new government be like? Neither the ex-priest nor the general thought it wise to decide that point just then, for fear of disagreements. It was understood that there would be a temporary Consulate of three members. Two of them, Siéyès and Bonaparte, would hold the power. For the third, a figurehead, Roger-Ducos, would serve. Siéyès took it for granted that on grounds of age and experience he would have precedence over his colleague, that, in fact, the management of the state would be his while Bonaparte attended to the army. Bonaparte played to that illusion in his confederate. He was deferential towards Siéyès and seemed ready to agree to almost anything. He knew that there was enough vagueness in the arrangements to enable him to recover a free hand once the opportune moment came.

Final decisions were made during the days following. For one thing, the coup was moved along to the 18th—it had been planned for the 16th. The plotters spent the time in winning sympathies for a change in government and in neutralizing a number of ambitious or wavering generals.

Bernadotte, the enigmatic, shifty, popular, dangerous, ever dangerous Bernadotte, was the chief worry. What would he do? Would he come out openly against Bonaparte? He was quite capable of doing so, the rogue! He was hand and glove with Gohier and Moulins. He had the backing of the Jacobin wings in the two Councils, and a strong following in the Paris garrison, which was deeply enmired in the hazy republican tradition. The whole revolutionary Left would rise en masse at a word from Bernadotte. All sorts of rumors were current as to his real attitude and most of them were not favorable to Bonaparte. In spite of their old comradeship in Italy, Bernadotte kept referring to Bonaparte as the "deserter" and the "mutineer."

Joseph Bonaparte and Bernadotte had married sisters. Joseph therefore felt free to go and have it out with him. He did not succeed in winning Bernadotte's support. The general did allow him to understand that he would keep hands off unless the government appealed to him.

At seven o'clock in the morning on the 18th of Brumaire, the drive, the garden, the inner court of the mansion on the rue de la Victoire were filled with army officers in full dress. They were busily going and coming, eagerly talking. Bonaparte was in conference in his study with delegates from the Council of Ancients. They had brought him official notification of his appointment to the supreme military command and of the transfer of the Legislative Body to Saint-Cloud. He expressed his thanks, issued a few orders, then mounted a horse and started for the Tuileries, in company with Murat, Lannes and Macdonald.

The weather was perfect, the sun bright. The cortège went down to the street with horses at a walk. Dignified, erect in their saddles, determined, enthusiastic, the generals and officers made a spectacular array in their long boots, white breeches, big hats with tri-colored plumes, and braided coats on which the gleam of gold had been softened by the dusting of many campaigns. They were followed by Sebastiani's dragoons, a corps on which Bonaparte could rely, knowing that they would stand by him to the death of their last man. Passers-by on the sidewalks drew back against the walls of the buildings. People in the windows saluted and waved their hands. There was not a sound from a human voice, though a breathless excitement pervaded the atmosphere.

Leading the procession, and some thirty feet ahead of his staff, rode Bonaparte on a black horse. He wore a plain blue uniform with two pistols in his belt. Haughty, his shoulders thrown back, his face darkly tanned by the sun of Egypt, he held his eyes straight ahead. Spangles of sunlight seemed to play about his person.

He was welcomed with some cordiality by the Ancients. He addressed them briefly, then went down into the gardens of the Tuileries to review the troops that were drawn up there. Siéyès and Roger-Ducos now joined him. Barras had sent a secretary, Bottot, to represent him. Arriving in the presence of the soldiers, Bonaparte turned rudely on Bottot:

"What have they been doing with this France which I left so brilliant? I left peace, I find war. I left victories, I find defeats. I left the millions of Italy, I find impoverishment and confiscatory taxes. What has become of a hundred thousand Frenchmen, who were all my comrades in glory? They are dead!"

Bottot was terror-stricken and took to his heels. Frightened in his turn, Barras hastily wrote his resignation at the suggestion of Talleyrand and Admiral Bruix, and went into hiding at Grosbois. There came not a sound from the city. Bernadotte had not moved.

So the first act in the coup d'état ran off like clockwork.

The second almost came to grief. On the morning of the 19th, Bonaparte went to Saint-Cloud and there joined Siéyès and his other friends. The Councils went into session at two o'clock, the Ancients in the luxurious Gallery of Apollo, the Five Hundred in the Orangerie. The two bodies were stewing with an excitement which was definitely hostile to Bonaparte, especially in the Five Hundred. He decided to appear before them and face the music.

He went first to the Ancients. Nervous, stage-struck, he spoke haltingly, disconnectedly:

"Citizens: You are sitting on a volcano. . . . I have come to your rescue. . . . I hear calumnies all about me . . . talk about Caesar, talk about Cromwell! . . . There is no time to lose. . . . You must act promptly. . . . I stand ready here to execute your decisions. . . . Let us save liberty! . . ."

"How about the Constitution?" interrupted Linglet.

Taken aback, Bonaparte stopped. His bronzed cheeks flamed. Finally he shouted:

"The Constitution! But you have destroyed the Constitution yourselves. You violated it on the 18th of Fructidor! You violated it on the 22nd of Floréal! You violated it on the 30th of Prairial! The Constitution! . . ."[1]

Once more he halted, flustered. He was conscious of shrinking to nothing in the presence of those lawyers, a

[1] [Allusions to political battles which had purged the Directory of unpopular figures on May 11 and June 18. For the 18th of Fructidor, see above, p. 46.—A. L.]

race of men that he despised. He felt powerless. What more than anything else tied his tongue was his terror at finding himself so inadequate to the situation. Logically, he should have denounced the anarchist plot, since his ostensible purpose was to ask for extraordinary measures to deal with it. But he knew perfectly well that no such plot existed. So he merely stammered:

"I feared for the Republic. I have joined my brothers in arms. . . ."

Then beating his hollow chest, he protested:

"I am not an intriguer. You know me well. I believe I have given proof enough of my devotion to the country. If I am a traitor, it is for you, all of you, to be my Brutuses."

Bonaparte knew how to talk to soldiers. He was out of his element in haranguing an assembly of politicians. Pandemonium was let loose in the hall. Motions and countermotions were shouted at a president who was powerless to preserve order. Finally in the hubbub Bonaparte began to speak again. He had suddenly remembered a sentence that he had one day hurled at a divan in Cairo:

"Remember! I march with the god of Fortune and the god of War!"

The assembly booed as one man. It felt insulted. Bonaparte had not sensed that words that had laid Arabs full length on the floor before him had no such potency over Frenchmen.

Bourrienne gave a pull at one of his coattails:

"Come, General, let's get away. You don't realize what you're saying . . ."

Bonaparte made a gesture that might have been taken as a salute, then he withdrew.

The moment he was across the threshold he recovered his nerve. He hurried to the Five Hundred.

The chair was held by Lucien Bonaparte, but he had not been able to steer things. The hall was in an uproar. Most of the representatives were on their feet, standing around the room with their backs to the stone walls. Draped in scarlet togas in Roman style they were shouting and gesticulating. Bonaparte slipped in among them, his hat in his hand. For a time he passed unobserved. Then suddenly a mighty shout arose, and it seemed to nail him to the floor:

"Down with the Dictator! Down with the tyrant! Outlaw! Outlaw!"

Lucien stood wildly ringing his bell for order. To no avail! Ten, a dozen, a score of deputies were upon Bonaparte. They had him by the collar and were shaking him, howling insults into his face. The strain on the collar cut off his breath. He paled and was about to faint. He would have fallen had not Murat with his grenadiers seen his peril and rushed in, elbowing their way into the press about him, thrusting the deputies aside and tearing him free from the hands that clutched him. It was a humiliating scuffle between soldiers and deputies that left uniforms and togas in rags. The spectators poured over the balustrades of the grandstands and joined in the mêlée. The little troop that had rescued Bonaparte backed away with its booty towards the door. He was outside, at last, half fainting. "Outlaw! Outlaw!" came the chant of three hundred hoarse voices. "Outlaw!" The cry that had spelled doom for Robespierre!

LUCIEN BONAPARTE
From the Portrait by Lefevre

Clear, sharp, sonorous, hammered syllable by syllable, it poured through the doors and reached the troops: "Outlaw!" As Bonaparte walked past the soldiers not a cheer rose from their serried ranks.

He felt that the game was up, but he none the less refused to resort to force. He could rely on his own men—but how about the Council Guard? To persuade it to turn on the representatives of the law some legal pretext would be necessary.

Just then Lucien sent Frégeville, a deputy, to warn Bonaparte that unless the session of the Five Hundred were broken up, he would not answer for the consequences. Bonaparte sent a detachment of soldiers to fetch Lucien.

On his brother's departure, Lucien had tried in every possible way to avoid putting the motion to outlaw Bonaparte to vote. He talked as president, he tried to talk as a deputy. Jostled, pummeled, he did not budge an inch, standing his ground frantically, gaining minute after minute with sentence after sentence. Finally, however, he was overborne by sheer numbers. But he did not lose his head. He tore off his robe, cast it upon the speaker's desk with his blue cap and his tricolored scarf, and declared in a tone of helpless misery:

"I give up trying to get a hearing! There is no liberty here! I hereby lay aside, in sign of mourning, these emblems of the people's magistracy!"

A tumult of boos was his answer.

But the door opened. An officer, followed by ten soldiers appeared. Thunderstruck, the Assembly fell silent. The soldiers dragged Lucien from the speaker's desk to which he clung desperately. They carried him off, without a move on the part of the deputies to resist a kidnaping that transferred from them to Bonaparte the visible symbol of legality.

The general sat mounted on his horse on the esplanade beyond the terrace, along which Serurier's infantry and Sebastiani's dragoons stood deployed. A thunder of applause had greeted his appearance there. His eyes shining, sunken, his face bleeding from the scratches he had received, he galloped up and down in front of his soldiers, shouting words of fury that sent their hearts leaping in rhythm with his hate. He was accusing the Five Hundred of trying to murder him. Lucien appeared, surrounded by his rescuers. He leapt upon a horse lent by a dragoon and dashed to his brother's side. Standing up in his stirrups in front of the grenadiers of the Directory, he cried in a thundering voice:

"Soldiers of the Republic: The President of the Five Hundred declares to you that the immense majority of that Council is temporarily under terror from a few armed members who have seized the speaker's desk. Threatening death to their colleagues they are forcing through the most atrocious measures. I declare to you that those shameless brigands have been bought with English money. They have come out in rebellion against the Council of Ancients and are trying to outlaw the general who has been commissioned to execute its decrees. . . . I entrust to you warriors the deliverance of that majority. . . . Those brigands no longer represent the people. They represent the knife!"

A wordy, nonsensical speech that was to be recognized as such by nightfall! At the moment it served to pull Bonaparte out of his pickle. The grenadiers were swept off their feet, persuaded. Lucien reached for a sword and resting the point on Bonaparte's breast proclaimed, with grandiloquent ferocity, that he would shove it home were his brother ever to make one move against Liberty. The guard answered with a hearty cheer for Bonaparte. Murat had brought up the infantry and the dragoons to listen to what was being said. His men took up the cry and it became uncontrollable. It ended as Bonaparte suddenly ordered the charge. A rolling of drums, brutal, harsh, filled the court. Murat lined up a column of grenadiers and placed himself at its head, his sword drawn. They marched on the Orangerie at double quick.

The drums continued to roll. The Five Hundred sat listening on their benches. The tumult drew nearer. Silent, they looked into one another's eyes. The audience vanished from the stands like water running out of a vase. Now the high vaulted windows of the Orangerie shook with the drumbeats, and a clatter of military heels on the pavements was plainly audible. Soon the grenadiers appeared, four abreast, with fixed bayonets. The drums continued beating. Murat's sonorous voice made itself heard above the clangor:

"Citizens, you are dissolved!"

The members rose in a body and shouted:

"Long live the Republic! Long live the Constitution of the Year III!"

On the speaker's platform a number of deputies shook their fists and admonished:

"Soldiers, you are soiling your laurels!"

The drums continued beating. A throng of red-togaed

deputies backed slowly away with shaking fists before the press of grenadiers:

"Grenadiers—forward!"

The members vanished as if by magic from the speaker's platform. Murat stood up on a bench:

"Soldiers, clean that rubbish out of the place! (*Fichez-moi tout ce monde-là dehors.*)"

The grenadiers crossed their bayonets. There was a clatter of over-turning chairs. In unseemly disorder the members scattered, seeking any way out. In groups of five, six, they leapt through the open windows, terrified, grotesque, tossing aside their red togas, their plumed caps, their insignia. Night was falling. A torch appeared here and there, smoky, tragic. The drums continued beating.

The rest was routine. While the guard watched at the gates of the château, the conquerors legalized their victory. Lucien appeared before the Ancients and announced the dissolution at his order of the Five Hundred. The Ancients proceeded to designate three "consuls," Bonaparte, Siéyès, Roger-Ducos. As an afterthought, in order to preserve all possible appearances of regularity, Lucien decided that it was better to have the ratification of the Five Hundred also. Saint-Cloud was combed for such deputies as had not fled. Hustled into the Orangerie again they submissively approved the acts of the Ancients. At two in the morning the new consuls took their oaths of fidelity to the Republic, and Bonaparte went back to Paris, worn out, in a raging fever, but with France in his hands.

CHAPTER VIII

The Consulate

THE FOUR AND A HALF YEARS OF THE CONSULATE, November 11, 1799, to May 18, 1804, are the most brilliant, perhaps, in all French history. A regenerate country stepped forth from a morass of blood and mire before a Europe of whom new victories had at last exacted respect. At home it was a matter of political and administrative reorganization, of religious peace, of economic revival. Abroad it was glory and then more glory. One has to go back to the youthful days of Louis XIV to find such resurgent vitality, such splendor.

The France that Bonaparte took in hand on the morning of the 20th of Brumaire had a pulse so weak as scarcely to be detectable. There was chaos everywhere. Trade and industry were at a standstill. Only an eighth of the man-power that had been employed in 1789 was still employed. The peasants had torn up the paved roads to provide stone walls for their newly acquired lands. Bridges were everywhere out of repair. Cultivated fields had become brush and marsh. Fleets of vessels were rotting at their moorings in the ports of Le Havre, Bordeaux and Marseilles, which were themselves clogged with shifting sands. The hospitals were short of bandages.

The army, which had been giving such a magnificent account of itself, had disintegrated. Left without food and without pay the soldiers were deserting in groups, sometimes to swell the ranks of the bandits who levied toll on the great highways of the south and west. Brittany and the Vendée were defying the Republic to come and conquer their deserts. The public treasury was empty. On the first day of the Consulate it developed that the Republic had just 137,000 francs in cash at its disposal! It had paid no pensions and no interest on loans for two years. The public was discouraged, indifferent. The depression that had set in in 1789 had been too long and too severe. Other less resilient countries might have succumbed to such a trial. France did not succumb. Her flesh bruised and torn, she still kept to her feet.

Bonaparte pulled her together. Under his strong hand she molded herself into a new, her modern, form. He set to work the morning after the coup d'état and began to demonstrate that his keen and practical intelligence, his enormous capacity for work, were as serviceable in matters of government and administration as they had been in war.

His first step was to discard the famous constitution which Siéyès had been compiling. He found it too involved, too vague. It would tie his hands to a futile system of representation. He forced through another which gave him the title of First Consul and virtually autocratic power. Siéyès was disappointed, hurt. He sulked and then resigned, Roger-Ducos going with him. Bonaparte replaced his two colleagues with a Second Consul, Cambacérès, and a Third Consul, Lebrun. They did not count as against the First Consul, but they were splendid executives in the departments of justice and finance. Suffrage was narrowly limited, and the three elective bodies, the Tribunate, the Legislative Body and the Senate, were reduced, by the very complexity of their interlocking, to mere cogs in a machine of which Bonaparte was the sole motive power. The Constitution of the Year VIII seemed to set up a sort of Roman Republic. Actually it set up a monarchy, leaving the country the merest semblance of freedom.

The new constitution was proclaimed by a message from the Consuls. Bonaparte wrote most of the text:

"Citizens: The Revolution remains fixed on the principles which inspired it. It is now over." The government's policy would be "to endear the Republic to its citizens, win respect for it abroad, inspire its enemies with fear."

Those were not words only. The policy was carried out to the letter and at once. A plebescite gave Bonaparte three million votes against 1500. Strong in that approval, he centralized administration much more compactly than it had been under the old régime. In that direction he went even farther than the Convention had gone. There were to be a prefect and a general council in each department, and a mayor and a municipal council in each commune. Everything tapered up to Paris, which appointed and removed. The courts were organized along the same lines: justices of the peace, trial courts, appellate courts, with a supreme Court of Revision. The jury system was installed for crimes and misdemeanors—a reminiscence of Constituent Assembly reforms. In order to complete the legislative program of the Revolution, of which he felt himself to be the heir and said as much, the First Consul appointed a commission of eminent jurists, Tronchet, Bigot de Préameneu and Portalis, to blend in a Civil Code all laws and precedents bearing on the legal status of individuals and on their social relations. Along with Cambacérès he took an active part in the work of this commission. Other codes —the Code of Civil Procedure, the Code of Criminal Information, the Code of Commerce, finally a Penal Code, gradually rounded out this monumental edifice (which became complete in 1810). It still forms the basis of French private law, and many modern countries have imitated it.

In the field of finance the new régime retained the former taxes of the Constituent Assembly and the Directory—taxes on real estate, on personal property, on trade licenses, on doors and windows. There were custom duties and stamp taxes on registries, contracts and other documents. To facilitate credit operations, Bonaparte established the Bank of France, which discounted commercial obligations and issued a paper currency that was guaranteed by funds of precious metals. Higher education, finally, was also centralized as a prerogative of the State. The University of France had jurisdiction over secondary schools and institutions of professional and higher learning. Primary education was left to private initiative. This last was a singular omission. It indicates that the government was not eager to propagate enlightenment among the masses.

The ministry which Bonaparte gathered about him contained men as opposite in views as Carnot and Talleyrand, Lucien and Fouché, Decrès and Gaudin. That showed the concern of the First Consul to unite all parties in one association. He would have nothing to do with Jacobins, Moderates, Royalists. He wanted "Frenchmen short and simple." "To govern in the interests of a party," said he shortly after the Brumaire coup, "is in the end to become its slave. They will not catch me there. I am strictly *national*."

Outstanding in the administration were two figures, Talleyrand, Minister of Foreign Relations, and Fouché, Minister of Police. Bonaparte inherited them from the Directory and he kept them—he kept them for a long time, for too long a time, in a sound appreciation of their capacities, in gratefulness for services rendered, in fear, also, of the intrigues they would all the more easily weave about him and against him if they were ever driven into opposition.

For that matter they intrigued just the same. They intrigued under the Consulate. They intrigued under the Empire. At all the critical junctures which Napoleon was to face he found them both ready to upset him and provide a successor for him if he stumbled. Those two men were the only ones in Bonaparte's entourage who could really be called statesmen. They had political temperaments, ideas, general views. They were always looking ahead, far ahead. In spite of the crushing superiority of "the chief," they managed to cut out important positions for themselves. At the peak of his power, first the Consul and then the Emperor always knew that he had to reckon with them.

Charles Maurice de Talleyrand-Périgord was a member of the most ancient nobility. He had been bishop of Autun. Believing neither in God nor in the Devil, neither in King nor in The People, he saw nothing inconsistent with his cloth in saying Mass at the Festival of the Federation in 1789. However, he had an eye to his neck and to his ease, and without seeming to emigrate he slipped away from France to the United States and did not return till the Terror was good and over. Mme. de Staël pushed him into the Ministry of Foreign Relations through Barras. He was probably the first to discover Bonaparte. It was he who warned Bonaparte in Egypt that the moment for his return seemed to have come. From then on he helped the "man on horseback" in every way possible to work the coup d'état.

Talleyrand was a man of a disdainful, indolent intelligence, but it was acute and in all respects of a high order. From the tip of his clubfoot to his powdered hair he was and remained an aristocrat. In a rage one day Napoleon was to call him "a silk stocking filled with s—." That came pretty close to the fact. Talleyrand was a bundle of vices. No promise ever worried him, no emotion ever swayed him. His needs, which were boundless, he covered by graft and peculation carried to unprecedented extents. But he was never without his graceful manner or his death's-head smile which gave pause even to Napoleon the Almighty. At the time of Brumaire he was forty-five, with an immense experience of things, men and countries. He knew the old diplomacy, its ways, its methods, its language. After the storm of the Revolution he was about the only man left in France who could still talk to Europe. Himself incurably lazy, he had a faculty for making others work. Of an imperturbable coolness, with an instinct that was quick and unfailing, that accomplished cynic might have become an

TALLEYRAND
From the Portrait by Prud'hon

admirable public servant for his country had he been able ever to think beyond himself, his own interests, fortune and power. He went along with Napoleon's policies as far as Tilsit. Then when the master's eyes were opened to his double-faced dealings, he was to turn traitor without once losing his outward semblance of devotion, coldly betray the Emperor and wait for a turn of the wheel of Fortune that would lift him to the top rank again and—who could say?—leave him as regent and virtual king of France.

Fouché offered a perfect contrast to Talleyrand. Of petty bourgeois origins, he had been an Oratorian novice, though he had never gone as far as the vows. Under the Terror he distinguished himself by a free use of grapeshot at Lyons, then to save his own neck he wove the plot that sent Robespierre to the guillotine. After a number of dubious twistings and turnings he crept obscurely into public office under the Directory and came to appear to everyone, Bonaparte included, as a master detective, as the genius of the police. A bloodless individual, with thin closed lips and the eyes of a fish, Fouché was in fact a versatile though slippery person of immense ability and, when occasion required, of tireless energy. Orderly, accurate, hard-working, keen, he was a hard man indeed ever to catch napping. His sense of what was going on never failed him—nor his good judgment either. He knew the strong points and the weak in everyone about him. He was eager to help the right people, created obligations on all sides, then watched for his chance and took it without being troubled by the slightest remembrance or scruple. The Revolution stamped him as a Jacobin. In the councils of the Empire he was to represent the old spirit of the Convention and he derived a strange power from it, which was to win him consideration from one régime after the other. However, for lack of a free stage he was never to display his capacities to the full. Napoleon was always suspicious of him, though he could not help paying tribute to his talents. He was to dismiss him and then take him back again—a twin mistake; for men like Fouché must either be coddled or be shot. They can be used only as long as they know that they are under a firm hand. A moment too late and they have already betrayed and ruined you.

CHAPTER IX

Marengo

Bonaparte could not conceive of order apart from security. France could catch her breath and become great only in a quiet Europe. At the moment two enemies were still in the field against her, Austria and England. Russia to all intents and purposes had deserted the coalition.

The First Consul offered peace to the two foes, but, with the whole country behind him, he wanted a peace that would not come too high. "This war," he wrote nobly to the King of England, "has been ravaging the four quarters of the globe for eight years. Is it to be everlasting? Is there no basis on which we can come to an understanding? Our two countries are the most enlightened in Europe. They are far stronger, far more powerful, than their safety and independence require. Do they not feel that peace is the first of their needs as well as the first of their glories?"

Pitt was head of the British cabinet. He replied with a demand that the brother of Louis XVI be recalled to France and placed on the throne. Vienna made the same demand. Bonaparte could do nothing but fight.

The Austrians were in the field before Strasburg and in the direction of Nice and gave signs of taking the offensive. Bonaparte put Moreau at the head of a hundred thousand of his best men, ordered him to march through southern Alsace to Basel, where he would cross the Rhine. In Italy Masséna was directed to hold Mélas with the remnants of Joubert's army, which had been beaten at Novi. The general shut himself in at Genoa, gained time, and so allowed Bonaparte to mobilize a reserve corps of drafted troops and get them to the foot of the Alps.

In order to take the Austrians off guard, Bonaparte made a surprise march into Italy by way of the Great Saint-Bernard, dragging his guns and baggage wagons through deep snow over an incredibly difficult terrain. Despite a brief delay before a fort at Bard, he soon overran all the enemy outposts. He was in Milan, triumphant, and had re-established the Cisalpine Republic before Mélas, still on the Var, had any idea of what was going on.[1]

Cut off from his bases, Mélas came hurriedly marching east with 77,000 men and more than a hundred guns. Bonaparte had 25,000 men and fifteen guns. He received the shock on the plain at Marengo (June 14, 1800).

The evening before the battle Bonaparte had imprudently separated Desaix's division from his army. He hastened to recall it, but before Desaix arrived the engagement was all but lost. Mélas was so sure of the outcome that he reported a victory at Vienna, while a mysterious courier set out for Paris with word that the Consul had been defeated. After six hours of brutal fighting Bonaparte ordered a retreat. But just then

[1] [Bonaparte left Paris on May 6, 1800, and was in Milan on June 2. The army crossed the Alps May 15-23.—A. L.]

Desaix came on the scene with his men fresh. That re-inforcement decided the battle. The Austrians gave ground and left the field to the French.

Desaix was killed as he came charging into the battle. After the victory an officer asked the Consul why he was so sad. Bonaparte replied with brimming eyes:

"It's Desaix! What a day if Desaix were here for me to embrace him!"

Discouraged, Mélas signed a truce at Alessandria. Bonaparte left the command in Italy to Masséna and made haste to return to Paris. The city lighted up on news of his arrival. It was in fact time. Fouché, a group of generals who had scented disaster, and even Bona-parte's own brothers, were making plans to replace him. A glance from the First Consul was enough to set them in order, but he was never to forget that in spite of all the love and trust that the country had shown him, his power depended on the issue of a battle. From that mo-ment his constant thought was of so binding himself to France that the knot would withstand even a serious reverse.

While the second campaign in Italy was resulting in victory, Moreau had won at Hochstädt and Feldkirch. Would those occurrences bring the peace that all Europe longed for? England would not consent to it. She ad-vanced two million and a half pounds to Austria and negotiations were broken off. The fighting began again in Germany. In spite of his inferiority in numbers, Moreau kept the Archduke John guessing by skillful marches and counter-marches and finally fell upon him and beat him decisively at Hohenlinden. Thence he marched on to Salzburg and Linz, and Vienna was in danger. Meantime Augereau was invading Bohemia and Macdonald was advancing in the Tyrol.

The Emperor Francis was terrified and ordered that negotiations be reopened. Cobenzl tried to dispute possession of the Rhine to the French but Bonaparte settled the question. In a speech before the Legislative Body he declared: "The left bank of the Rhine will be the frontier of the Republic. If good faith is again violated, we shall go on to Prague, Vienna and Venice." Austria yielded. A treaty was signed at Lunéville, February 9, 1801. By it Campo-Formio became a thing of the past. France was left mistress of Italy as far as the Adige, while Austria resigned supremacy over the German league. The French monarchy had never dreamed of obtaining such a peace. It remains the most glorious that France has ever dictated.

Bonaparte's popularity soared on high. The country, to use an expression of the days of the League, was infatuated, rather than in love, with him. Not only had he made France the leading power in Europe. He had restored the country's natural productivity and resourcefulness. Good times were returning. Factories were reopening. Men were at work repairing bridges, roads, canals. With money in the Treasury, bondholders began receiving their interest again. Exiles were flocking home. Their properties, which had been seized under the Revolution, were going back to them. Religious pacification was in sight. Conversations had been opened with Rome the day after Marengo.

Nevertheless that was a dangerous moment for the First Consul. On the Left a shifting, formless opposition was organizing through a fusion of old revolutionary

THE BATTLE OF MARENGO
By Général Lejeune

elements with everybody else—ambitious ministers, jealous generals, impatient tribunes, who were enraged at seeing Bonaparte gaining in power and consolidating it. Siéyès, Fouché, Carnot, Benjamin Constant, La Fayette, Bernadotte, Masséna, Augereau, were all busily at work. Meanwhile the Royalists plotted time after time to rid themselves of the one obstacle which, they thought, still stood between them and a Bourbon homecoming.

Early in the Consulate they had an idea that Bonaparte might lend himself to a re-establishment of the monarchy. The future Louis XVIII, then Comte de Lille, wrote to him from Prussia, where he was living as a refugee, urging him to play the rôle of Monk. The First Consul declined:

"Monsieur, I am in receipt of your letter. I thank you for the many kind words which you have for me personally. However, you should not think of returning to France. You could do so only by marching over a hundred thousand dead. Sacrifice your personal interest to the peace and well-being of France! History will place the act to your credit."

Bonaparte had attained power in open combat. It was folly to imagine—as Josephine, right at his side, was imagining—that he was the man to sell out for a title and a fortune in money.

In exasperation at the spectacle of so many exiles returning to Paris and deserting to the government, the Royalist leaders decided to make an end of the business. In the early evening of the 3rd of Nivose (December 24, 1800), Saint-Réjant, Carbon and Limoëlan, all of the Chouan party, set off a powerful bomb in the rue Saint-Nicaise while the First Consul was passing on his way to the Opera. By a mere chance he escaped, but twenty people were killed and fifty hurt by the explosion.

Bonaparte was angry at the time with the Jacobins. He at once charged them with the attempt on his life. Fouché vainly pleaded. Bonaparte retorted:

"Nobody is going to pull the wool over my eyes. The Chouans, the exiles, have nothing to do with this business. I know who did it. I will catch them, and they are going to get what they deserve."

He was, in fact, as severe as he was unjust. A hundred and thirty-two prominent republicans were arrested, put aboard ship and deported to the Seychelle Islands, whence very few of them were ever to return. All the same Fouché proved his own point. He arrested Saint-Réjant and Carbon and their confessions amply proved that the plot was Royalist. That did not induce Bonaparte to change his decision, however. He was mainly concerned to rid himself of the Left opposition, which was the one he had most reason to fear. Any pretext that served that purpose was good enough.

However plainly the followers of the old régime had manifested their attitude towards him, the First Consul did not abandon his policy of reconciliation. The frontiers were opened wider and wider to exiled Frenchmen; and soon, July 16, 1801, over the heads of an anti-clerical opposition which was powerful in the legislative assemblies and at the Institute, he concluded the Concordat.

That act, which liberated hosts of consciences, reproduced in its essentials the old concordat of Francis I. The Pope recognized the seizures of Church properties, which had become properties of the state. In compensation bishops and priests were to receive salaries from the government and bishops were to be named by agreement between the government and the Holy See. This measure brought the whole French clergy under the thumb of the executive power. Badly received by many army men and civil employees, who still remembered the days of the Supreme Being and the Goddess Reason, the concordat was hailed with joy by an immense public majority. Despite its many omissions and defects, the document was to guarantee religious peace to the country for a full century.

Only England was still left at war with France, but now that she had to do the fighting herself her resolve seemed to waver. She had managed to drive the French out of Egypt as soon as Kléber had been assassinated. She had retaken Malta and was in possession of the French colonies. However, her treasury was empty and her people, over-burdened with taxes, were calling for peace. Bonaparte had had the brilliant and noble idea of sending home eight thousand Russian prisoners with new uniforms and new guns. Czar Paul was delighted with the gesture and came forward as an outspoken admirer of the First Consul. The Czar's League of Neutrals was beginning to look like a serious menace to England. Bonaparte meantime had gathered a light fleet at Boulogne and Nelson had not succeeded in destroying it. Fear was as great in London as it had been in Vienna. Pitt, the unchangeable enemy of the French, was therefore driven from power and his successor, Addington, at once opened negotiations with France.

CHAPTER X

The Peace of Amiens

T HE RESULT WAS THE TREATY OF AMIENS, WHICH WAS signed March 25, 1802, by Joseph Bonaparte. It was a capital moment in the history of Europe. For the first time since the outbreak of the Revolution peace reigned over the whole Continent. England recognized the French Republic, restored its colonies, promised to evacuate Malta and Egypt. There was no mention of Italy and the left bank of the Rhine. Implicitly the treaty asquiesced in those conquests.

The settlement was hailed with enthusiasm on both sides of the Channel and no one was more sensible to the greatness of the moment than Bonaparte himself. In a proclamation "To the French" he cried: "At last you have in full the peace that you have deserved by your long and high-hearted endeavors. . . . Let us crown the glory of battle with a glory that is sweeter to our citizens and less fraught with fear to our neighbors. Let us teach the rising generations to love our institutions and our laws. . . . Let us carry into the workshops of agriculture and the arts the eagerness, the steadfastness of purpose, the firmness that have astounded Europe at all our critical moments. . . . Let us be a bond between the peoples that are about us and an example to them."

In those words Bonaparte was not speaking for himself alone. He was voicing a yearning of the nation. He was never to strike a loftier note. Having finished the most fearful revolution that the world had witnessed, France was laying aside her arms and taking a seat, radiant, at the fireside of Europe. Abroad the glory of the First Consul was such that it wrung admiration from the enemies of yesterday. Beethoven was quite in the current in dedicating his "Heroic Symphony" to him. At home the country was satisfied in virtual unanimity with a government that was recovering some of the better of the old monarchical institutions and founding a new order that was sounder, more logical than the old, and better adapted to modern needs.

However, all that structure was very fragile. It rested on one man who had received his mandate for a limited period. Issuing from such troublous times the country was hungry for stability. Bonaparte was not unaware of that. He desired an extension of his magistracy, but was loath to ask for it—a false step might break his hold on public opinion.

A year before Lucien had prompted the servile pen of Fontanes to write a pamphlet called "A Parallel between Caesar, Cromwell, Monk and Bonaparte." It had aroused such bitter criticism that the First Consul had seen fit to remove his brother from his post as Minister of the Interior. In the assemblies, the government, the army even, many important men were opposed to any extension of Bonaparte's powers. Tronchet, who had defended Louis XVI at his trial, remarked to Cambacérès one day:

"This young man is starting out like Caesar. I am afraid he will end like Caesar."

Partly, perhaps, out of shrewd instinct, partly out of devotion, Cambacérès was trying to please Bonaparte in everything. He may have been sincere. He was an intimate of the First Consul and was better aware than anybody else of the man's superiority. He therefore undertook to manage the delicate matter on the occasion of the legislative ratification of the Treaty of Amiens. Fouché blocked him, however. Manipulated by the Minister of Police the Senate refused to grant more than a ten year extension to the First Consul. Bonaparte was dissatisfied and about to refuse when Cambacérès, who was a resourceful legalist, thought of another expedient. He pledged the Council of State in advance and then had it call for a plebiscite on the question, "Should Napoleon Bonaparte be Consul for life?" The response of the people (August 2, 1802) was more enthusiastic than had been foreseen. The affirmative won by 3,568,000 votes to 8000. France was paying the man who had saved her, and wholeheartedly!

Proclaimed Consul for life by the Senate, Bonaparte proceeded to amend the Constitution of the Year VIII, introducing electoral colleges with life terms,[1] stronger prerogatives for the Senate, reduced powers for the Tribunate (which became a sort of pendant to the Council of State), a Privy Council, the right of the First Consul

1 [To simplify the election mechanism "electoral colleges" made up of notables were designated by universal suffrage to vote on national issues. Communal or local colleges comprised 10 percent of the total electorate, departmental colleges ten per cent of the communal colleges.—A. L.]

to designate his successor, power of amnesty and pardon to the Consul, and a consular civil list of six millions. A king in fact if not in name! Such had Bonaparte become for France and for Italy. Safe henceforth against all intrigue, satisfied with his grandeur and with the country's confidence, he had only to think of the new glory that was to spring, as he thought and hoped, from the achievements of peace.

It was in fact a glorious year. The Legion of Honor was founded to replace the old royal orders. Society came to life in the capital. Paris was a humming, booming city. The budget was balanced that year at the 1789 level, with a surplus of 500 millions, which surtaxes raised to 625 millions. The farmers were in a flourishing condition. Far-reaching enterprises in housing were launched to provide work for veterans retired from the armies. New towns were springing from the ground, and old ones were carting away their ruins and rebuilding. The colonies were set in order again. General Decaen was despatched to India. The revolt of the blacks in Santo Domingo was crushed. Louisiana was beginning to amount to something. Such the record of that marvelous year. France eagerly stretched her rested limbs, took a deep breath and smiled.

Peace was necessary—but would it last? England looked upon the settlement of Amiens as a mere truce. In signing it Addington had actually said: "Let us conserve our strength for some future occasion when we can resume the offensive successfully." The boom in French industry was a nuisance to British manufacturers. That was why, with an eye to protecting French trade, the First Consul had declined to sign a commercial treaty with England.

Bonaparte's colonial outlook was viewed with anger in London. The Commons heard mention of "a Gallic colossus towering over the new world with one foot on the Amazon and the other on the Mississippi." France was still in Antwerp and Amsterdam, for Holland had not as yet been evacuated. All that was a worry to England, and it was not in the English tradition to enjoy worrying. Foreseeing a resumption of hostilities, in fact seeking pretexts for resuming hostilities, the cabinet at St. James did not execute essential clauses in the Treaty of Amiens. It held on at Malta, which it had promised to restore to the Knights. It was still pensioning the Bourbon princes and harboring the Chouans—chief among them, Cadoudal. It was allowing Royalist pamphleteers to insult the French government.

Bonaparte thought he had been fooled. Perhaps he should have been patient, allowing time to heal old wounds, soften animosities that had long been keen. But he was young. Such power as he held could not have failed to intoxicate the soberest head. He replied to the bad faith of the British by measures which alarmed Europe, provided England with new allies and so enabled her to tear up the treaty with more assurance. He tightened his grip on Italy by annexing Piedmont. He forced Switzerland to transact her foreign affairs through him. By negotiations that were to result eventually in the *Recès de l'Empire,* he suppressed ecclesiastical domains on the left bank of the Rhine and organized that territory as part of the French system.

The tension between London and Paris grew. The governments debated, the embassies threatened. Talleyrand sent Addington a veritable ultimatum. War plants were strengthened on both sides. On March 13, 1803, in the presence of the diplomatic corps, Bonaparte laid angry hands on Whitworth, the English envoy, shook him and cried, his face flaming:

"So it's war you want? We have been fighting for ten years. You want us to fight for ten years more? Curses on people who do not keep their agreements!" And as he strode from the room he called back: "Malta or war!"

War was unavoidable. He was now convinced of that. He therefore changed his plans at once. The French navy was too weak. It could not cope with the English fleets. He gave up his colonial ambitions, accordingly, selling Louisiana to the United States for 54 millions and recalling the army in Santo Domingo. However, he made a last desperate effort to preserve peace. Whitworth had already received his passports and was on the way to Calais when he was handed an offer for England to keep Malta for ten years. He made no answer.

When Whitworth reached London, the English capital broke into warlike enthusiasm. Pitt addressed the Commons with a bitter, contemptuous denunciation of France. Fox spoke in admiration of Bonaparte, but his rejoinder had no effect. On May 16th an Order in Council laid an embargo on all French ships in the ports of the United Kingdom—a flagrant violation of the law of nations. To it the First Consul replied by ordering the arrest of all English subjects in France and directing Mortier to occupy Hanover, a hereditary possession of King George III.

After all that, war was the only alternative and it would be a fight to the finish. All Europe understood that. In the terrible duel that was to ensue between the mistress of the seas and the master of the Continent there was to be neither truce nor quarter. All the trickery, all the tenacity, all the wealth that England had at her disposal was to be called into play to destroy her enemy. Coalition was to succeed coalition. Napoleon was to win in vain. English hatred was always raising new armies against him, until one day, dashing across an exhausted Continent, the great captain was himself to stumble, and England was to find herself in a position where she could rally all peoples against French tyranny. So after a debauch of genius, with several serious mistakes, deserted by a Fortune of whom he had received too much and was presuming too much, assailed by too many enemies, badly served, betrayed, worn out, Napoleon was to sink to the ground.

CHAPTER XI

The Duc d'Enghien

WHERE COULD HE STRIKE—AT ONCE, DECISIVELY? HE thought of the plan he had been considering before his departure for Egypt. He would put it into execution now—he would make a descent on England and dictate terms to that nation of conceited peddlers in London itself! He proceeded to concentrate 150,000 men in a great camp near Boulogne, and in all the ports of France he began to fit out ships, buy fishing boats, build scows for the transportation of men and artillery. He himself was more often to be found in Boulogne than at the Tuileries, personally training recruits and rushing the other work along. He had won the wholehearted support of Holland, the worried assistance of Spain and Naples, the paid neutrality of Prussia. He figured that all would be ready in six months. By midwinter the French army would be scaling the chalk cliffs of Dover! "The Channel? It's just a trench!" he cried to Cambacérès. "Have the courage and in one jump you are over!"

The English public was for a time amused, but in the end the magnitude of the preparations made an impression. Not since the days of the Armada had English shores been actually threatened. Now the English could see that there was at least a trace of danger, for if the French troops once succeeded in getting ashore all would be lost —there was no army in England that could cope with them. Already a legendary figure "Boney" became a nightmare.

In the face of the danger Pitt and his ministers countenanced tactics that were truly unworthy of the nation for whom they acted. It was conceivable that if Bonaparte could be put out of the way France would slip back into revolutionary anarchy and become powerless. Now Cadoudal and other Chouans in England had organized a plot against the life of the First Consul. The English ministry decided to co-operate.

The plan was simplicity itself. Cadoudal and a number of armed men would waylay Bonaparte on one of his trips to Malmaison, scatter his escort and kill him. With Bonaparte dead, a number of generals and senators who were anti-Bonapartist in secret would set up a provisional government with Moreau, the victor of Hohenlinden, for a temporary blind. Moreau would open the door to the Bourbons. Bonaparte had always refused to be Monk. Taking the Consul's place, Moreau would definitely end the era of revolutions and restore peace to Europe and France to her rightful kings.

Moreau's attitude was not known for certain. A pompous, spineless, uxorious sort of person, he was much more concerned about his wife's comforts and state of mind than with anything else. To sound him out the conspirators disinterred a "ghost of '92," Pichegru, who, before betraying the Republic, had served with Moreau on the Rhine.

Conveyed by an English ship Pichegru landed on the Norman cliffs near Biville towards the end of 1804. Cadoudal had been in hiding for some months at Chaillot. Pichegru joined him and together they called on Moreau.

Moreau was willing to assume power in Bonaparte's place, but he refused to have anything to do with recalling the Bourbons. Cadoudal was disappointed.

"So he wants to be boss too! Well, Blue for Blue, I prefer the one who's there to this sucker (*jean-foutre*)." [1]

But Cadoudal did not lose heart on the main issue. He would play out the game with his band of Chouans and allow events to decide the outcome in the political field.

In spite of all the goings and comings to and from the capital, the Consular police were long deaf and blind. Bonaparte had suppressed the emergency, or political, detective force on becoming Consul for life, thinking it wise to make some gesture of trust in the public. Fouché was given a seat in the Senate in compensation for the post he had lost. But he kept his *limiers*, his ferrets, at work all the same and continued making reports to Bonaparte. He caught wind of the conspiracy. The air, as he put it, was full of knives. Bonaparte must have believed him, for he said to Réal, Councilor of State in Fouché's place (but with far fewer brains): "The émigrés are at it again!"

Curiously enough, he himself, guessing at a hazard, picked out the thread that led to unraveling the snarl. At his order a number of Royalist agents were picked up,

---

[1] [The soldiers of the republican armies were known as "the Blues."— A. L.]

arrested and tried. One of them, Quérelle, before stepping in front of the firing-squad, revealed Cadoudal's presence in Paris and the general outline of the Chouan's scheme for taking the Consul's life. He named Bouvet de Lozier as one of the leaders in the enterprise. Lozier was arrested before long and talked freely, mentioning the collusion between Pichegru and Cadoudal, the advances that had been made to Moreau, the imminent arrival in France of a Bourbon prince, whose presence was to keep up the courage of the assassins and give the signal for their attack on the Consul.

On a report by Réal Bonaparte ordered Moreau's arrest (February 15, 1804). Not that he believed the general guilty in the strict sense of the term. He did not like Moreau but he thought him a good officer for the army. For his own part he was even inclined to overlook the whole matter.

However Moreau was touched in his pride and he stiffened. He lied and he lied—"like an idiot."

"Well," said the First Consul, "if he won't make a clean breast of everything with me, he'll have to take his chance in court!"

In order to get hold of the elusive Cadoudal, Pichegru and their gang of cutthroats, the roads leading from Paris were closed tight for three days. The public was alarmed and not knowing what it was all about feared a new Terror. Finally, on February 26, Pichegru was caught and packed away with Moreau into the Temple. The next day three more of the chief conspirators were arrested, including Polignac and Rivière. Chased like a rat from hole to hole, Cadoudal kept free till March 9 and then managed to kill a policeman before he was pinioned.

A huge man, with a fat, jolly, honest face, Cadoudal confessed everything without wincing. The fact of the plot and its seriousness were apparent to everybody. Bonaparte was deeply stirred. The chance of assassination he had discounted as incidental to his dictatorship. What impressed him rather was the far-reaching political character of the plot, which seemed to strike not only at his life but at the whole structure of the France that had issued from the Revolution. He therefore resolved to paralyze his enemies by a spectacular reprisal.

All the confessions were in agreement that a prince was party to the conspiracy and waiting on the frontiers of France. A report of Talleyrand noted the presence of the young Duc d'Enghien, the most energetic of the Bourbons, at Ettenheim in the Duchy of Baden. Was he the prince for whom the conspirators were waiting? An investigation was opened at Ettenheim. Hastily and incompetently conducted, it indicated, mistakenly, that the Duc d'Enghien had had a number of interviews with General Dumouriez. The name of the notorious traitor crystallized the wavering impressions of the Consul.

"Am I a dog," he cried hotly, "that they think they can knock me on the head in the street, while my enemies are sacred beings? They attack me in my person? I will pay them in the same coin."

He decided to seize the Duc d'Enghien and bring him to trial.

In the deepest secrecy he consulted the men at the Tuileries—Cambacérès, Lebrun, Talleyrand, Fouché,

Murat. Lebrun was shocked at the proposal. Cambacérès disapproved.

"What are you talking about, sir!" cried Bonaparte, measuring Cambacérès from head to foot. "I refuse to be considerate of people who send assassins to kill me."

Talleyrand supported the Consul's view in the most emphatic manner. "Sound policy," he declared, "requires punishment without exception." He judged his own case with the Bourbons lost beyond recall. It served his purposes, therefore, that the First Consul should cast the corpse of a Bourbon prince between himself and the past. Talleyrand guaranteed that the Grand Duke would swallow at the violation of the territorial sovereignty of Baden. Fouché added another consideration: The execution of a Bourbon would please the old Left and make the Consul's position absolutely secure in France.

Bonaparte ordered Ordener and Caulaincourt to cross the Rhine with 300 dragoons and bring the duke in. They obeyed without asking any questions. Seized at Ettenheim, the young prince was conveyed first to Strasburg and then to Vincennes, where Murat had assembled a court martial. Bonaparte had directed Savary to appear there and make sure that the procedure was regular and the verdict certain. His earnest caution had been: "See to it that everything is over before morning. The sentence, of which there can be no doubt, must be executed at once."

Zealous, but stupidly literal, Savary hurried to Vincennes. The prince was asleep. He was awakened and hurried before the court. General Hulin, one of the old French Guards who had mutinied on July 14, 1789, and joined in taking the Bastille, acted as judge-advocate.

The prince was questioned. He answered "with noble assurance" and even with an air of bravado. He had, he said, participated in no plot against the life of the First Consul—he scoffed at the idea as insulting. He did admit that he was receiving a pension from England, that he had fought in the field against the Republic and would do so again. "I have supported the claims of my family. My birth, my rank, my personal opinions, make me forever the enemy of your government."

In a sense of pity, perhaps, Hulin cautioned him against making such frank avowals. The duke shook his handsome, curly head:

"I appreciate the honorable intentions of the court. Unfortunately I cannot avail myself of the evasions suggested."

Twice, however, he requested an interview with the First Consul. Such an audience would have saved his life. The requests were ignored. Even as he was being returned to his cell, the officers were condemning him to death "for having borne arms against France." Hulin scribbled a hasty verdict, leaving it legally incomplete. Following his orders blindly, Savary urged an immediate execution.

A grave was hastily dug in the moat of the fortress. It was raining. The prince was led out into the cold night to a spot near the grave. He could see it plainly. An officer read the sentence of the court, holding the paper in the light of a lantern. For one last time the duke asked to speak with the First Consul or at least to write to him. The request was again refused. He then asked for a priest.

"No monk stuff!" came the voice of an officer from the dark.

"How horrible to die at the hands of Frenchmen!" said the young man quietly.

He lowered his head for a moment in what seemed to be a prayer. Then he stepped in front of the platoon of eight grenadiers.

"Order fire!" called Savary.

"Fire!" echoed the lieutenant in charge of the platoon.

The eight muskets blazed. The last of the Condés lay dead on the ground (March 21, 1804).

While his body was being buried coffinless in the grave, Savary leapt upon his horse and galloped off towards Malmaison.

All that evening Cambacérès, Josephine and Hortense had been begging Bonaparte to spare the young man. He listened to them in a silence that was long unbroken. Then the idea of a spectacular forgiveness suddenly struck his imagination. He despatched an order to Réal to hurry to Vincennes and subject the prince to a last questioning. Réal, however, had been worked on by Talleyrand and Fouché. He "did not receive the order in time." So at least he said to Savary, whom he encountered on the Vincennes road. By that time everything had been over for some hours.

When Bonaparte heard of what had happened his face, to believe Méneval, his secretary, blanched, betraying the utmost stupor. That his sorrow was sincere there can be no doubt. But he pulled himself together in a flash. There had been a slip, but a leader, especially the head of a state, had to take the responsibility for the acts of his subordinates. He could punish them if he chose, but he could not shift the blame to them. Since what had been done could not be undone, the First Consul elected to claim the execution as a pondered act of policy. He declared as much in an address to the Council of State. To intimates in whom he sensed a feeling of reproach he exclaimed haughtily:

"Those people were bent on killing the Revolution in my person. I was obliged to defend it. I was obliged to vindicate it. I have shown how far we are ready to go in that direction. . . . Unfortunately we have no time to be polite. I have shed blood? I had to shed blood. Perhaps I shall have to shed some more blood. . . . I am a statesman. I am the French Revolution. I shall uphold it."

The more striking the example, he figured, the greater would its effects be. And he figured correctly. Fouché has been falsely credited with a remark to the effect that the execution of the Duc d'Enghien was worse than a crime—it was a blunder. It may have been a crime. It was not a blunder. Not only was the power of the First Consul strengthened. There were to be no more organized conspiracies against his life. The Jacobins, for their part, applauded. As for the Royalists some of them holed in, others rallied with greater courage than ever. Chateaubriand used the distressing tragedy as a pretext for withdrawing from the Consular diplomatic service and retiring into a sulking opposition. But Talleyrand gave a ball three evenings after the rainy night at Vincennes. The greatest names in the French aristocracy and the ambassadors of the proudest powers crowded in throngs about the First Consul. Everything was giving way before the fortunate soldier who had not hesitated to shed royal blood in defense of his mission.

CHAPTER XII

The Emperor of the French

THE DEATH OF THE DUC D'ENGHIEN HAD ONE CONSE-
quence that was immediate and direct. It rushed public
opinion and Bonaparte himself in the direction of restoring monarchy.

There had been much talk already of raising the First
Consul to the dignity of Emperor.[1] The idea had long
drifted about at loose ends. It now seemed to be the one
guaranty of continuity that Bonaparte's government
could obtain. The Life Consulship was just a stage. It
could have lasted for a long time still without any great
harm, but an imperial organization of France would

---

[1] [The term "Emperor" as used by Napoleon and the French of his time,
went back, like many conceptions of the French Revolutionary period, to an
early Roman connotation. The *imperator* was a Roman general, who, however, within specified limits of time and space, exercised absolute power in
the name of the State. Beginning with Augustus, who had been a general,
the term acquired the concept of heredity. Under Augustus' successors the
"emperor" became the hereditary administrative head of an agglomeration
of peoples or nationalities though command of the army was never wholly
absent from the concept. In the Middle Ages the term was almost wholly
"bureaucratized," to indicate administrative headship of a multiplicity of
peoples. Dante's emperor had almost no military attributes, being the titular
head of a world morally united under the peace of God. Napoleon thought
of himself as emperor "by grace of the people and the army"—the Roman
military conception, with a tinge of democracy and a stress on the thought of
hereditary succession. The modern British Empire is a concept of the medieval type. Mussolini's is an imitation of the British, with a military tinge
which, however, is not supplied by the emperor, nor even by the Head of the
State, but by the emperor's generals.—A. L.]

116

undoubtedly strengthen and prolong the Consul's reconstructive efficacy. If Bonaparte were an hereditary sovereign his régime would not be at the mercy of the first intrigue of politicians or of the knife of the first assassin.

The earliest to be convinced of the desirability of the change was Bonaparte himself. He had been thinking of a throne for two years, but without confessing it to anybody, even to Josephine, who was a convinced Royalist and had always discouraged the idea of his making any usurpation. Now at a moment when everything was ripe for favoring his great ambition, he was reluctant to manifest it—he could not. Cambacérès had been his usual helper in such circumstances, but Cambacérès would not serve this time. He was against any empire. Times, he thought, were still too close to the Revolution to admit of restoring a throne. Besides, he was in no great hurry to step down from his rank as Second Consul and become a mere subject.

Fouché saw his chance and volunteered to perform the task of mediation which Cambacérès could not assume. Fouché was sorry he had opposed the Life Consulship. That mistake had cost him his post as Minister of Police. He would get it back, he figured, if he helped to make Bonaparte emperor.

No "interpretation of a people's wish" was ever more effective than Fouché's. He had worked up a considerable influence in the Senate, but he also represented the Jacobins, the party which could be expected to offer bitter opposition to a resurrection of monarchy even with a new dynasty and under another name.

Fouché went to Malmaison, saw Bonaparte and urged

him to accept a crown in response to a public demand of which he, Fouché, could give full assurance. Such a step would guarantee permanency to the achievements of the Revolution and mean quiet for France. "A dictator can disappear, a sovereign never, for the moment he dies his successor ascends the throne."

The First Consul allowed Fouché to talk without once breaking silence. Silence seemed to Fouché to be all that he needed. He set out to get the press in hand and had a number of electoral colleges vote petitions and resolutions. Then, seizing the moment when the Senate was debating a report by the Chief Justice on the activities of English spies, he moved and secured the passage of a resolution praying the First Consul "to complete his work by making it as immortal as his glory."

On receiving the message Bonaparte still pretended to be doubtful. He consulted a number of friends among the generals, notably Soult, and sent out "feelers" to the courts of Austria and Prussia—Russia seemed to be tying up with England—as to whether they would recognize him under a new status. They made haste to answer in the affirmative, thinking rather of their skins than of the puckery taste in their mouths. The First Consul thereupon replied to the Senate, in a language that seemed appropriate to the occasion, that it was for that assembly "to speak its full thought." That was the moment for a sometime Conventionist, Curée, to turn his trick. On learning of the death of the Duc d'Enghien Curée had exclaimed: "Good! Bonaparte is still doing Convention!" He now rose and brought before the Tribunate a motion calling "Napoleon Bonaparte to the throne, with his descendants, under the title of 'Emperor

FOUCHÉ, DUC D'OTRANTO
From the Portrait by Dubufe

commissioned to govern the French Republic.' " The debate was conducted publicly. Carnot, virtually alone and with rare nobility of spirit, opposed the motion in the name of liberty, advancing very sound considerations against the proposed step.

The motion, however, was adopted by a great majority and sent up to the Senate. The Senate made a number of amendments of detail, specifying, among other things, that the Empire should be hereditary "in the Bonaparte family" and that the Emperor should have the right "to adopt his successor" (May 3, 1804).

Six high dignitaries were created about the sovereign, glamorous posts designed to satisfy the ambitions of Napoleon's relatives and of the two Consuls who were losing their jobs. So Joseph Bonaparte was to become Grand Elector, Louis Bonaparte, Constable, Cambacérès, Arch-Chancellor of the Empire, Lebrun, Arch-Treasurer, Eugene de Beauharnais, Arch-Chancellor of State, Murat, Grand Admiral. Sixteen marshals were to be named, to satisfy the outstanding military leaders—Kellermann, Jourdan, Suchet, Masséna, Murat, Augereau, Berthier, Brune, Ney, Lannes, Bernadotte, Davout, Lefebvre, Soult. A number of high court positions, further, would perhaps revive the lost splendors of the old royalty: Cardinal Fesch, Napoleon's uncle and archbishop of Lyons, became Grand Almoner, Talleyrand, Grand Chamberlain, Caulaincourt, Grand Esquire, Ségur, Grand Master of Ceremonies. There was even one strictly new idea: Duroc, Napoleon's most intimate friend and most trusted confidant, became Grand Marshal of the Palace.

On May 18, 1804, the Senate went in a body to Saint-

Cloud to pay its respects to the new emperor. Napoleon received the senators with Josephine at his side. Dressed in his ordinary military uniform, he was calm, grave. Cambacérès was the first to address him as "Sire" and "Your Majesty." That was in process of proclaiming him "for the glory and well-being of the Republic—Emperor of the French!"

A great shout arose and it was taken up by the crowds that churned in the gardens and courtyards: "Long live the Emperor!"

Napoleon answered with a dignity that came natural to him. Ten years before that young man with the severe expression had been a captain of artillery hurrying to take a job at Toulon that he thought himself lucky to get. At Saint-Cloud he seemed always to have sat on a throne.

Satisfaction in France was all but unanimous. By that time the Revolution had come to seem just a bad dream. The Terror, the proscriptions, the invasions, hard times, lay hazy in a distant past. The nation had risen to its feet, brushed off its clothes, licked its wounds. A despotism of genius was surely better than a distracting play of factions. The country now rallied as one man behind its regenerator. The plebescite sanctioned the Empire by three and a half million votes to two and a half thousand.

Ten days later, on the 28th, the trial of Cadoudal and Moreau opened. Pichegru had strangled himself in his cell at the Temple. Had he been helped to do so? There was nothing improbable about such an assumption. The police force of those days was an assortment of rogues. Mme. de Staël remarked ironically: "Bonaparte is so unlucky! All his prisoners die on his hands!" Neverthe-less Napoleon was both surprised and disappointed at Pichegru's suicide. The man had been a mere figurehead, but his absence was a great embarrassment to the prose-cution. He was the link between the Royalists and Mo-reau. The sessions were noisy and tumultuous. Cadoudal now denied points that were essential to proving an attempt at assassination. On other points he refused to say anything, in order to help one accomplice or an-other. Moreau denied ever having thought for a moment of a dictatorship. His demeanor was a blend of haughti-ness and embarrassment.

On June 10th the court pronounced its sentences: death for Cadoudal and nineteen others, among them Armand de Polignac and Rivière; for Moreau, two years in prison. Moreau's sentence angered Napoleon. He had hoped for death. Not that he ever dreamed of allowing the head of a rival soldier to fall into a basket on a scaf-fold. With his deep sense of the theatrical he had counted on making a spectacular pardon and so recouping for the opportunity he had lost with the Duc d'Enghien. The act would have balanced things in the public mind and contributed to his popularity. Balked this second time, he at least spared the general any imprisonment and allowed him to sail for America. Bitter, a man of no real greatness, the victor of Hohenlinden was not to return till 1813. Then he was to lead the Allies against his country and fall at Dresden, struck down by a French cannonball.

As for the Royalists the Emperor was at first disin-clined to spare any of them. But Josephine and Hortense brought Mme. de Polignac into his presence at Saint-

Cloud and she fell weeping to her knees before him. Murat intervened for Rivière. The Emperor commuted both their sentences. Cadoudal went to the guillotine on June 28th and died, undaunted, with a cry of "Long live the King!"

The sensational trials, meantime, had upset public calm. The atmosphere was uneasy, nervous. The politicians were worried about their futures under the Empire. Napoleon kept a close eye on developments and sought to reassure everybody. He made no changes in his ministries. The lower bureaucracy had silently slipped through the Revolution from the old régime and given continuity to public administration in the most tragic crises of the nation. It was allowed to go on with its work, unchanged. A man of habits Napoleon did not like new faces. He knew the art of picking men, training them and keeping them. There were excellent ones among them—Gaudin in Finance, Fontanes as Grand Master of the University, Maret as Secretary of State, Regnier in Justice, Daru in War. Talleyrand was surrounded by a truly admirable staff and continued on in Foreign Relations. The police, however, had been in weak hands during those somewhat disquieting moments of transition. Napoleon owed something, nay much, to Fouché. He could do no better than restore him to the general superintendency of police. The sometime Conventionist was, within a few months, to make of it the supplest, subtlest, and most burdensome instrument of power that had ever weighed upon a European nation.

CHAPTER XIII

Coronation

On December 2, 1804, at eleven in the forenoon, all Paris was at the windows or standing in lines along the streets—and with Paris all the curious of France and Europe. The rumble of cannon answered the clanging of bells. Napoleon was to drive from the Tuileries to Notre Dame, where the Pope was to crown him. Lines of troops hedged the sidewalks to hold back the crowds. It was one continuous cheer as the cortège rolled past at a slow pace on a cold, cloudless day.

First came Murat, dressed as gaudily as an opera general, leading companies of carbineers, chasseurs of the Guard, cuirassiers, mamelukes. Next came carriages bearing the high dignitaries, then, after an interval, a coach of glass and gold, topped with geniuses holding up a crown and drawn by eight cream-colored horses with white trappings. Behind the coach windows the Emperor could be seen, bowing now to right and now to left in acknowledgment of the cheers, which came in waves and spurts as new crowds caught sight of him. He offered a profile that was noble, austere, altogether imperial. He was dressed in scarlet velvet, stiff with gold. His cap had plumes. On his left sat Josephine in an ivory satin gown that glittered with diamonds. Made up with endless and priceless art she seemed as young as one could wish and she kept smiling happily. In front of the imperial couple sat Joseph and Louis, glum, indifferent, bored.

Just ten centuries before, Charlemagne had gone to Rome to fall on his face before the Pontiff and receive the imperial crown from pontifical hands. Today the Pope of Rome had come to Paris to crown the soldier of the Revolution! A sensational reversal indeed! How had the Pope ever been brought to it?

The negotiations had in fact been long and difficult. Altogether contrary at first, the Sacred College had finally come around to demanding, in exchange for an unprecedented favor, a long list of substantial advantages—a return of the Legations, attenuations of the Organic Articles, the elimination of divorce from the French Civil Code. In Paris the opposition was strong, however unexpressive. The assemblies were still filled with anti-clericals and Terrorists. The people had grown unused to church functions. The army regarded the whole ceremony as so much tomfoolery. The Royalists cried aloud: Rome was deserting the dynasty of St. Louis to kneel before the murderer of the Duc d'Enghien! Devout Catholic that he was, Joseph de Maistre, the future author of *The Pope,* would soon be writing: "The crimes of Alexander VI are less revolting than the apostasy of this insignificant successor of his—Pius VII!"

But Napoleon was bent on an anointment, perhaps with the thought that it would link him to the most solemn monarchical tradition. In virtue of it a right that he held from the sword would become something resembling divine right. He insisted, he pressed, often imperious, always adroit, never promising anything, never refusing anything, but dangling before the pontiff's eyes hopes that were as vast as they were vague and hazy. A simple soul and pure Pius was ready to forgive anything to the "restorer of the Church in France." He had liked Bonaparte ever since Tolentino. In spite of the disappointments and persecutions that were eventually to come, he was to love Napoleon always, and, after the Emperor's fall, he was to manifest his abiding affection in many touching ways. He allowed himself to be persuaded at last, resigning himself to the long, tiring journey. He started out in poor health, to be prodded along the way by solicitous messages from Napoleon. "They drove the Holy Father at a gallop," Cardinal Consalvi was to remark, "like an almoner bidden by his master to say Mass."

To sidestep questions of precedence, Pope and Emperor met in the forest of Fontainebleau, Napoleon finding himself there by prearranged chance on a hunt.

In spite of the endearments and subtle attentions that Napoleon rained upon His Holiness, new difficulties arose at once as to the forms of the ceremonial. The Emperor wanted anointment and blessing from the Pope but he insisted on crowning himself. His crown he owed to the nation and the army. He refused to receive it from the Church. Pius thought he had been made a fool of, but he had come so far, he was being so splendidly entertained! After all, a mere matter of form! What was the harm in letting the Emperor have his way?

Napoleon found most unexpected difficulties and annoyances within his own circle. He had made princes of his brothers and stuffed them with titles and incomes, but there was no limit to their greed, no end to their intrigues. "To listen to you people," he finally cried, justifiably enraged, "one might think I had defrauded you of the inheritance of our father the king!"

Joseph, for his part, was jealous of his younger brother and struck a Jacobin pose, voicing sentiments of insulted democracy (without once forgetting, meantime, to pocket incidental profits). "He refuses to be a prince!" sneered Napoleon. "Does he think the state is paying him two millions to parade up and down the sidewalks in Paris in an afternoon coat and a tall hat? . . . You don't run a country that way! . . . Or does he think he's going to get my job? Let him try! He will find that I am grounded on solid rock!" Louis was moody and suspicious. He refused to allow Napoleon to adopt the son that he, Louis, had had by Hortense and to designate the boy as the successor to the throne. As for Lucien and Jerome, they had "married like idiots" and were not admitted to the imperial circle. Their banishment had angered Letizia, now become "Madame Mère," and in protest she lingered far from the capital, refusing to witness the apotheosis of the glorious son to whom she and her brood owed so much.

Napoleon's sisters, finally, were a nuisance of an altogether special kind. He found himself quite at a loss to deal with their greeds and their complaints. Elisa had been married to Felice Bacciocchi, Pauline to Prince Borghese, Caroline to Murat. They fought tooth and nail to become Imperial Highnesses, insisting on as good treatment as their brothers, as Hortense. Napoleon could only let them have their way. "With her," he said, speaking of Caroline, "it's always a pitched battle. To get a little chit in my family to understand what it's all about I have to make a speech as long as I do before the Council of State to get a measure passed. . . . And then they are always talking about my dying. . . . If I did not find some bit of sweetness in my domestic life I should be too unhappy to bear up!"

The Bonapartes were all in league to prevent the coronation of Josephine. Their hatred of "the intruder," "that fast Creole," never slackened. As a matter of fact Josephine's conduct had of late been most exemplary. She was acting up to her new position to perfection, her one shortcoming in that regard, being her failure to provide the Emperor with an heir. But the Bonapartes talked, and they set everyone else to talking, of a divorce. Such attacks really overreached their aim. Napoleon refused to throw his wife away. "It is more than I can do," he said to Roederer. "I have the heart of a human being. I am not the cub of a tigress."

So Josephine was to partake of the anointment and become Empress. By an adroit maneuver she got more than that—she got a religious celebration of her marriage, a thing that Napoleon had always shunned but which she felt would bind her husband to her by an indissoluble tie. When all other arrangements were in order she secretly confided to His Holiness that her marriage had not as yet received the blessing of the Church. The Pope threw up his hands in horrified dismay. The imperial couple living in sin! He declared he could not officiate at the coronation unless the religious marriage had been properly celebrated in advance. Napoleon, outwitted, knew that on such a point the priest's conscience would not compromise, and he shuddered at the scandal that any postponement or abandonment of the coronation would cause. Cardinal Fesch was directed, therefore, to obtain the necessary dispensations, and then privately, without witnesses, he gave the imperial couple his belated benediction. So it was that the next day Josephine was able to depart in all happiness for Notre Dame, sitting at Napoleon's side and feeling certain in her woman's heart that she was to share in the hero's whole future.

The procession reached the Archbishopric at eleven o'clock. There Napoleon donned his imperial robe—purple velvet lined with ermine and sprinkled with gold bees. Surveying himself in it he could not help whispering into Joseph's ear: "Joseph—if only our father could see us now!"

Salvos from batteries of artillery were making the capital shake, and the great bell of Notre Dame was booming deafeningly. The Archbishop met the sovereigns on the pediment in front of the cathedral portal and then the company marched in to the rhythm of a military hymn, the Bonaparte sisters carrying Josephine's train, and doing it in very bad humor.

The nave was packed with all official France—senators, state councilors, tribunes, generals, admirals, high magistrates, members of the Institute. Visiting foreign princes and the ambassadors had seats in boxes. The Emperor's group consisted of his marshals and high dignitaries, the officers of the crown and the chamberlains, all in splendid uniforms, while the princesses and ladies-in-waiting glittered in the candlelight in costumes veritably of fairyland.

The ceremony unfolded majestically in accord with

the ancient royal rite. Napoleon himself had overseen every detail, aided by the Comte de Ségur, Grand Master of Ceremonies and a learned and fastidious observer of the traditions of the old monarchy. The Emperor was, to be sure, a man of the Revolution and on the whole was far from repudiating that ancestry. But deep down he belonged to the old régime and was moreover a Frenchman of the far south, in fact an Italian, in many of the strands in his sentimental fiber. He believed in grand official spectacles and in their beneficent influence on the public. At all times he manifested the interest and the talent of the stage-director in fashioning the settings for his public acts.

He received the triple unction from the pontiff, kneeling before the altar. Then he rose and, mounting the altar steps, took in hand a simple coronet made of laurel leaves in gold, and set it upon his own head in a manner and with a gesture that bespoke his full self and all his glory. The Empress was still kneeling at the foot of the sacred podium. Slowly, his face pale, impassive, handsome, Napoleon stepped down one of the three steps towards her and laid a light diadem upon her brow. She rose. Just then the Bonaparte sisters spitefully dropped Josephine's heavy train and she stumbled under its sudden weight. But righting herself she joined her husband and, side by side, they walked to their thrones. The Pope gave them each his blessing, then, after embracing the Emperor, he turned towards the dazzling congregation and intoned: *Vivat Imperator in aeternum!* A response of thunderous applause came.

Napoleon then proceeded to take his oath, on the Catholic Gospel:

"I swear to keep the territory of the Republic intact; to enforce the Concordat and freedom of worship; to uphold equal rights, political and civil liberty, and the irrevocability of sales of public properties; to levy no imposts and lay no taxes except as prescribed by law; to maintain the institution of the Legion of Honor and to govern with sole view to the welfare, happiness and glory of the French people."

A high pontifical Mass was sung and then the portals of the basilica were thrown open again. Under a sinking winter's sun the procession filed out into flag-draped streets where the crowds acclaimed with one continuous roar the military chieftain who, by a twin miracle of genius and fortune, had taken the place of the Capets and become the first-born of the Church, the Lord's Anointed.

Six months later Napoleon was to don another crown. As Emperor of the French he could hardly remain a mere president of the Cisalpine Republic. It was not the easiest of matters to arrange, but after cautious negotiations with the Consulta at Milan North Italy agreed to become a kingdom. At first Napoleon had no idea of assuming that throne himself. He thought it best to be moderate in view of the state of mind in Europe and especially in Austria where Emperor Francis II could only be alarmed for the Hapsburg dominion over Venice. He therefore offered the Iron Crown of the Lombards to his elder brother. Joseph, however, was wary, fearing lest acceptance might damage his eventual claims to the Empire. Louis, on being sounded out, vetoed a proposal whereby his infant son would become King of Italy, leaving him as mere regent. Bored, an-

THE CORONATION OF NAPOLEON
By David

noyed, Napoleon finally compromised by taking the title of King of Italy himself, exercising power through his stepson Eugene. The two states, Italy and France, were explicitly declared to be separate.

He crossed the mountains, therefore, taking leave of Pius at Turin. The Pope journeyed homeward loaded with gifts but disappointed at having gained little otherwise except a promise here and there as to some detail. In the end the influence of the Cardinals was to ripen that dissatisfaction into portentous results.

Revisiting the field of Marengo Napoleon watched from a grandstand a sham battle that reproduced the victory which had restored Italy to French control. He made his second triumphal entry into Milan and then, some days later, in the cathedral covered with banners and bunting, he set the Lombard crown upon his own head, pronouncing the famous formula: "God gave it me! Woe to anyone who lays hand to it. (*Dio me la diede. Guai a chi la toccherà*)" (May 26, 1805).

His energetic demeanor was profoundly stirring to the congregation. There was to be no mistake about it. After centuries of bondage the fair land of Italy had been delivered from slavery. Out of a paste of triturated principalities and municipalities Napoleon had molded a nation of which he was quite as proud as of France. Italy had been the prize of his first and most dazzling campaign, the episode that had made his fortune. Across the Alps, moreover, he felt and showed that he felt himself Italian. His supple, plastic genius adapted itself to peoples and races by an instinctive mimetic process and he was ever striving to master their basic, essential ideas.

"I ended the Vendée business by becoming a Catholic," he said to Roederer one day. "I got my hold in Egypt by becoming a Mussulman. I won public opinion in Italy by turning Ultramontane. If I were ever to govern a nation of Jews I would begin by rebuilding Solomon's temple."

Genoa was now annexed to the new kingdom, ostensibly at the request of the Doge. That would prevent the English from remaining there and using the Genoese harbor as their base against southern France. The Bourbons in Naples were henchmen of the British cabinet and secretly arming. The Emperor threatened to dethrone them and they made haste to apologize. The Kingdom of Etruria was being ruled by a Spanish princess. She became a vassal to the King of Italy. Napoleon further bestowed the sovereignties of Lucca and Piombino upon his sister Elisa. That brought the whole peninsula very firmly under his control.

CHAPTER XIV

Ulm

WHILE NAPOLEON WAS THUS INCREASING AND CONSOLI-
dating his power, the fear that he inspired in the other
countries in Europe was also growing. At the time of
the coronation he sent conciliatory allocutions to England and Austria. He sincerely wanted peace. He needed
peace. Peace alone could lend permanency to his conquests and personal power. But Pitt's government did
not want any such peace. The English could not get used
to seeing France at the mouths of the Rhine and Scheldt
and mistress of the Continent. With untiring patience
and ingenuity, therefore, Pitt kept at work on a new
coalition.

As a counter-move, the moment the Treaty of Amiens
was repudiated, Napoleon returned to his great project
of a descent on Dover. He established headquarters at
Boulogne in July, 1804. "Around me here," he wrote to
Brune, "I have 120,000 men and 300 pinnaces that are
awaiting only a fair wind to carry the imperial eagle
to the Tower of London."

Really they were waiting for more than that—they
were waiting for the coming of the squadron from

Toulon, where the French navy had been mobilizing.

It was in command of Admiral Latouche-Tréville, a skillful and energetic sailor. He had received orders to go through the Straits and make the Channel. Meantime Admiral Ganteaume, who was blockaded in Brest, would create a diversion by making a sortie and attacking the vessels of Lord Cornwallis. The English fleets were patrolling the coasts from Amsterdam to Cadiz. The French ships were inferior in numbers, in armaments and in the training of officers and crews.

"Never mind!" said Napoleon. "Give us a clear Channel for six hours and we are masters of the world."

On August 16th, in order to communicate his own enthusiasms to his troops, Napoleon distributed eagles and crosses of the Legion of Honor at a muster of the whole army. The invasion of England should have preceded his coronation, according to his original plan, but an unforeseen misfortune had interfered. Admiral Latouche-Tréville died just as he was about to sail from Toulon. He was replaced by Admiral Villeneuve, a brave man in action certainly, but not of ready decision in council. The new orders which he received from the Emperor assumed a dash and audacity that he was far from possessing—in fact they were utterly foreign to his character. He was to collect the fleet of Spain, an ally of France, at Cadiz and make all sail for Martinique. There he would be joined by the fleet of Missiessy from Rochefort and the fleet of Ganteaume from Brest. Napoleon foresaw that in fear for their colonies the English would divert a large naval force to their protection; but this fleet would reach the Antilles on a wild goose chase, for meantime, the French navy, sixty vessels strong, would be sweeping the Channel. Its arrival off Boulogne would be the signal for the Grand Army to embark.

The plan was gigantic in range and it was complicated, but after all it was workable. All it needed was a little luck with favoring winds and seas. Napoleon kept the secret tight. In order to mislead the English more thoroughly he made a journey to the Rhineland and struck a pose of reverie before Charlemagne's tomb. He lingered at Milan to reshape Italy. He multiplied receptions, spectacular festivals, parties, at his court. His confidence was boundless. Fortune had always been with him. She would not fail him this time! Decrès, at the Navy Ministry, knew the fleet and the sort of leaders it had. He warned, he made objections. Napoleon gave him a dressing down and refused to allow him to answer back. Decrès, alas, was right.

Villeneuve got away from Toulon without opposition on March 30, 1805. That fulfilled the first item in his orders. He also united with part of the Spanish fleet and made the Antilles, where he found Missiessy waiting. Ganteaume, however, had not broken out at Brest and one fleet of Spanish ships allowed itself to be blockaded at Ferrol in Galicia. The Emperor thereupon ordered Villeneuve to return. Villeneuve obeyed. Arriving off Spain he missed a chance for a brilliant victory at the Azores. "My despair doubles at the evidence of your trust in me," Villeneuve wrote unhappily to Decrès. "I cannot hope for success, whichever way I turn." Frightened at so much responsibility, lacking in resolution to begin with, Villeneuve did not drive on the Channel. He crept for safety into Cadiz.

His spirits high, Napoleon waited and waited, imagining that Villeneuve must be somewhere off Brest. "England's hour is striking," he cried. "We are going to avenge Poitiers, Crécy, Agincourt!" The ships and scows at Boulogne were made ready for the crossing. Troops, horses and guns were assigned to the exact spots they were to occupy on the boats. But no lookout reported Villeneuve. What was the man doing? "Admiral," wrote the Emperor on August 21, "I hope you are off Brest. Hurry! Do not lose a moment! Combine all my fleets and enter the Channel! England is ours!"

Impatient, Napoleon kept his glass to the horizon. Not a sail in sight! Then suddenly the exact news came. Villeneuve was not even on the way. He had gone into hiding at Cadiz! For fear of playing for such high stakes he had thrown the game away! Napoleon's rage was a terrible thing to behold, and in the presence of Daru, inspector general of the armies, he gave full and long vent to it: "Villeneuve is a coward and a traitor. He would sacrifice anything to avoid risking his skin!" For the first time he had failed of a major purpose. The descent on England would have to be postponed, perhaps abandoned!

Then suddenly his anger cooled. In a flash his mind had deserted the sea and turned back towards the Continent. They had formed a new coalition? He would smash it and make Austria foot the bill! He would strike at England by entering Vienna! To Daru, over one stretch of time of several hours' duration and with amazing clearness and foresight, he dictated his plan of campaign and then and there commanded the Grand Army to break camp at the Pas de Calais and march on the Rhine.

While Napoleon was gazing at the sea at Boulogne, the Continent had gradually been rising against him. Czar Alexander I had been busy promoting and organizing a new system of alliances that aimed to fell the Corsican and reduce France to her historic boundaries. The Czar, a young man, grandson of Catherine the Great, owed his throne to the murder, committed doubtless with his knowledge, of his father. On his ascent he aspired to resume the rôle as arbiter of Europe which his grandmother had played so successfully of yore. Piqued at French power and personally jealous of Bonaparte's renown, he professed great horror for the encroachments of France in Italy and Germany and openly broke with the First Consul on receiving news of the execution of the Duc d'Enghien.

He made a first move to cover his tracks by putting himself forward as a mediator between France and England. That offer, as is now known, rested on an understanding with Prussia (May, 1804) and on a military agreement with Austria (November 6, 1804). It was altogether hostile to Napoleon. For the rest the Czar wasted no great amount of time in passing from a neutrality that had its savor of blackmail to avowed hostility.

On the 11th of April, 1805, he signed a treaty with Pitt, with a view to forming a general alliance that would "restore to Europe a peace of which she was being deprived by the inordinate ambition of the French government." The campaign was to be financed by English gold. Pitt guaranteed to pay the Czar an annual subsidy of 1,250,000 pounds sterling for each 100,000 men that the Allies should put into the field. Napoleon was to be requested to evacuate Italy, Switzerland, Holland, and

Germany. If he refused war was to be declared and its successful conclusion would further strip France of Belgium and Savoy and leave her within the frontiers of 1789. The Allies would dispose variously of this booty. Prussia would get the Rhineland. Austria would recover her Italian properties and expand in the Balkans at the expense of Turkey. Piedmont would annex Genoa and the province of Milan. Poland would be patched together again and handed over to Russia. A conference to be held at the end of the war would fix details within these general lines, no peace being signed until a mutual agreement had been reached.

The idea in all this was to bring France to harsher and harsher terms. The treaties of Vienna of 1815 were already present in the Anglo-Russian agreement of 1805. With this basis for the coalition established, the next problem was to secure the acceptance of the Continental powers. Sweden agreed out of hand. Gustav IV detested the Emperor whom he refused to style otherwise than as "M. Napoleon." Prussia and Austria were harder to bring around. Though his personal sympathies were with France, King Frederick William was fearful of Alexander and Napoleon equally. He thought the safer play for him was to gain as many advantages as possible from so tangled a situation through a policy of alert neutrality. Negotiating with Russia, therefore, he was all honey and smiles for the new Emperor of the French. Napoleon was perfectly aware of the Prussian game, however, and kept on his guard. He sought to weaken the tightening noose by detaching Frederick William from it, and in order to alienate him from England offered him, through Duroc, the Duchy of Hanover, which belonged by hereditary right to the British ruling family. "We've got to win Prussia," he said. "Let's throw her a bone to gnaw." Frederick William was perplexed. Hanover was certainly a pretty bribe. It tempted him. But there was Russia! Russia had to be considered! Meantime, not knowing just whom he was going to fight, he put an army of 80,000 men in commission.

Still sore from their two thrashings at Napoleon's hands the Austrians were far from resigned to the loss of Italy and only awaited a fair chance to begin another war. However, while military preparations were being hurried in Vienna, the Emperor Francis observed a most cordial and in fact most solicitous demeanor towards Napoleon. He sent a personal representative to attend the Iron Crown ceremonies in Milan. Recommending that move Cobenzl wrote: "The gesture, in itself inexpensive, will prolong Bonaparte's sense of security down to the time when he learns that the Russians are on the march." But Alexander kept the pressure up and, considering himself ready for the fray in any event, Francis unmasked himself on August 9, 1805, and openly joined the coalition. On September 7, without a declaration of war, he sent Mack, one of his best generals, across the Inn to invade Bavaria. The move was designed to catch Napoleon napping.

The Corsican was far indeed from being caught. With one eye on England he had been watching Europe with the other. He was a genius of the first order in making calculations. Whenever he formed a plan he unfailingly considered the chances of its miscarrying. "If my admirals prove to be nincompoops," he wrote to Talleyrand, at a time when he was still looking for Villeneuve off Boulogne, "I'll break my ocean camp here, enter Germany with 200,000 men and not stop till I've touched home-base at Vienna. . . . I shall not allow the Austrians and Russians to combine forces. I shall strike them before they make a junction." He proceeded that early to demand subsidies of Holland and to order Junot to raise soldiers in Spain. Bernadotte was occupying Hanover. Napoleon directed him to move nearer the probable center of operations, while Masséna went to Italy to guard that approach. Since the Bourbons of Naples were a slippery lot in the best case, he sent Gouvion-Saint-Cyr to call their attention to their promises with 20,000 men. Duroc was still in Berlin working at the King of Prussia for an open alliance with France; but meantime Napoleon had won the princes of the German south and, after some hesitations, Bavaria, Baden and Württemberg sent contingents to swell the ranks of the Grand Army.

Over that army Napoleon had watched with a patience and a systematic application that brooked no distractions. It had risen to 186,000 men with 350 guns. Following a conception altogether novel Napoleon had broken it up into seven distinct army corps, each possessing its own infantry, artillery and cavalry, and each maintaining its independent, autonomous existence. In command of them were Bernadotte, Marmont, Davout, Soult, Lannes, Ney and Augereau. A reserve cavalry force, 30,000 strong, was entrusted to Murat. Napoleon commanded in person a Guard that was made up of the flower of the army. It too had its own cavalry and artillery and in battle stood ready to deliver the decisive thrust at the point which the Emperor in person should select. Napoleon counted on the energy, endurance and dash of his troops and it was a sound calculation. For more than a year they had been trained at Boulogne to the most exacting maneuvers. Full of fire, tired of the long wait, confident of themselves and of the capacity of their leaders, they were eager for action.

This was not so markedly the case behind the lines, in Paris and in the provinces. One more war! War with all its private mourning and hardships and its social dangers! The bourgeoisie—businessmen, manufacturers, merchants—did not dare complain too loudly, but it viewed the outbreak of another conflict with definite alarm. For some months hard times had been making themselves felt again. The business at Boulogne had cost untold amounts of money. Public finance was over-strained. Stocks had fallen and were falling. Specie had gone into hiding. Deposits at the Bank of France had virtually ceased. On returning to Paris on the 4th of September Napoleon noted an atmosphere of coolness and grumbling. He got little applause along the streets and that was something he was not used to and did not like. He proclaimed a number of measures—they were strictly necessary, to tell the truth—among them conscription pushed down to the youngest classes, the recruits to be distributed among concentration camps to the north and east; then forced loans to the public treasury. Those decrees were not calculated to revive his popularity.

He, however, was certain of a quick and smashing victory.

"Within a fortnight," he kept repeating, "I will have

beaten the Russians, the Austrians—and the bears on Exchange (*joueurs à la baisse*)!"

But before leaving for the army he thought it wise to make an appeal to the nation's heart. He went before the Council of State and declaimed:

"I go to crush the odious House of Austria which I should never have spared. . . . While I am engaged in faraway Germany the nation must be responsible for itself. . . . It must revive its old energies. It must show all Europe that it is one with its leader. . . . I am the nation's work. The nation must uphold me."

The language had a flavor of '92. It was to recur readily to Napoleon in the critical hours that the future held for him. Like Antaeus touching his mother Earth, he seemed to gain new strength from the ideas and the rhetoric of the Revolution.

He was at Strasburg, ready for work, on September 27th. The army in full force was spread out along the Rhine. "Soldiers:" read his order of the day, "Your Emperor is among you. You are naught but the advance guard of the great people. If necessary it will rise as one man at my call to confound and dissolve this new league which the hate and the gold of England have woven. Soldiers: Ahead of us lie forced marches that we must make, fatigues and privations that we must endure; but whatever resistance is set in our way, we shall overcome it. We shall not rest till we have planted our eagles on the enemy's soil."

The army deployed between Mainz and Strasburg and crossed the Rhine. Mack was at Ulm with 80,000 men. He expected the French to debouch through the Black Forest. Instead Napoleon made a long turning movement up the valleys of the Neckar and the Main, and his various divisions met on scheduled time at Donauwerth, squarely in Mack's rear and between him and Vienna.

Napoleon established headquarters at Augsburg. His procedure was now simple. He marched his army up either bank of the Danube with the design of shutting the Austrians up in Ulm. Mack was outnumbered two and a half to one. Perceiving his peril he tried to break free either into Bohemia or into the Tyrol. Battles at Günzburg, Haslach, Memmingen and Elchingen hurled him back, however, from north and south, and he was obliged to retreat into his fortified camp at Ulm (October 11-14). Ney showed a demonlike bravery in the battle at Elchingen and came off with immortal honors.

Completely cut off now, with no hope of succor, Mack could not make up his mind what to do next. The Archduke Ferdinand, his second in command, tried a desperate sortie and, in spite of heavy losses inflicted upon him by Murat's cavalry, succeeded in piercing the French lines and making his way to freedom. Mack finally became resigned to his fate and sent Prince Lichtenstein to Napoleon's headquarters to negotiate a capitulation.

Admitted to the Emperor's presence Lichtenstein asked for a free passage for his troops to Austria. Napoleon refused:

"Why should I consider such a proposal? You are mine within the week without conditions."

Mack could only accede. On October 20th the gates of Ulm swung open. Napoleon took up a position on a rocky hillock under the Michelsberg, and the various corps of his generals were deployed along the neighboring hilltops to witness the spectacle. Mack and his staff first appeared. Hat in hand he delivered his sword to Napoleon. The Emperor received him cordially and gave him a place at his side. For five hours then the Austrians marched past in review, led by their officers. As they stacked their muskets in piles, the Emperor would from time to time warm his hands at an open fire: 62,000 prisoners, 80 flags, 200 guns! The campaign had lasted fourteen days.

That evening Napoleon wrote to Josephine: "I have carried out my plan. I have destroyed the Austrian army by plain marching. Now I am going after the Russians. They are lost."

CHAPTER XV

Trafalgar

THE DAY AFTER THE SURRENDER AT ULM THE FRENCH navy was virtually destroyed at Trafalgar. The weakling Villeneuve had gone into hiding at Cadiz; but he had been frightened by reports of Napoleon's wrath and by a warning that he would probably be relieved of his command. He therefore made up his mind to retrieve himself, if possible, by a victory. Leaping from abjection to boastfulness, he wrote to Decrès: "If the French navy has been wanting only in boldness, as is charged, the Emperor will soon be satisfied. He can count on most striking successes."

Villeneuve spent the month of September repairing his ships and resting his crews for a sortie. Counting the Spanish fleet under Admiral Gravina, he had forty ships at his disposal. Nelson was cruising along the Spanish coast in somewhat smaller force (32 units). The best sailor in the British navy, Nelson was a cold, persistent, energetic, dashing commander. He sincerely hated France and dreamed of freeing his country of the nightmare of the invasion. He had taken every measure required for preventing Villeneuve's escape.

The Franco-Spanish fleet sailed out of the port of

Cadiz and headed south, moving in line parallel with the coast. Nelson was waiting off Cape Trafalgar. With the idea of taking advantage of his superiority in numbers Villeneuve tried to outflank the British, but the Spanish vessels were slow moving and badly manned. Their line became strung out too thinly. Nelson saw his adversaries' mistake and proceeded to take advantage of it. He ordered an attack in two columns, one commanded by Admiral Collingwood, the other by himself. For his order of the day, Nelson signaled: "England expects every man to do his duty."

His twin blow struck the French line fairly and cut it into three sections of 15, 5 and 20 vessels. The fight was on. For six hours it lasted in a heavy wind and sea. The Spanish ships were bad sailers on the wind and had soon drifted out of range to leeward. Collingwood was the first to score, causing ten French ships to strike their colors. Nelson had a harder fight. The *Redoubtable* engaged his *Victory* close at hand and tried a boarding operation. A musket ball struck Nelson on the left shoulder and stretched him dying at the foot of his mainmast. However, he remained conscious long enough to learn of his victory. It was complete. Dismasted, sinking, veritable wrecks, seventeen French and Spanish ships were in English hands. One other had blown up. Taking advantage of the storm fifteen French ships managed to escape and return to Cadiz.

Villeneuve had made a brave fight, but he was a prisoner. A few months later he committed suicide, unable to survive a defeat which may have saved the honor of the French flag but which left the English permanent and undisputed masters of the seas. Trafalgar was, in fact, to prove decisive of Napoleon's destiny and of the destiny of Europe. Freed of the danger of invasion England was to be at liberty to devote all her resources to the struggle on the Continent. Napoleon could no longer hope to strike her down at home. He was to see himself in the guise of a new Sisyphus condemned ever to roll his rock, to pile victory on victory. Successes on the field often gave momentary hope to himself and to France, but they could have no lasting effects as long as the main enemy was left untouched. Trafalgar, moreover, was to lead Napoleon in the end to his deadliest error —the mad attempt to enforce the Continental Blockade.

The importance of the disaster at Trafalgar was not apparent to anyone during those first days. Eyes were concentrated on the plains of the Danube where the fate of the coalition was being worked out. England went into public mourning for the hero who died on the *Victory*. Pitt himself—destined very soon to vanish from the scene—was much more depressed by the defeat at Ulm than encouraged by the victory off the coast of Spain. Napoleon received the news calmly and ordered that the importance of the action be minimized in the French press, which should ascribe the losses of the French ships principally to the storm.

CHAPTER XVI

Austerlitz

ALL THE SAME, HE FELT THAT A RAPID DECISION WAS NOW more urgent than ever. Ulm had been just a preface. The Austrian and Russian forces were getting nearer to each other every minute. Francis II had recalled the Archduke Charles from Italy, where he had been beaten at Caldiero by Masséna. Prussia was wavering more and more in her neutrality.

On the outbreak of hostilities Napoleon and Alexander had each demanded free transit for their troops across Prussian soil. Between the two fires Frederick William had been unable to make up his mind. Napoleon simply ignored the king's predicament and marched his troops through Anspach on the way to Ulm. That emphatic violation of sovereignty had inclined the Prussian ruler towards the Czar; but the main pressure came from his wife, the beautiful Queen Louise, a consistent hater of Napoleon. Frederick William resolved to break with France. Mack's defeat supervened, however, to give him pause. Thereupon Alexander hastened to Potsdam in person and browbeat Frederick William into giving his word. The king took the painful step on November 3. He would offer his mediation to the belligerents and in

148

the probable case of refusal by France would join forces with the coalition.

On receiving the news about Prussia from Duroc, Napoleon hurried his march across Bavaria. Before him lay only the Russian army of Kutusov. Kutusov, however, decided that he was too weak and retreated. Crossing the Danube he headed north into Moravia where the Allies had now agreed to concentrate. That left the Austrian capital completely unprotected. Hoping to overtake the Russians Napoleon pushed on along the road to Vienna, advancing down the right bank of the Danube with the bulk of his army, while Mortier kept pace along the other shore. In three weeks' time the Grand Army had marched through rain and snow from Ulm to the Austrian capital, always looking for the invisible enemy. "Our Emperor," said the soldiers, "has a new way of making war. We fight not with our arms but with our legs." Murat with his cavalry was the first to reach Vienna—taking grave risks, to tell the truth. The city had seen no enemy in arms since Sobieski drove away the Turks in 1683. The bridges having been seized, Vienna capitulated on November 13. The Emperor made formal entry and slept the night in the imperial palace at Schönbrunn.

He lingered there only two days, however. Turning back towards the northeast he burst by forced marches into Moravia to find the Austro-Russian army settled in the neighborhood of Olmütz some seventy miles from Vienna.

The Czar and the Emperor Francis had 95,000 men at their disposal. Napoleon had been obliged to secure his bases in the conquered territories with numerous garrisons. He had less than 80,000 soldiers left.

He entered Brünn on November 20, in spite of Bagration, and put his footsore men into camp. The two sovereigns were still waiting for the Archduke Ferdinand, who had escaped from Ulm, and for the Archduke Charles, who was hurrying up from Hungary with Masséna on his heels. They thought it might help to pass the time if they wheedled Napoleon with pretended proposals of peace. The French Emperor did not take unkindly to the idea. He was worried about Prussia and preferred an amicable settlement to further fighting. Prince Dolgoruki, speaking for his Russian master, demanded the surrender of Italy, the Rhineland, Belgium. . . .

"What, Belgium too?" cried Napoleon ironically. "Why—here we are in Moravia. You wouldn't get Brussels if you were on Montmartre!" And he dismissed the Czar's favorite disdainfully: "Go and tell your master that I am not in the habit of being trifled with in this way."

On November 30th he wrote to Talleyrand, who had remained in Vienna on his order: "There will probably be a battle with the Russians tomorrow—rather serious. I have done a good deal in an effort to avoid it, for I consider it a useless waste of blood. . . . Don't be alarmed. I am in a strong position. I am sorry for all that it is going to cost and to no great purpose."

The ground was of his own choosing. He hastily evacuated the town of Austerlitz as though he had suddenly been struck with alarm but found himself forced to fight a defensive battle. That stratagem worked. It lured the Austro-Russians out upon the broad plain of Pratzen.

Napoleon's plan, however much it may be simplified, remains a masterly conception. Austerlitz was his "model battle," the high point in his genius, his most glowing victory. The position he had taken could hardly fail to tempt the enemy to turn his right and cut off his line of retreat on Vienna. The moment the enemy had weakened his center Napoleon would fall upon it in force and crush it. Over-confident, imprudent, Kutusov made haste to do just as Napoleon foresaw. "We're not just winning a battle," the Russian officers were saying. "The battle is already won. We must surround the French army and force it to lay down its arms—the army and its Emperor." Joyously Napoleon saw the Russian columns advancing on Telnitz. "They are walking into the trap!" he cried, late in the afternoon of December 1st when the Russians were in their new positions. "Before sundown tomorrow that army is mine!"

"All day long he has been on horseback," Rovigo relates, "looking over his army in person, regiment by regiment. He spoke to the private soldiers. He inspected each battery of guns and light artillery. He gave instructions to all the officers and to the cannoneers. Then he went to the field hospitals and inspected arrangements for the transportation of the wounded." He had discussed all the various possibilities of the battle with his generals, giving them each definite and very detailed directions. The lieutenants read before each company of men a proclamation which he had dictated from his carriage:

"Soldiers: I shall direct your battalions in person. I

shall keep out of range if you succeed, with your usual bravery, in throwing the enemy lines into disorder and rout. But if victory should at any time seem doubtful, you will see your Emperor exposing himself in the front line."

As evening fell Napoleon dined with his staff. He was strangely calm and strangely gay. In that circle of intimates he seemed to have forgotten the fight that was to begin at dawn. He discussed Corneille and the theater at some length. "The problem is to be eager to live and yet to know how to die. . . . Political life should be a great motive in modern tragedy. . . . It is a mistake to imagine that tragic subjects have all been worn out. There is no end to their number in the requirements of policy. That is a fatality as imperious, as relentless, as the fatality of the ancients."

His thoughts drifted back to early days in his career and to the campaigns in Egypt and Syria. He followed his reverie aloud:

"Yes, if I had taken Acre, I would have adopted the turban and dressed my army in baggy breeches. After that I would have used it only in dire extremities, making it over into my sacred battalion, my Immortals. I would have finished the war with Turkey with Arabs, Greeks and Armenians. Instead of fighting here in Moravia, I would have won a battle on the Issus, turned myself into an Oriental despot and come home to Paris by way of Constantinople."

He smiled as his fancy played, his countenance taking on a very striking nobility of expression.

"If it is a question of going to Constantinople," suggested Ségur in a low voice, "we're on the road again!"

To get some rest Napoleon went and lay down in a little shelter that his grenadiers had built for him. Soon he had fallen into a deep slumber. When Savary came to report a skirmish between outposts, he was obliged to shake the Emperor to waken him. Napoleon rose, mounted a horse, and rode out with Soult into the foggy night. Silently he visited the bivouacs and reconnoitered the Russian positions. His soldiers recognized him. To light his path they made torches of straw and set them on fire. The whole army lay bright under the glow. A great shout—"Long live the Emperor!"—went up and spread from one end of the line to the other. One of the "grumblers," as the veterans of the Revolutionary wars were called, stepped up to Napoleon and said, answering the order of the day:

"Sire, you will not have to expose yourself. I promise you, on behalf of the grenadiers of the army—you will have to fight only with your eyes. Tomorrow we are going to bring you the flags and the artillery of the Russian army as a present for the anniversary of your coronation."

Delighted, Napoleon went on his way. For those rough simple souls he was not just the Emperor—he was the nation visible in person. They admired him, they loved him, they were happy to die for him. And he loved them too. Always solicitous of their comfort, he understood their fatigues and their sufferings and instinctively found words that would set the tears to dripping down upon their long mustaches. In the great moments he was one with them in mind and heart. From their courage and their spirit of self-sacrifice he expected a victory that was now more necessary than ever. At the very moment when the army was raising that prolonged shout, Paris was fretting and disorganizing. Cambacérès and Joseph were proving wretched administrators. They were squabbling over their respective powers. At that distance Napoleon could see the fragile nature of the structure he had reared. To use words of Albert Sorel, it was beginning to look as "though the Emperor were compromising the Empire." Yes, he was just a military dictator. At the first defeat he would find ambitions, rancors, hatreds, which success was for the moment muzzling, rising behind him and nipping at his heels. On his side, really, he could count only his genius and the loyalty of those soldiers who were shivering about the camp fires there.

On the morning of the 2nd the fog lifted, and the plain, the villages, the fir-clad hills, the Goldbrook and its ponds, lay bright under an unclouded sun. The Emperor reviewed the lines for one last time.

"Soldiers," he repeated, "we must finish this campaign with a lightning blow that will humble the pride of our enemies."

They answered by waving their caps on the ends of their bayonets.

The enemy attacked Telnitz and Sokolnitz, as Napoleon desired. Davout nailed the Russians there for three hours, while Soult and Vandamme were storming the plateau of Pratzen. By nine o'clock they had driven the Russians back and were masters of the high land. Napoleon followed with the Guard. Kutusov then tried a desperate effort. He sent the Russian Guard, which had been held in reserve near Austerlitz, to recapture the plateau. It was a frightful hand-to-hand combat in which

THE BATTLE OF AUSTERLITZ
By Naudet

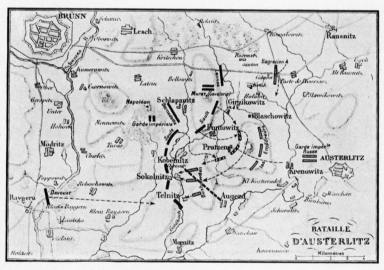

MAP OF THE BATTLE OF AUSTERLITZ

angry howling men sabered and shot each other at arm's length. Finally the Russians gave way and fell back into the ravines. Meantime, on the wings, Murat had dispersed the Austrian cavalry and Lannes had dislodged the infantry of Bagration. The Allied left was still holding under Buxhöwden. The French came crashing down upon it from the high ground on Pratzen. The Russians broke in rout, trying to escape across the ice-covered ponds. The French artillery played upon the ice, which gave way under their weight.

The battle ended at nightfall in a driving snow-storm. 23,000 Austro-Russians lay dead or wounded, 20,000 were prisoners. The two emperors were in flight, almost unescorted, towards the castle of Holitsch. There they holed in. The French had lost a total of 8000 men.

Napoleon rode back and forth over the battlefield. "It was already dark," writes Rovigo. "He had ordered silence that the cries of the wounded men might be heard, then he would ride immediately in their direction, dismount at the side of a wounded man and give him a glass of brandy from the flask that he was never without. I was with him that whole night. He stayed out very late on the battlefield. His personal bodyguard spent the whole time gathering up capes from the bodies of dead Russians to spread over wounded soldiers. He had a great fire built near each man whom he found, sent orderlies in all directions to hunt for a stretcher-bearer and did not move on himself till the aid had arrived. Then he would detach a picket from his own escort and order him not to leave the wounded man till the latter was safe in a hospital."

Napoleon has been portrayed as an insensitive despot.

How deeply he was stirred by what he saw that night appears from the 30th communiqué from the Grand Army, which was drawn up at his dictation:

"Never was a battlefield more horrible. From the middle of the great ponds one could hear the appeals of thousands of men who were beyond any help. . . . One's heart bleeds. . . . May so much unhappiness and the spilling of so much blood fall at last upon the heads of the treacherous islanders who are responsible for all this."

To his soldiers he addressed a thrilling expression of gratitude:

"Soldiers: I am pleased with you. You have adorned your eagles with boundless glory. When everything required for the happiness and prosperity of our country has been achieved, I shall lead you back to France. There you will receive my tenderest solicitudes. My people will hail your return with joy, and you will have only to say, 'I was at Austerlitz,' to hear in answer, 'There is a brave man.'"

Two days later Emperor Francis appeared at a French outpost at Poleny Mill to ask for an armistice. Napoleon received him as he alighted from his carriage and embraced him. The two sovereigns stepped into the mill to confer.

"This," said Napoleon, smiling, "is the sort of palace Your Majesty has been compelling me to live in for the past two months."

"The environment seems to agree with you so well that you can hardly owe me any grudge on that score."

A truce? Napoleon was perfectly willing to agree to one. However, he demanded that the Allies separate first.

"The Russian army is surrounded, but I am anxious to do a favor to the Emperor Alexander. I will let the Russian army pass if Your Majesty assures me that it will evacuate Germany and Poland and return to Russia." If Russia agreed to an immediate peace, Napoleon would ask for no territorial indemnities, for he would find his hands free to turn against England.

Alexander hedged, however. He would go no further than ordering his generals to quit Austrian territory. Napoleon was already thinking of an alliance with Russia and was anxious to get a mortgage on the future. He sent back to the Czar the members of the Russian Imperial Guard who had been taken prisoner. That gracious gesture angered the French staff.

"To let them go today," cried Vandamme, "is to see them in Paris six years hence!"

A far-sighted prophecy! It missed only in respect of the date.

Talleyrand went to Brünn to talk peace with the Austrian envoys. Napoleon settled at Schönbrunn. Thither he summoned Haugwitz, the Prussian minister, who had called on him some days before Austerlitz to demand acceptance of Prussian mediation.

Napoleon had sent Haugwitz back to Vienna at that time. He was not being fooled by Frederick William's tortuous policy, but still he did not know just what sort of agreement Potsdam had reached with the Czar. His purpose at the moment was to frighten Prussia off and prevent her from joining Russia and the English. He received Haugwitz with a scowl. When the minister began to congratulate him he retorted:

"Those are compliments which Fortune has redirected!" And he launched out into a denunciation of Prussia's double-dealing.

Haugwitz was terrified by the Emperor's rage, for Napoleon was a genius at staging diplomatic scenes. The ambassador could hardly believe his ears when suddenly he heard Napoleon propose that Prussia accept Hanover in exchange for a formal alliance to be concluded then and there. Actually Haugwitz signed the agreement the following morning and then rushed away for Berlin to obtain his king's ratification. The document called for the cession of Anspach to Bavaria and of Neuchâtel and Clèves to France. In compensation Prussia got the hereditary domain of the English kings in Germany, so increasing her territory and her population by a fourth.

The conference with the Austrians at Brünn soon moved to Pressburg. Talleyrand was for dealing gently with the Hapsburgs. His thinking went back to the old lines of Choiseul and Vergennes, who were always working for a Franco-Austrian alliance. But Napoleon was tired of Austrian duplicity and bent on settling accounts with Vienna once and for all. His terms were ruinously harsh. Francis II pleaded in vain. The French army was sitting in the heart of his states and Napoleon threatened to resume hostilities. The Emperor could only yield. At Pressburg on December 26th his plenipotentiaries ceded Venice, Friuli, Istria and Dalmatia to France, and the Tyrol, the Voralberg and Swabia to the electors of Bavaria and Württemberg. Austria further agreed to pay an indemnity of forty millions. Stripped of her possessions in Italy and Germany, she thus gave up one-sixth of her population.

From Vienna also, and again over Francis's protests,

Napoleon decided to settle accounts with the treacherous Bourbons of Naples, who, in spite of their pledge of neutrality, had called the English and the Russians to their aid during the Austerlitz campaign.

"Soldiers:" he proclaimed magniloquently. "The dynasty at Naples has ceased to reign. Its existence is incompatible with peace in Europe. . . . March! Cast into the waves these insignificant battalions of the tyrants of the seas, if it shall be that they dare await your onslaught."

It had already occurred to him that Naples might provide a good throne for his brother Joseph.

With the Naples matter off his chest, Napoleon hurried away to Munich where Josephine, courted and pampered by the princes of Germany, was waiting for him. He concluded a marriage for Eugene de Beauharnais with the princess Augusta, daughter to the King of Bavaria, and then moved on towards France by way of Strasburg.

The whole campaign had lasted three months.

CHAPTER XVII

Emperor of the West

NAPOLEON CAME BACK IN TRIUMPH. WHAT MARENGO
had done for the Consulate Austerlitz did for the Empire. "The people's joy," wrote Cambacérès, "was more
like a frenzy." But Napoleon did not partake of it. In-
ternal problems required every particle of his attention.
To set home affairs in order again he bent his neck to the
yoke.

The business depression had begun in the autumn of
1805 and had grown steadily worse during his absence.
Barbé-Marbois, a complete failure as an administrator,
had allowed the speculators to fatten on disgraceful prac-
tices which had exhausted credit and emptied the treasury. The Bank of France had quintupled its paper, so
causing an inflation panic. A number of banks, the
Récamier institution among them, suspended payments.
Napoleon removed Barbé-Marbois the morning after his
return from Vienna, replacing him with Mollien. He
obliged the manipulators, notably the famous Ouvrard,
to repay eighty millions into the public cash-box. That
money, supplemented by the forty millions from Austria
and a heavy contribution from Spain, checked the panic
and the currency recovered.

His next thought was for public works—projects in the Roman style were always on his mind. He seemed able to think of everything, little and big, at one time: a column in the place Vendôme to be made from captured guns melted down; an arch of triumph at the Carrousel by Percier and Fontaine; another arch, of monumental proportions, for the place de l'Étoile; the Louvre to be completed and connected with the Tuileries; St. Mark's square to be completed in Venice; foundations for a Stock Exchange Building and for a Wine Market; new streets—the rues de Rivoli, Castiglione and de la Paix; a new town, Napoléon-Vendée, afterwards to become La Roche-sur-Yon; new harbors—Antwerp, Cherbourg, Brest, La Rochelle; reconstructions—Lyons had been knocked to pieces during the Revolution; new canals—the system uniting Belgium and northern France; new roads—an admirable network of highways, bringing the remotest frontiers of the Empire into touch with one another. This colossal activity was to continue during all the reign. Between campaigns Napoleon was ever at work, choosing plans, devising ways and means, inspecting results. The achievement of the Emperor in public works has never been adequately studied or appraised, but one may say from a casual glance that it was not the least useful nor the least grandiose of his career.

Industry began to prosper under a high protective tariff—silk at Lyons, broadcloth at Elbeuf, linens at St. Quentin, woolens at Roubaix. Napoleon gave large orders for such factories, in that respect going back to a policy of Colbert but with broader views and a more potent impulse. The Emperor would tolerate nothing about him, even the gowns of the women, that was not

French. An exposition of manufacturing products was opened at the Louvre, and Napoleon personally decorated Oberkampf, who had invented a process for printing cloth, and Delessert, who had submitted to him a tentative plan for replacing colonial cane with home-grown beet sugar.

Under the handicap of the English blockade trade remained sluggish, but to do what he could for it Napoleon opened credits and founded Chambers of Commerce in the principal French cities. Agriculture for its part was flourishing. The peasant was now working enthusiastically on lands which he had bought as national property and was no longer afraid of losing. Production quintupled in almost all crops. It was good living in the provinces, the one harassing specter being the draft. The army had been weakened by the many campaigns. Effectives had to be built up again. 450,000 men were under arms, 150,000 more in recruiting or reserve camps, another 100,000 outside France. The Grand Army, always on a war footing, counted 130,000 infantry, 30,000 cavalry, 10,000 cannoneers, all with war experience. It was the most impressive military machine that the world had so far seen.

Napoleon was hoping that he would not need to use it very soon. He had not given up entirely the idea of a raid on England—he was not to abandon that hope till late in his reign. He had merely postponed it indefinitely. A political change had taken place in London and Napoleon saw a chance that peace might come of it. The irreconcilable Pitt had died and Fox had succeeded him. Napoleon respected Fox and Fox admired Napoleon. Shortly after Fox assumed power an adventurer approached him with a plan for assassinating the French Emperor. The Premier not only had the man arrested but notified Talleyrand of what had taken place. Napoleon thanked Fox personally for that loyal gesture. Fox had courageously and consistently deplored the repudiation of the Treaty of Amiens. He suggested opening negotiations again. The Emperor was delighted. He could feel sure of nothing so long as England remained his enemy. He was ready to leave Malta to the English, and the Cape which they had seized from the Dutch. He would even restore Hanover, finding some compensation for Prussia elsewhere. There remained one obstacle, however—the commercial rivalry of the two nations. Napoleon was unwilling to make concessions in the field of trade. He wanted to go on protecting the industries he had founded. Had Fox been sole master of English policy, the negotiations would probably have borne fruit even in the face of that difficulty. But Fox had to deal with his colleagues in the ministry. They were basically hostile to any accord with France and always found a thousand ways to block progress. Conversations dragged along. The English cabinet, for one thing, was loath to treat apart from Russia. That obstacle disappeared of itself. The Czar sent d'Oubril to Paris of his own accord. In April, 1806, it really seemed as though a general peace were in sight.

Napoleon selected that moment to carry out a project that he had long been pondering and which would make his empire the driving center of an array of vassal states that would taper up to him with close-knit ties. He would re-create the great Empire, less along Roman than along early Medieval lines. That would leave Napoleon not merely a French sovereign. He would be Emperor of western Europe, holding control of the Mediterranean to boot. Born a Corsican, steeped in classical traditions and now freshly influenced by memories of Egypt, he remained a man of the Mediterranean in sentiment and in his manners of thinking. He was still, as he was ever to remain, a Corsican in his sense of clan. He wanted to make his brothers rulers of kingdoms which he would annex or create. He knew the qualities of his kinsmen as well as their deficiencies and weaknesses; but however many mistakes they might make, they would, he thought, be faithful in view of common ties of blood—more faithful, at any rate, than outsiders. Owing everything to him, they would have to be subservient to his will.

On March 31st, 1806, he named Joseph King of Naples, and on June 5th, Louis Bonaparte King of Holland. Murat, Caroline's husband, became Grand Duke of Berg. On a minor plane, Elisa, already Duchess of Lucca, received Tuscany, while Pauline became Duchess of Guastalla. The Emperor then went on to distribute other principalities as prize-money, so to say, to the men who were filling leading posts at his side and were entitled to shares in the booty of conquest. So Talleyrand became Prince of Benevento and Berthier Prince of Neuchâtel. Bernadotte was a traitor at heart, as Napoleon well knew. But he had married Désirée Clary, Joseph's sister-in-law, and Napoleon was always treating him too considerately on that account. Bernadotte became Prince of Ponte-Corvo. Twenty duchies were further provided to recompense high civil servants and the marshals. Napoleon already held the title of "Mediator of Switzerland." That gave him virtually the same power over the Helvetic Federation that he held over Italy. To cover the French flank on the east, he worked on the princes of western Germany to form a Federation of the Rhine. Bavaria, Württemberg, Baden, Hesse, the Grand Duchy of Berg and eleven other states so came into league with a capital at Frankfurt. The Federation declared itself the perpetual ally of France and proclaimed Napoleon its Protector.

So after seven centuries and a half of existence the old Holy Roman Empire came to an end. Francis II was asked to drop his empty title as Emperor of Germany and rest content with being Emperor of Austria. All this shuffling of titles was a merely symbolic reflection of a social revolution in Europe that was real enough. The transformation, in fact, was profound and permanent. Napoleon's theory was a blend of concepts going back through the Revolution to the traditional organization of Europe. All Europe, he thought, should ultimately coalesce into a more or less close federation which would function under the hegemony of France. So the United States of Europe would come into being, an organization possessing uniform laws and customs but with due account being taken of differences in race and climate. There would then be no more wars. As was the case with the *pax romana* in the Roman world which he admired, so under a *pax napoleonica* in a European world thus constituted, civilization would soar to unpredictable, truly limitless heights. Napoleon was not unaware that several human lifetimes would be required to carry out a program so far-reaching. But he thought that the most difficult step was the beginning and he stood ready to devote his own life to making the start. His successors would find the going easier. They would simply have to do the fusing and the consolidating.

In these basic conceptions Napoleon was reviving the system of Charlemagne. The Pope was to be closely bound to the Emperor. Napoleon did not intend to touch the spiritual prerogatives of the pontiff, but he did think of himself as the temporal suzerain of the Holy See. As King of Italy he was to be at home in Rome. "All Italy is to be subject to my law," he wrote in February, 1806. And he reiterated to a number of ambassadors: "The Pope is my vassal."

The Pope, however, would not agree to this appropriation of his sovereignty. Pius VII was not a great mind. He was what might be called a great soul. In the face of objections from the Sacred College he had showered favors on Napoleon's head. He had signed a concordat that gave Napoleon greater power over the bishops of the Church than any king had ever had before. In spite of the claims of the old dynasty, he had gone to Paris to anoint the Emperor. After that, he had been treated ungratefully, as he thought, and disappointment had followed disappointment. Napoleon began to behave not like a dutiful son but like an arrogant master. Now the Pope could recognize no master other than God. Pius was a simple, devout, unassuming, frugal monk. He certainly did not want any possessions, any dotations, for himself. But he did think of himself as the steward of the Church domains. He would not surrender them, because he did not see how he had a right to surrender them.

The Pope was guilty of some breaches of tact in his

dealings with Napoleon. While the Emperor had his hands full with the campaign that was to end at Austerlitz, Pius suddenly demanded the evacuation of Ancona. Napoleon rejected the proposal angrily: "Those people counted me dead already!" he wrote to Fesch. Later on the Pope declined to recognize Joseph as King of Naples, on the ground that "that crown emanated from the Holy See." The Emperor leapt to his feet: "Your Holiness is sovereign in Rome, but I am Emperor of Rome." "There is no Emperor of Rome," Pius replied. "There can be none such without depriving the pontiff of the authority that he exercises in Rome."

So the conflict opened. It was embittered by minor difficulties. The Pope objected to the introduction of the Civil Code into Italy, as recognizing the principle of divorce which the Church abhorred. At the instance of the Cardinals he created embarrassments for Elisa and Pauline in their duchies. Finally he refused to bar Englishmen from his territories.

Napoleon could not have been pricked in a more sensitive spot. Should he reply to the challenge by an assertion of force and decree the annexation of the Papal States to the Kingdom of Italy? That was a serious business. He would think it over. . . . For the moment he had to give all his attention to the negotiations with Russia and England.

Somewhat by surprise Talleyrand had obtained a treaty from d'Oubril, the Russian ambassador in Paris. It only required ratification by the Czar. Unfortunately the talks with the English were not getting on. Lord Lauderdale was a great stickler for niceties and very mistrustful. He had taken Lord Yarmouth's place in

Paris, judging the ambassador too pro-French in his sympathies. The stumbling-block was Sicily. Napoleon wanted the island for Joseph. England would not consent to stripping that last rag from the backs of the Neapolitan Bourbons.

Then something unforeseen occurred, and it threw everything into the air. Fox died. The death of one individual has rarely had such an important influence on the course of world events. "Fox's death," Napoleon was to say at St. Helena, "was one of the strokes of bad luck in my career. Had he lived, we would have come to terms." From that moment the war party had a clear field in the British cabinet. Discussions dragged along for some days still; then Napoleon broke them off and handed Lauderdale his passports. "In a brain-storm" (*accès de folie*) Prussia had declared war and Russia had torn up her own treaty and joined Prussia. So there was no help for it. The Emperor had to get his army together once more and go out and force upon his enemies a peace which they refused to give him in Paris.

CHAPTER XVIII

Jena

THE ATTITUDE OF PRUSSIA ON THE EVE OF AUSTERLITZ should have indicated to Napoleon that his victory only had induced Prussia to become an ally of France. But Napoleon cherished astonishing misapprehensions in regard to Prussia. However clear-headed he was as a rule, sentiments and habitual ways of thinking sometimes misled him. He thought he had won Frederick William by the gift, actually very dangerous and humiliating, of Hanover, a property filched from an ally of Prussia. But Napoleon had grown up admiring the great Frederick and professing high esteem for the Prussian army. Like most men of the Revolution he regarded Prussia as a natural friend of France. All the same the Prussia that he had treated with consideration and enriched was in the hands of a military clique that hated him. Queen Louise was the soul of the antagonism. "Napoleon," she declared, "is just a monster that has crawled out of the slime." On recalling his representative, d'Oubril, from Paris, the Czar had urged Frederick William to join him "in restoring peace to Europe," and especially for the purpose of reducing France to her former power.

At the time when he created the Rhine Federation

the Emperor had been at some pains to inform Berlin that he had no objection to the King's forming a similar association of states in north Germany and taking the presidency of it himself, even, if he desired, with the title of emperor. Frederick William was afraid and hedged. Then suddenly his ambassador in Paris, Lucchesini, sent word that in order to make his deal with England, Napoleon had indicated willingness to ask Hanover back from Prussia. A loss without compensation, an unbearable insult! The wavering monarch felt that he had been duped. At the same moment, a rumor began floating about that Poland was to be reunited. That would deprive Prussia of the Polish provinces which she had gained at the last partition. Anti-French feeling ran high at court and in the army. A council held at Potsdam decided to mobilize the army, and when the news spread generally abroad a fever of pride and folly seemed to sweep all Prussia: The homeland of Frederick II owed it to herself and to Europe to "overthrow the disturber of the universe"!

The Berlin cabinet began by demanding the withdrawal of all French troops quartered in Germany. Napoleon was not averse to that. He was thinking of mobilizing the Grand Army somewhere near Paris for a great holiday celebration. But the fact of Russia's repudiating her treaty caused him to suspect, and not without reason, that a new coalition was in the making. However he was loath to reopen hostilities and showed himself ready to find some compromise. "Let Russia send her soldiers home," he wrote to the Prussian ambassador, "and the French will withdraw across the Rhine, but not before." "War between our two countries," he added, "would be a monstrous thing." To these conciliatory moves Prussia replied by an ultimatum, calling on Napoleon to evacuate German territory by the 8th of October, 1806.

The excitement of Queen Louise and the Prussian generals went to unheard-of lengths. Young German officers whetted their sabers on the steps of the French Embassy, while a colonel, addressing them, shouted: "Sabers are not necessary for these French dogs. Clubs are good enough." Napoleon was with Berthier when the Prussian note arrived. He shrugged his shoulders and remarked: "We have been challenged to the field of honor. No Frenchman ever missed such an appointment. I shall be in Saxony tomorrow."

Not a moment was to be lost, in fact. Under the influence of the Spanish queen's disgraceful favorite, Manuel Godoÿ, Spain seemed about to turn against France. The Dutch were restless because of the resumption of war on the seas. Italy was rumbling because of disappointments at Rome. The British had landed in the Kingdom of Naples. The Czar was mobilizing with noisy publicity. Napoleon hastened to muster the Grand Army, 170,000 strong, in the neighborhood of Bamberg in Franconia, then he threw it upon Saxony in three columns. After a number of successful skirmishes the left column, under Lannes, defeated Prince Louis of Prussia at Saalfeld (October 10th), the prince losing his life in the engagement.

Then the Prussian high command seemed strangely to lose its head. Instead of sticking together to face the French the two principal Prussian generals, the aged Duke of Brunswick, the veteran of Valmy, and Prince

Hohenlohe, separated. Napoleon debouched into the plain of Jena on October 13th.

He could not have been calmer. "The business is going beautifully," he wrote to Josephine, who had accompanied him as far as Mainz. "With God's help, things will have a terrible look, I imagine, for the poor King of Prussia. Personally I pity him for he's a good soul. The Queen is at Erfurt with him. If she wants to see a battle she will have that cruel pleasure. I am in wonderful health. I have gained in weight since my departure. Nevertheless, what with horseback, carriages and other means of conveyance, I have been doing from fifty to sixty miles a day. I go to bed at eight and am up again at midnight."

Forces were about evenly matched at Jena—40,000 French against Hohenlohe's 46,000 Prussians. During the night the Emperor and the Guard, along with Lannes, occupied the steep-sided plateau called the Landgrafenberg. It was a magnificent position, commanding a view of the whole countryside. Napoleon personally discovered a path for getting the artillery up. When it proved to be too narrow the sappers broadened it by cutting away the ledge, the Emperor holding a lantern for them to work by. He did not move away till he had seen the first guns dragged up by man power and put in their places. Then he made a tour of the front lines and so carelessly that one of the French pickets, mistaking him for a Prussian, took a shot at him. Returning to his tent he fell asleep on his little iron cot. He was awakened at five.

"Well," he said to Soult, "are we going to lick them?"

"Yes," the marshal replied, "if they are there. I'm afraid they won't be."

In fact, it would have been the most obvious common sense on Hohenlohe's part to decamp on finding Napoleon before him, and join Brunswick. But he thought he had to deal with the corps of Lannes and Augereau and was bent on giving them a lesson they would remember.

On catching sight of the Prussians in the early morning light Napoleon cried out for joy:

"By jove, they stayed! It's going to begin!"

He rode to the front lines and chatted familiarly with the officers and men who crowded around, explaining the situation of the two armies: "Today," he concluded, "we've got to destroy the famous Prussian cavalry on our squares, just as we crushed the Russian infantry at Austerlitz."

"Send us in!" cried the men, their morale high.

Two little skirmishes cleared the approaches to the Landgrafenberg, and then the real battle started. The Prussian grenadiers marched as coolly and in as good order as they would have on parade. Their volleys were badly aimed; but Ney, impatient, charged before receiving the order and was repulsed. Then Napoleon gave them Lannes. The Prussian lines gave way at almost every point, and Murat's cavalry turned the recoil into a rout, the Prussians fleeing in a disorganized mob along the road to Weimar. Hohenlohe was wounded but made his escape. By late afternoon, 20,000 prisoners and 200 cannon were in the hands of the French. At the same hour, at Auerstädt, Davout attacked the Duke of Brunswick. Bernadotte, out of jealousy, refused to support

Davout and the battle, bitterly contested, was more costly than the one at Jena. Davout lost 10,000 men, a third of his effectives. But he was finally able to beat off the attacks of the enemy cavalry and his counter-attack, though made in greatly inferior numbers, completely crushed the army of the duke, who fell mortally wounded by a ball of case shot.

Prussia collapsed, and never did a country in misfortune show more abject terror or more servile abasement. Hohenlohe capitulated at Prentzlow on October 28th. Blücher had boasted that he was "digging a grave for every last Frenchman on the Rhine." Actually he imitated Hohenlohe at Lübeck on November 7th. Frederick William had not a soldier left between the Rhine and the Oder.

By that time Napoleon had already entered Berlin. The population lined the sidewalks in masses to see the conqueror pass. They were sad but they admired. The imperial Guard led the procession, then came Napoleon on horseback, in the uniform of a simple chasseur. A little behind him rode the marshals, Berthier, Davout, Augereau, Duroc. The king had humbled himself to the point of ordering the authorities "to have an eye to the Emperor's comfort in the palace where he should elect to reside and to entertain him there as a respected guest" at the expense of the Prussian treasury. He had asked for a truce the morning after Jena. "You are too great a man," he wrote with no great dignity, "to lose your respect for me because of the outcome of a single battle." Napoleon was in no hurry to answer, and when he did reply the terms were so harsh that the cringing king could not bring himself to accept. He took refuge in East Prussia, the only province he still had left, hoping to delay until help from Russia should enable him to treat without too flagrant dishonor.

The people about him also changed from arrogance to discouragement, though the Prussians ascribed their defeat less to the valor of the French than to defects in their own social system. One of the king's officers wrote to his family: "If one could use just one's muscle against the French they would be no match for us. They are small, insignificant creatures. Any one of our Germans could whip four of them. But they become supernatural beings under fire. They are carried away by an indescribable enthusiasm of which one notes no trace in our soldiers. . . . What can one hope to do with peasants who are led under fire by nobles, whose dangers they share without ever sharing in their passions or their rewards?"

At Berlin Napoleon reassured the magistrates and maintained strict orderliness among his troops. He showed severity only towards the nobles who had premeditated the attack on France and carried it through. He even considered making an example of the Prince von Hatzfeld, head of the municipal government in the capital, who had written a letter informing Hohenlohe of the positions of the French army. He ordered Hatzfeld shot. Hatzfeld's wife threw herself in sobs at Napoleon's feet. He handed her her husband's letter. "That is your husband's writing?" he asked. She bowed her head, finding no answer. Finally he added: "Well, madame, suppose you burn it. I should never feel strong enough now to have your husband punished."

Napoleon wrote to Paris from Berlin ordering the

construction of a Temple of Glory (it was eventually to
become the Madeleine). The bridge across the Seine
opposite the Military School he ordered renamed in
honor of Jena. He had declared the Prussian army the
best in Europe, and to have destroyed it in two mighty
strokes filled him with measureless joy and pride. Nothing, he thought, would be able to cloud his glory after
such a feat.

"This time," he wrote to Cambacérès, "I am going
to deal with my enemies in such a style that it will be
the end of them." By enemies he meant the Russians
and the English. The former he intended to run down
in the marshes of the North. He was counting on smiting
the English with a fatal paralysis by barring them from
the Continent. "The sea would be conquered by the
land." He drew up and signed his famous Berlin Ordinance on November 21. It instituted the "Continental
Blockade." "The British Isles are declared in a state of
blockade. All trade and all dealings with them are hereby
forbidden."

His whole policy was henceforward to revolve around
that capital decree. The fate of Europe was pinned to it.
The die was cast. The only alternatives now were victory
or death. It was to be a hazy, indefinite struggle both in
space and in time, a pitiless hand-to-hand from which
either England would issue, strangled, gasping for breath,
a petitioner for peace, or else Napoleon would fall on a
battlefield, overwhelmed by the foes which English gold
would have mustered about him.

For his own part he had no doubt of the outcome and
in no distant future. Under the spur of success Illusion
was carrying him away at full gallop. Talleyrand had

led him into mistakes already and was to lead him into still others. He did not stay him from making this one, indeed he urged him to the extreme decision.

The Continental Blockade was the basic, the supreme mistake in Napoleon's career. To enforce such a blockade rigorously (and without strict enforcement it was a mere jest) armies of customs' guards were not enough, nor even the connivance of governments. A strange paradox: In order to make the blockade effective, in order to close the choke on that far-flung economic net, Napoleon needed to control the seas, and that control he was never to possess. Compelling him to rule Europe under an iron law, the decree of Berlin was to force him into a series of encroachments and acts of violence which were gradually to array most of the countries of the West against him. While France was struggling to subdue them in order to enforce the blockade England organized against her not merely a coalition of princes but—much more dangerous—a coalition of peoples. From the Pandora's box that was opened at Berlin were to fly forth the wars of Spain and Portugal, the spoliation of the Pope, the unification of Holland, the great Russian campaign and the disasters that were to come of that disaster. A grinding nine years' wastage of men and of hearts that was to find its ruinous end at Waterloo!

CHAPTER XIX

Eylau and Friedland

MEANTIME THE CZAR WAS STILL ON HIS FEET. THE FATE of Prussia had not cowed Alexander. He made a first move to rouse Austria again against Napoleon. The Russian ambassador at Vienna was Pozzo di Borgo, a sometime henchman of Paoli the Corsican. Pozzo di Borgo hated Napoleon on those old scores as only Corsicans could hate. Francis II explained to Pozzo naïvely: "If I declare myself now I can only expect to have Bonaparte on my hands with all his strength. . . . I speak frankly: I shall delay fighting as long as possible." Napoleon also was working at him, offering him Silesia, which Frederick the Great had wrested from Maria Teresa a half century earlier. Silesia could be exchanged for Galicia. There again Francis answered inconclusively and in order to be ready for any eventuality he began secretly to arm.

Napoleon wanted Galicia in order to reconstitute Poland. That country had been partitioned for the second time only thirteen years earlier. In Napoleon's eyes it was the real bulwark of the West and he regarded the partition as "an inexcusable imbecility." He thought of undoing the mistake for the incidental reason that Polish gratitude and enthusiasm would supply him with no end of first-rate soldiers. As regarded Russia the redemption of "the martyr nation" was a threat well calculated to bring the colossus to terms; and he added force to the threat by urging Turkey to attack the Czar. Soon, he thought, Alexander would be caught in a vise.

To provide for unforeseeables, the Emperor called out the class of recruits maturing in 1807 and drew from his reserve camps seven regiments of infantry and a fine cavalry force made up largely of Italians. This army he billeted on Prussia, and Prussia, bled white for the purpose, paid the other costs. He was soon ready to advance into Poland.

Murat occupied Warsaw on November 28th, 1806, acclaimed by the populace in a delirium of patriotic hopefulness. The Emperor, however, held off. He knew how shifty, how untrustworthy, how divided the Poles had always been, and he was unwilling to proclaim their independence till they had risen of their own spontaneous accord against their oppressors. As soon as his feelings were known the high Polish nobility made haste to form a provisional government under Prince Poniatowski, and glorious banners that had been in hiding since the partition began to float once more over battalions of young men who went into training under French instructors. Napoleon entered Warsaw in person on December 18th. An immense throng watched all night in awed silence under the windows of the liberator, and in the morning there was but one voice and one soul to welcome him. Never in history had a conqueror been received with such devout homage. Preoccupied as he was with the intricacies of policy Napoleon could not help feeling the throb of aspiration that pervaded the air about him. "This is really a people," he said to Duroc. "We must try to do something for them. They deserve it."

General Benningsen, commanding the Russian army, had added the driftwood from Prussia to his forces and taken the offensive. Napoleon crossed the Bug and ordered an attack on him. A sudden and unseasonable thaw supervened. Rain washed the frost out of the ground and the troops often moved about with mud up to their knees. A number of skirmishes turned to the advantage of the French—Czarnovo, Nasielsk, Soldau. Lannes won a pitched battle at Pultusk. However, Benningsen was a good strategist and made a successful retreat, which deprived the victory of any great significance (December 23).

Napoleon returned to Warsaw on January 1, 1807, to go into winter quarters. He had concluded that the decision had to be postponed till spring. Benningsen, on the other hand, thought the cold weather was in his favor and resorted to a bold plan of operation. He began a turning movement along the Baltic coast, screening his maneuver behind the lakes and forests of East Prussia. His idea was to take Napoleon by surprise and cut him off in Warsaw. Ney, however, with his usual imprudence, had driven ahead in the direction of Königsberg. He stumbled into Benningsen on the march. Retreating, he notified Napoleon.

The ground had hardened again in a severe and prolonged cold. Poland and Prussia were just one immense snow-covered plain. Napoleon decided to resume the campaign and finish it by one overwhelming blow. He picked the flower of his troops to outflank the Russians and drive them into the sea. Benningsen sidestepped at Jonkowo and fell back upon Eylau, with the Emperor hot upon his heels. Suddenly on the evening of February 7th, beyond Eylau, the Russians halted and lighted their bivouacs. They had decided to make a stand— 80,000 of them against 54,000 French.

The engagement opened at daybreak on the 8th of February, on a snow-covered battlefield under a cloudy sky. Napoleon stationed himself in the cemetery at Eylau on a high knoll. The two armies stood for a long time under a grilling artillery fire, making no movement except to close ranks as the solid shot tore gaps in their lines. Finally Augereau attacked Benningsen's left, charging in the face of a wind that filled the air with driving snow. He was received with a withering fire. Blinded by the snow his men finally recoiled, after losing two-thirds of their number.

"Are we going to let those people eat us up?" called Napoleon to Murat.

Murat charged, using his whole force of cavalry, twenty squadrons strong, straight at the enemy's center. The terrific impact shook the wall of Russian infantrymen. It cracked at one point. A terrifying hand-to-hand ensued. Benningsen ordered his artillery to play upon the confused mass of men regardless of whether French or Russians were killed. Finally the Russians gave way and fled into the woods. Napoleon had been holding the Guard in reserve in the cemetery. A Russian column suddenly appeared and attacked it there. Napoleon directed the formation of the squares in person and went from gun to gun cheering the cannoneers. One of them held up a pair of swollen, frost-bitten hands. Repeating a gesture he had made at Toulon, Napoleon took the ramrod and loaded and aimed the piece. The Russians came on, to be shot down almost to the last man, though they sold their lives dearly.

Meantime, lashing at the snow with his whip and striding over the graves in the cemetery which were now covered with fresh corpses, the Emperor was watching anxiously for Davout to turn the enemy's left. But suddenly 8000 Prussians, who had eluded Ney, arrived on the field to reinforce the Russians. The battle was begun all over again. Evening was just falling on that spectacle of butchery when Ney also arrived. He had heard the cannonading and made for it across the snow-clad fields. Benningsen was discouraged and ordered a retreat. He had lost half his army. He had yielded the battlefield. One could hardly say that he had been defeated.

Napoleon was well aware of that. As he rode over the plain the next morning among the thousands of mounds raised by the snow-covered dead, he was seized with a sort of despairing sorrow. "This spectacle," he exclaimed, "is of the sort to inspire princes with a love of peace and a horror for war." And in an intimate letter to the Empress he confessed: "My soul is appalled at the sight of so many victims."

He was free to assert in his communiqué that he had won a victory. Benningsen did not admit defeat and Europe believed Benningsen. Vienna started intriguing with a will. Spain advanced along the road to betrayal. Even the cringing Prussia began to take heart. The Emperor for his part was disappointed. Eylau had not ended the war. It had been a gigantic give-and-take. Hemmed

MURAT

From the Portrait by Gérard

in by winter five hundred miles from his bases, the French giant seemed to be tottering.

Napoleon, however, did not brood for an instant. He sent Ney and Murat to harass the Russian retreat as far as Königsberg. When Benningsen was safe within his entrenchments, Napoleon withdrew his men behind the Passarge river into camp. That was to cover Dantzig, which was being besieged by Lefebvre. Adapting his ideas to the climate, the season, the terrain, Napoleon gave up the war of maneuver for the war of position. Camping himself in a sort of barn at Osterode, he set to work to reorganize his army. He had hardly more than 80,000 men left. The remainder of the Grand Army was scattered over all Germany, from the Rhine to the Vistula. March proved to be a very cold month, and provisioning was difficult, but for all their hardships, the troops lost none of their spirit or good humor. The Emperor's presence seemed to make up to them for everything.

With an astonishing agility of mind that displayed all his greatness Napoleon continued to manage the Empire from a distance of seven hundred miles. Paris had suffered a shock at tales that pictured Eylau as a great disaster. Stocks fell on Exchange. Napoleon scolded Fouché for not managing, or even trying, to put an end to such talk. He kept in touch with work at the Council of State and even directed it through auditors, who reported on the doings of the ministers. He wanted Paris to be gay, with plenty of celebrations and festivals. The public, as well as trade, needed such things. To provide work for the unemployed he applied several millions from his reserve funds to orders for cloths, furniture and

art objects. At the same time he gave a thought to the
Academy, which was finding fault with the Revolution
and therefore with his own origins, to the Opera where
there was bickering and quarreling, to the academy for
young ladies at Écouen, for which he drew up a cur-
riculum. He banished Mme. de Staël, brought Ricord
home from exile, extended help to Berthollet, advised
and scolded his brothers, Joseph and Louis, apprentice
kings who were beginning their reigns with acts of fool-
ishness.

Joseph had written to him complaining about minor
irritations that he had suffered on arriving at Naples.
Napoleon replied: "The officers of my staff have not
undressed for two months, and some of them for four.
I myself have not taken off my boots for two weeks. . . .
We are buried in snow and mud. We are living on po-
tatoes and meat, without wine, brandy or bread. We
make long marches and counter-marches without any
sort of comforts, and we fight ordinarily hand-to-hand
under a rain of grape. The wounded are carried off on
sleds and lie exposed to the weather for as many as 150
miles. It seems to me a sort of bad jest to compare the
places we are in to your beautiful Naples country, where
you have wine, bread, bedclothes, society and even
women. We have destroyed the Prussian monarchy. Now
we are fighting the rest of Prussia, the Russians, the
Kalmuks, the Cossacks, and the tribes of the North who
invaded the Roman empire of yore. We are waging war
in all its ferocity, in all its horror. As a result of all these
hardships everybody has been more or less sick, except
me. I have never been stronger. . . . Osterode, March 1."
The King of Prussia thought that Eylau furnished

him with an opportunity to come to terms, but Napoleon stuck to his demands. He would return no territory east of the Elbe. On April 1, he transferred his headquarters from the barn in Osterode to the castle at Finkenstein. He was very properly worried at the demeanor of Austria, who was raising troops and filling her magazines. He felt ready to make very considerable concessions, in Silesia, in Dalmatia, in order to obtain Austrian neutrality. The court at Vienna found a compromise between its hatred and its fear of France in an offer of mediation. It proposed to make advances not only to Russia and Prussia but to England. Napoleon sensed a veiled threat in the proposal, but he accepted, in the thought of gaining time.

He had further strengthened his army by calling out the class of 1808. The effect in France was bad, tending to increase uneasiness; but Napoleon was able to count on sixteen new regiments and so to build up a reserve force in Germany to deal with Austria, if need required. The Rhine Federation, Holland, Italy and even Spain supplied other contingents, and five legions of drafted men guarded the coasts in France.

Meantime two considerable successes contributed to a weakening of the enemy's morale. The English had sent a fleet to the Dardanelles to force the sultan Selim to drop his alliance with France. Admiral Duckworth destroyed a Turkish flotilla in the Sea of Marmora, but on arriving before Constantinople he found the city so well fortified by General Sebastiani that he had to sail for the Dardanelles again. There his fleet was exposed to a grilling cannonade and suffered heavy losses (March 3, 1807). Three months later (May 26th), as though in presage of the decisive campaign that was about to open, Marshal Lefebvre overcame the heroic resistance of Dantzig. The Prussian garrison marched out of the city with the honors of war on a pledge not to serve again for a year against France.

The army received the news with great joy. It had rested from the hard campaign of early winter and having been strengthened in all its departments by the Emperor begged impatiently to be led against the foe. Napoleon, however, bided his time. The moment did not seem to have come till early June. Then on the 6th he wrote to Fouché: "Within a week after you get this letter all will be over."

The good offices of Austria had been rejected by Russia. Puffed up over his pretended victory at Eylau Alexander had persuaded Frederick William to break off his overtures for peace, assuring him that he would be restored to the whole of his dominions since the coming battle would be the end of Napoleon. The two monarchs sealed their alliance at Bartenstein. England promised a subsidy of a million pounds, and 20,000 soldiers who would debark in Pomerania. The evident interest of the Allies would have been to wait till they could fight at their full strength. But Alexander's eagerness forced Benningsen to start at once.

Ney was encamped at Guttstadt. Benningsen slipped along the foggy roads of East Prussia and attacked him on the 5th of June. Ney retired along the Passarge. A lively engagement took place at Heilsberg, where Murat and Soult inflicted heavy losses on the Russians. Benningsen then tried to shake free by a rapid march on Königsberg. Napoleon sent Lannes to stop him at Friedland.

At that point the marshal's men withstood with rare fortitude the shock of the whole Russian army.

But Napoleon was near at hand. He reached Friedland in the afternoon of the 14th of June, a Sunday. He saw at a glance that the Russians were in a bad fix, with their backs to the Alle.

"It's a lucky day!" he cried. "The anniversary of Marengo!"

As it was already late his seconds suggested that the battle be postponed till the morrow.

"No, no!" he answered. "You will never catch an enemy making such a blunder twice."

And he ordered a general attack at once.

The center, held by Mortier and Lannes, was to remain on the defensive. Ney was to charge the Russian left commanded by Bagration.

"That's the key to the situation," said the Emperor to Ney. "Go in, head down, and break into that pack at all costs. Don't think of your flanks. Don't think of your rear. I shall be there with the Guard to take care of all that."

As soon as Ney had done his work, Mortier and Lannes were to take the offensive and push the enemy back into the river.

The plan ran off like clock-work. The Russians fought doggedly but in vain. Ney "roared upon them like a lion." Bagration was thrown off balance, gave ground, and finally broke in disorder across the Alle, blowing up his bridges behind him. It was then Gortchakov's turn. Lannes and Mortier rushed him with fixed bayonets. Shattered by grape, mashed by cavalry, his lines gave way, the Russians fleeing in rout across the river.

Many of them tried to swim and were drowned. Having lost 25,000 men and all his guns, Benningsen fled towards the Niemen. The French had lost only 7000 between killed and wounded.

The battle had begun at five in the afternoon. It was over at ten o'clock, ending in a complete victory, "as decisive as Austerlitz," wrote Napoleon, "or Jena." He slept on the battlefield while joy-crazed grenadiers milled about him. In the morning the French started in pursuit. Soult was soon in Königsberg, the last redoubt of Prussia, Frederick William hurrying away to Memel. The French reached the Niemen on the 19th. Camped on the other shore they found an exhausted, discouraged Russian army begging for a truce.

CHAPTER XX

Tilsit

I T WAS SIGNED BY BENNINGSEN AT TILSIT ON JUNE 22. Three days later Napoleon met the Czar on a raft anchored in midstream in the Niemen. The two sovereigns embraced as they came together, the troops applauding. Then they stepped into a tent that had been pitched on the raft and spent an hour in private conversation.

"If your trouble is with England and only with her," the Czar is said to have begun, "we can easily come to an agreement. I have as much reason to complain of England as you have."

"In that case peace is made," Napoleon is supposed to have answered.

"The Czar is a young, kindly, and very handsome emperor," he wrote to Josephine on the day of the meeting. Later he was to say of him: "He is a Greek of the Low Empire." Those two sentences mark the limits of his experience, as he passed from a first impression of enthusiasm to an ultimate disgust.

Alexander was a complicated soul, one of the most incomprehensible of which history makes mention. Nervous, sensitive, almost feminine, he was not so much

189

treacherous as uncertain. Eager for glory he dreamed of power the way young men dream of love, but he never took his eye off realities, never lost an opportunity to seize an advantage. Having murdered his father in intent if not in act, he set out to be a reforming czar. Then suddenly he removed the liberal influences that had gathered about his early beginnings and became a despot again. He had hated and despised Napoleon. Now he admired while still envying him. On leaving one of the conferences at Tilsit, in which the great soldier, whom he had been wheedling with servile flatteries, had shown such generosity towards him, he wrote to Catherine, his sister: "God has saved us. Instead of having sacrifices to make we are coming out of this struggle with a sort of glory. But what will you say of all these doings? I, spending whole days with Bonaparte, and hours and hours in private conversation with him! I ask you—isn't it all something like a dream? . . ."

His aim was to charm Napoleon. "With all his genius," he said, "the man has his weak spot—vanity." And he did charm him in fact, by his frank address, by his eagerness to agree, by the bitterness he manifested towards his recent allies. He was playing the part of the gallant knight, the hero of the sentimental novels. A trace of sentiment remained in Napoleon from his boyhood and it was touched by such poses. He needed a powerful, trustworthy ally in his terrible struggle with the English. Who could better serve the purpose than this monarch whom he judged "a naïve and charming young man"?

To win the Czar over entirely he pushed concessions to the point of endangering his own schemes. He sacrificed Sweden and Turkey without a murmur, traditional allies of France towards whom sound policy would have counseled consideration. Alexander was free to conquer Finland and dismember Turkey as he saw fit—"Constantinople excepted." More serious still, Napoleon abandoned, out of regard for Russia, the idea of reconstituting Poland and giving her her independence. The plaints of Maria Walewska, of whom he had become enamored in Warsaw, the bravery of Polish soldiers who had offered their lives to him in the recent campaign, a sound instinct of his own that warned him that Poland was indispensable to the normal balance of Europe, all vanished before his eagerness to obtain a hold on Alexander with a view to subduing England.

In exchange for all the favors he extended, what did he ask for, after all? He asked for the Czar's adherence to the Continental Blockade! Alexander agreed willingly. If London would not accept his mediation, he would declare war on England and force Austria to do likewise. Prussia would foot the whole bill, though, "at the request of His Majesty the Emperor of all the Russias," Napoleon consented to return something better than half of Prussian territory, leaving the kingdom with five millions of subjects instead of an original nine. Of the two vast Polish provinces which Napoleon retained he formed an autonomous state to be called the Grand Duchy of Warsaw. He offered the throne to the sometime Elector of Saxony who was to have the title of king and enter the Federation of the Rhine. Hanover and Hesse-Cassel, the Prussian provinces in the west, he fused into a new kingdom for his young brother Jerome, who so became "King of Westphalia."

A good but awkward soul wretched in his misfortune, the King of Prussia could do nothing but argue and complain. Queen Louise vainly tried to obtain better conditions from the conqueror. She came to Tilsit and received Napoleon several times, begging with tears in her eyes for at least the restoration of Magdeburg to Prussia. She even went so far as to throw herself at his feet. The Emperor lifted her up chivalrously but did not yield. Then at dinner she was given a seat opposite him and brought herself to a supreme effort. She drew a rose from her corsage and held it out to Napoleon, beseeching:

"Sire, this rose—for Magdeburg!"

He took the rose and kept Magdeburg. "The Queen of Prussia is really charming," he wrote to Josephine that evening. "She is winsome and coquettish with me. Do not be alarmed, however. I am a piece of waxed canvas—I shed all that. It would cost me too much to do otherwise."

Louise was to die two years later, "unconsolable for having called misfortune upon her country."

Having brought all of central Europe under his control by these treaties, Napoleon took his leave of Alexander in the firm belief that he had won a sincere friend. But at just that time the Czar wrote to his mother, a bitter enemy of everything French, who exercised a manifest influence over her imperial son: "It is just as well that France should believe that her interests are harmonious with Russia's." A private avowal of his duplicity! Napoleon was to have public proof of the same duplicity in very short order.

He returned to Paris by way of Germany, having been

absent for ten months. The capital lighted up in his honor and erected triumphal arches of bay leaves. His troops saluted him as "Emperor of the West." After many hardships, after barely missing a defeat, he found himself more master of men than he had ever been before. Tilsit with its aftermath marks the high point in Napoleon's personal career and in the fortunes of the Empire.

CHAPTER XXI

Society Under the Empire

THE ADMINISTRATION OF THIS IMMENSE STATE, WHICH had been built up in a few years' time by an unparalleled series of victories, Napoleon did not entrust to his ministers. He governed it himself in all its infinite detail. He was even greater as a civil ruler than as a military chieftain, in that respect, indeed, deserving the greatest admiration.

Whatever may have been said on the point, he loved his country deeply. He had a simple and a very exalted conception of France. Child of a Corsica very recently annexed, he was eager to identify himself with the great, compact, high-minded French nation, become one in thought and in blood with the people which he was so proud to command. He thought of himself as an emanation of that people rather than as the head of it. "From Clovis down to the Committee of Public Safety," he said, "that is all one to me." His real passion, whatever the appearances to the contrary, was not war. War was for him, often, just a hateful necessity of which he had to take the greatest possible advantage. His ruling passion was power, power exercised with unremitting vigilance and with indefatigable application.

There had been and there will again be greater minds than Napoleon's. He was not a thinker. He disliked thought structures, systems, "ideologies"; but in the field of the immediate and the concrete he had an amazingly comprehensive, orderly, clear, discerning intelligence. In his view "high policy was nothing but common sense applied to important matters." Every question should be considered without preconceptions, on its own merits.

"What is all this talk," he asked, "about goodness, abstract justice, natural laws? The one basic law is necessity. . . . Each day has its problem, each circumstance its law, each person his nature." And nevertheless that great realist was a tireless dreamer of dreams. No human being ever had a more active imagination. "I am always living two years ahead," he said. That faculty, curiously combined with a clear perception of things as they were, enabled the soldier of fortune to become the most extraordinary handler of men that had appeared in the world since the time of Alexander the Great.

He compared his own brain to a well-kept dresser or filing-case. When he was dealing with a particular subject he opened the drawer that corresponded to it and closed the other drawers. When he wanted to sleep he closed them all. His unfailing memory made it easy for him to deal with men and to manipulate complicated legislation. He by no means reconstructed and remolded Europe, as has so often been said, by instinctive genius alone. He did it by severe and constant application. When still a young officer he set out to re-educate himself from the elements up. He was still ignorant of government and administration when he became First Consul. He had, to be sure, an instinct for such things, but

he also listened attentively and respectfully to men like
Siéyès, Talleyrand, Cambacérès, Fouché, Lebrun, Roederer, Regnault, men who did know and were in a position to teach him and steer him aright. Soon he knew
everything, was starting everything, directing everything,
and in the most varied fields.

No ruler ever worked so hard or with so much zest.
In addition to routine duties, such as receptions, audiences, interviews with diplomats, army reviews, Council
meetings where he sat in the chair, he kept up an enormous correspondence that covered the whole administration of the Empire. "I was born and built for work," he
commented, and he said to Roederer: "If I seem ready
for everything, prepared in advance to deal with the
most unexpected situations, it is because I have long foreseen things that might happen and have pondered deeply
what I would do before I was called upon to do anything.
I am always working. I work when I eat. I work as I sit
watching a play at the theater. At night I wake up and
work."

With his days entirely filled he often had to consult
his ministers at night. Eyes about him would begin to
blink or cheeks to pale, but he would cry: "Come, come,
gentlemen, let's wake up! It's only two in the morning!
We've got to earn the salaries the French people pay us!"
This continuous overdoing would have wrecked a less
sturdy constitution. It frightened his intimates. But let
his mother chide him for working too hard and he would
answer laughing: "What do you take me for, mother? A
chick of our old white hen?" Or let Corvisart try to for-
bid his working so late at night: "Poor Corvisart! He's
always chewing that cud! Yet I have shown him as plain

CAMBACÈRES
From the Portrait by Schopin

as two and two make four that I have to work at night to keep this shop running. The day simply is not long enough for it. I'd like to sleep more, but when the ox is hitched to the plow he's got to plow."

The interests of the state overrode everything else in his mind, and he watched them in the little things as well as in the big. Orderliness, a geometrical orderliness, was a prime need with him. It enabled him to act in every matter in a simple, regular, unbreaking rhythm and with the assistance of the best instruments. Near his desk was a cabinet that contained all the maps and drawings he needed for planning a campaign or drawing up a treaty. At his elbow he had reports and synopses, which were kept up to the minute, describing the situation in the army, in finance, in trade, in manufacturing, in imports and exports, in education. He turned to them time after time each day. On his person he always carried a scrap of paper on which he had scribbled the exact amount of money that France could dispose of on that date.

His first private secretary was Bourrienne, whom he discharged finally for accepting bribes. Then it was Méneval. After 1813, Fain alone had entry to his office. The first thing in the morning he would dictate letters, dispatches, communiqués, proclamations, walking up and down for hours with his hands clasped behind his back. Each matter was carefully considered. Not only did he ponder his orders, but—a trait essential in a good executive—he personally saw to it that they had been carried out, and he always judged how. The whole administration of the Empire went up to him and came down from him. A carefully locked briefcase brought him daily reports from each ministry. His filing chief, the tireless and ever dependable Secretary of State, Maret, kept all papers classified, registered and copied.

The next item on the day's program was interviews with ministers, grand dignitaries, directors-general. They were usually held in private. Only towards the end of his reign did the Emperor hold real councils of ministers. The ministers were really technical assistants, big "errand boys," as they had been in the days of Louis XIV. Infinitely jealous of power he kept his subordinates strictly confined to the work they were supposed to do. There was always one or more of them in the anteroom outside his office door, and with them visitors of all sorts, who had been called for special purposes—senators, state councilors, army officers, diplomats, prefects, newspapermen, foreign agents.

Barring rare exception, Napoleon kept the same assistants, both in the army and in administration, throughout the life of the Empire. He overlooked their faults since he had known them in advance. "By putting them in their right places," says Molé, "and asking of them only what they could do and knew how to do, he doubled their capacities and their success." Whether the given man came from one or another of the earlier régimes was of no interest to him. What he asked of an official in his service was that he should serve him and serve the country to the fullest of his knowledge and with all his energy. Did he fill the chief posts about him with inferior men, as has been charged, in fear lest superiorities should diminish his own prestige? There is nothing to that. Napoleon took the men he found available at the time of his assumption of power. His lieutenants were the generals who had fought for the Republic. His marshals were soldiers of the Year II—and what soldiers they were! Masséna, Ney, Murat, Davout, Bessières, Lannes, to mention only the greatest! Among his ministers Talleyrand and Fouché were altogether superior individuals. Cambacérès was a man of experience and shrewdness. Maret, Mollien, Roederer, Lebrun, Régnier, Daru, Molé, Regnault de St. Jean d'Angély, Pasquier, Montalivet, were administrators of genius.

Aside from the personnel which he gathered at the outset and which he retained down to the last moment possible, he found a breeding ground for the talent his bureaucracy needed in the Council of State. He followed the sessions of the Council all through the Empire. The Council voted measures and laws after singularly free and therefore productive discussion. Trémont relates: "As a youthful auditor I attended sessions of the Council at which the Emperor was in the chair for as many as seven consecutive hours. His stimulating influence, the prodigious discernment of his analytical mind, the clearness with which he could summarize most complicated situations, his carefulness not only in heeding but in provoking contradiction, roused the same sort of enthusiasm that he created in the army. The members were as ready to kill themselves with work as the soldiers were to die on the battlefield."

Napoleon's personal relations with his collaborators have also been clouded by diatribes and panegyrics. The truth is very simple. They were almost always conducted on terms of cordiality and trust. Napoleon dealt with the grand dignitary and the plain aide de camp on the same footing. It was always a man to man affair. Even personal disagreements did not spoil his good humor. As

Gohier puts it, "almost always the man whom he had scolded in the course of the day was the man he invited to dinner with him." All contemporaries are in agreement on the point. Says Méneval: "When a sharp retort struck the Emperor's mind, he most often was the one to give ground." And Rovigo remarks: "He had such a sense of fairness and devotion towards those whom he trusted that it was not only safer, it was wiser, to tell him everything. If he sometimes brooded for a time, when some friend would tell him the bald truth, he would always come back towards that person with greater trust and respect than before."

As time went on many of his seconds tired under the continuous strain to which they were subjected and became less submissive. They aged, became too rich, grew apathetic, mechanically executing orders that they had ceased trying to understand. At the end of the Empire Napoleon himself was no longer the watchful, patient master he had been under the Consulate. Knowing everyone better, seeing little about him except greed and lack of character, he became harder and harsher, as for that matter most human beings do. He was inclined by temperament as well as by his training as a soldier to be despotic. There can be no doubt that his Empire was the most tyrannical government that France has ever seen. From year to year power concentrated more and more in his hands. He suppressed the Tribunate, where a few germs of opposition still lurked. The Legislative Body and the Senate became mere boards of registry, decorative and servile. The Emperor drew up the budget. In 1813 he went so far as to determine what the taxes should be.

The press was closely muzzled. Sixty-six newspapers had been published in France under the Republic. The number dropped to thirteen in 1807. By 1811 only four were left. Their editors were appointed by the Emperor and not an article appeared without having passed the imperial censorship. Publications of books were also closely watched. Individual liberty was possible only within a deferential silence. Paris and the large towns were infested with spies. Under that form of dictatorship the police were supreme. There was the police of Fouché, but there was also Savary's gendarmerie, and a secret police in addition. An immense net was let down over the nation and prevented it from stirring. State prisons had been abolished by the Constituent Assembly. They were re-established by Napoleon. Anyone who seemed to be too noisy or who became notorious as an opponent was clapped under cover "as a measure of safety," on the Emperor's order, without trial. There were about six hundred such prisoners in 1807.

For all of Michelet and Taine, Napoleon was not inhuman. He did think that a power such as he held, a power born of the sword, would collapse unless it were firmly exercised. If anything, he was tender-hearted. A superficial eye, probably, often missed his real nature. The theory was that he was selfish, violent, ambitious, subordinating everything to his greed for power, stamping on his finer feelings in order to lock himself up in a barbarous tyranny. Certainly unpleasant moments are to be noted in him, bursts of anger, unfair retorts; but they are balanced and overbalanced by remarks of his that evince nobility, kindness, human understanding. It is too often forgotten that that insatiable grasper of power was an affectionate and dutiful son, a brother with too great a weakness for his brothers and sisters, an attentive husband, a considerate master, a generous friend.

His immediate family had known first straitened circumstances, then actual poverty, then, thanks to Napoleon, opulence. He was all the more attached to his people because of their misfortunes and because, afterwards, they depended altogether on him, owed everything to him. He was aware of their defects. He soon came to see how jealous his brothers and sisters were of him, how ungrateful, how far from understanding his real character. Their mistakes were to cost him dearly. In spite of that he was to remain devoted to them all his life long. The most varied commentators agree on this point. Says Metternich: "Napoleon had a great weakness for his family. A good son, a good brother, loyal to anyone in anyway related to him, and with those shadings that are conspicuous particularly in families of the Italian middle classes, he suffered from the foolish conduct of some of his people without ever mustering enough will power to halt it, even at times when it was to his most evident advantage to do so." "All of them," writes General Rapp, "filled cups of bitterness for Napoleon—all except his mother. Nevertheless he at no time ceased to shower wealth and honors upon them."

In the Bonaparte family the outstanding position always belonged to Madame Mère. Napoleon loved her, admired her, feared her. "She is an old-fashioned woman," he was to say of her. "She knows nothing of revolutions." In fact, Madame Bonaparte was entitled to the highest respect on the score of character. She underwent the most extreme reversals of fortune without ever

MADAME MÈRE

From the Portrait by Gérard

losing her balance. She had had a time of it bringing up her brood. Then, overnight, she found herself an Imperial Highness with a million to spend each year, the fine Brienne mansion, the Château de Pont, a little court. Napoleon manifested the greatest deference towards her on all occasions. He had few disagreements with her except in regard to expenditures. She had always been saving. Now she became frankly a hoarder and a miser. She was beset with fear lest a twist in fortunes would some day force her to come to the rescue of her children. She was always saying to Napoleon: "If you ever fall back on my hands you will be glad of what I am putting away now." The court at the Tuileries laughed aloud at the rough, homely Corsican expressions she never cured herself of using, but all who came near her paid homage to the uprightness of her manner of living. She was mainly interested in charities and her son gave her general charge of charitable institutions. She was too much under the influence of her brother, Cardinal Fesch, who was a wretched, base soul, in whom the Emperor was to find an ever relentless and underhanded enemy.

Joseph Bonaparte was Napoleon's elder by a year, and in the eyes of the dictator he was never to lose the prestige of that advantage. Attractive in appearance, intelligent, well-mannered, well educated, very vain, his outstanding defect was indolence. He was a cynic who was also a good fellow. He liked to live at his ease surrounded by friends and protégés, but at any rate sumptuously. Napoleon buried him in benefactions. His clannish spirit convinced him that from the mere fact that Joseph was his brother, Joseph could be trained and molded into a statesman. There he was, first a prince and then a general! At the first bake of kings he was on a throne in Naples, at the second, on a throne in Madrid. And was he grateful? Never in the least! He thought that all those favors were due to him on his merits, that he was called by his talents to posts on high. Apart from a few moments of exasperation Napoleon closed his eyes to Joseph's actual incompetence, his lack of courage, his breaches of self-control. How could he help doing so? He loved him too much. They had too many memories in common. In rebuking him he guarded his words with astonishing precautions. Joseph, for his part, disregarded such scoldings and went on doing as he pleased. In spite of an unending series of disappointments Napoleon long thought of him as his eventual successor. "I am thinking," he wrote as late as 1807, "that the habit of governing, your good mind and your fine native endowments will stiffen your character and make you better able to manage this great machine, in case the fates should grant you a longer life than mine." However angry he may have been with Joseph he would always close his letters on a note of affection: "In the midst of all that, keep well—that is the main thing." No lesson, however—and he was to have not a few of them—could ever humble Joseph's overbearing conceit.

With Lucien it was quite a different story. That gawky, loose-jointed, near-sighted young man, an overgrown boy, who "waved his arms like a peasant swinging a scythe," as the Duchess d'Abrantes remarked, was not bad material. Next to Napoleon he was the most interesting of the Bonapartes. Agile of mind, eloquent, taking to politics like a duck to water, he might have played an outstanding rôle in the Empire. Napoleon offered him thrones in Italy, Portugal and even Spain, but on condition that he break a marriage that he had contracted with Mme. Jouberthou. Lucien refused. He was in love with the woman and it was not a little to his honor that, ambitious as he was, he should have sacrificed position to that attachment. On many occasions, one as late as 1807 at Mantua, Napoleon vainly tried to bring the stubborn youth back into the fold. All through the Empire Lucien lived by himself, first in Rome, then in London (after he had been captured by the English in the course of an unlucky voyage). The break between the brothers seemed unhealable, when suddenly Fate provided the cure—misfortune. On the day when Napoleon tottered Lucien re-entered the imperial system and played an important part in it.

Napoleon was something more than a brother to Louis. A penniless lieutenant at Auxonne, living on three francs a day, he provided a home for this younger brother and educated him. Louis was probably the one he loved most, and the one certainly who most grievously disappointed him. Napoleon seemed unable to endure separation from Louis. He married him to Hortense undoubtedly to please Josephine, but also because he saw in that a way of having Louis happy and near him at home. Unfortunately things did not turn out just as he had planned. First a general, then governor of Paris, then a prince, then King of Holland, Louis raced up the whole ladder. But he was never satisfied. Sick, ill-humored, restless, jealous, he very soon rebelled against his brother, and forgetting that he was a king only through him and also that he was a Frenchman, he insisted that he could serve the interests only of the country of his adoption. Very shortly he was to quit the throne of Holland as a fugitive. Though denied by Louis, Napoleon continued to look after Hortense and the children. Louis himself would have had only to return to France to obtain forgiveness. He preferred rather to live out his life posing as a victim, and at the end, when Napoleon was at St. Helena, he was to write three fat volumes denouncing his brother's tyranny. "What, Louis too?" exclaimed Napoleon on opening the books. The *tu quoque* of Caesar! It was one of the last hurts that Napoleon was to suffer in this world.

Jerome, the Benjamin among the four brothers, was a mere child when Napoleon reached the Consulship. The difference in ages was reflected in their relations. Jerome was never lacking in respect for Napoleon and the Emperor always treated him as a favorite who was a bit of a rogue. Having never known poverty Jerome grew up as a prodigal aristocrat, extravagant but good-hearted. A sailor in the navy he deserted his ship in Baltimore to marry an American girl, Elizabeth Patterson. After that, however, he submitted to Napoleon's will and procured a divorce in order to marry Catherine, princess of Württemberg, and become King of Westphalia. In his little German kingdom he set out to enjoy life and there were few frivolities, prodigalities or scandals of which he did not become guilty. Napoleon tirelessly stuffed the ever-emptying purse of the young king, giving him, along with his scoldings, unending proofs of his affection and generosity. Jerome, for his part, was grateful at least. When the collapse came he stuck to his big brother, and so did his wife, Catherine. That good and faithful German woman became French and a Bonaparte at heart. She had the same admiration for the captive Emperor that she had had for him when he sat on his throne. Napoleon summed her up in a phrase when he said: "She has written herself into history with her own hands."

Of Elisa, the eldest of his sisters, Napoleon made a sovereign as early as 1804. Imperious, greedy, unattractive, she took the throne of Florence and kept the Emperor in hot water a good deal of the time by her abuses of her power. Foreseeing the fall of the Empire in 1813 she negotiated with Murat, in quest of ways and means for separating her interests from those of her brother.

Pauline, next in line among the girls, was beyond any doubt the most beautiful woman of her time. The delightful creature whom Canova immortalized was really nothing but a lover. "The prettiest woman one could hope to see, and the most irresponsible." So wrote Arnault. She had no more poise than a school girl. She chattered and giggled, giggled and chattered on any pretext or on none at all, mimicking the most important people and sticking her tongue out at Josephine when the latter was not looking. She was that way all her life long. Napoleon married her to a Roman prince, Camillo Borghese, and stopped at giving her the little duchy of Guastalla. He was much less lavish in gifts to her than he was to his other brothers and sisters, but he loved her and knew that she loved him. Pauline was the life of imperial society all through the Empire, ever the delight of the family and of the court.

Caroline was married to Murat. Like Elisa, she was a politician and an ambitious one. "Cromwell's head on a pair of pretty shoulders," Talleyrand said of her. The moment she became queen of Naples she began thinking of ways and means to save her throne. It was under her influence that Murat deserted Napoleon.

Napoleon gave boundless affection to Hortense de Beauharnais the moment he married Josephine. He pitied her and tried to cheer her in her unhappy marriage to Louis, petting and spoiling her children, especially the little Napoleon Charles. The boy came to be very close to the Emperor, whom he called "Uncle Bibiche," and often had luncheon with him. Lively, roguish, charming, when the little fellow would pass a grenadier in the courtyard at the Tuileries, he would call out: "Long live Nonon the soldier!" The Emperor sported with him, loaded him with toys, was always taking him for a walk. The death of the child in May, 1807, from an attack of croup, was a heavy blow. Had Napoleon Charles lived to grow up Napoleon would doubtless have designated him as his successor and would not have divorced Josephine.

Napoleon was just as affectionate towards his stepson Eugene, and covered him also with prerogatives, emoluments and honors, first as viceroy of Italy and then as son-in-law to the King of Bavaria. Eugene was to forget what he owed to Napoleon. Indeed among all those who shared most lavishly in the Emperor's bounty he was certainly the most ungrateful with the least excuse. The Second Empire tried to counterfeit an exemplary figure for him. Actually he was a mediocre person, as insignificant in talents as he was in character.

Napoleon evinced the same liberality, the same often excessive open-handedness towards his friends—for he had friends. Taine writes: "In the position which he

HORTENSE, QUEEN OF HOLLAND
From the Portrait by Gérard

achieved he was not called upon to consider anybody. People interested him only in so far as he could use them." That was a systematic view and therefore inexact. The Emperor, like the First Consul, showed a keen sense of friendship and a constant hunger for human sympathy and companionship. He observed to Girardin: "Do people think that things always go the way we want them to? Sometimes they go badly and we are crushed by their weight. Then it is that we have to open our hearts to someone—to do so is an overpowering need. But to whom can one trust one's inner secrets when one can look all around without seeing a soul of whom one can be certain as a friend?"

Well known are the favors he did to Berthier, whom he married to a Bavarian princess and made Prince of Neuchâtel; for Junot, who was bound to his intimacy by early memories of Toulon but who proved to be a scatterbrain as a man and an incompetent as a soldier; for Marmont, his favorite aide de camp who became a marshal and then a duke and was eventually to be Napoleon's Judas; for Lannes, who often addressed him impolitely and whose breaches of discipline he consented to ignore. Lannes was the only comrade of his youth who continued to say "thou" to him all through the Empire. In fact he always treated him as an equal. On the way home from Warsaw Captain Coignet heard the two men quarreling aloud at the head of the line of march. "The blood of one Frenchman," Lannes was saying, "is worth more than all Poland." Napoleon answered: "If you're not satisfied, get out!" "No," replied the marshal, "you cannot do without me." A number of his subordinates always preserved a surprising familiarity with him. "Lassalle, Junot, and Rapp," says Marbot, "told the Emperor anything that happened to enter their heads. Lassalle and Junot went broke every two years. They would go and tell Napoleon what they had been up to and he would always pay their debts."

Cambacérès, Talleyrand, Fouché, Lebrun, all the dignitaries, all the marshals and ministers, received gifts from him in addition to salaries and pensions that netted them immense fortunes, fortunes larger than any sovereign ever had dispensed. Berthier's income eventually reached a figure of 1,800,000 francs, Masséna's 1,500,000. It was almost the same story with Ney and Davout. Those figures would have to be multiplied by ten to get their value in the money of our time. Economical himself, Napoleon rained millions upon the people about him.

The men just mentioned were, one might say, instruments of governing; but there were the private, the personal friends too—Talma, Arnault, David, Isabey. Bonaparte had known Talma in the hard days, before Vendémiaire. At that time the actor had lent him money and books. Napoleon kept him as an intimate under the Empire, applauding his work on the stage, giving him wise counsel as to his art, gathering an audience of kings for him at Erfurt. He helped Arnault in the latter's literary career, just as he actively patronized the work of David and Isabey. Few rulers have shown themselves more appreciative and more generous than Napoleon towards the acquaintances of their early days or towards those who at any time or in any way helped or encouraged them. Mlle. du Colombier had received Bonaparte in her house at Valence when he was a lieutenant. Coming upon hard times and appealing to his good remembrance she at once became lady-in-waiting to Madame Mère, and her husband general manager of forests. Montalivet, also a friend of the days in Valence, became a minister. Old memories of Corsica account for the many favors he did to members of the Marbeuf family.

He manifested no trace of vindictiveness towards enemies. Bernadotte taxed his patience to the limit. The Gascon soldier could never forgive the Corsican for occupying a place which he might himself have seized. He was always mixed up in some intrigue, and Napoleon knew that perfectly well. He did not like Bernadotte and he mistrusted him. Nevertheless he buried him under promotions and titles. A word from Napoleon would have prevented Bernadotte from becoming heir apparent to the throne of Sweden. Napoleon never uttered the word. On the contrary, on Bernadotte's departure, he gave him a million and other precious gifts. Carnot maintained an attitude of frank and avowed opposition all through the Empire. Napoleon assigned him a pension of ten thousand francs as an ex-minister and gave him a large lump sum which was presented, in deference to Carnot's sensibilities, as "arrears on his salary as a general." Those who had harmed Napoleon at one time or another never suffered for it. Mme. Aubry was responsible for his losing a command in the artillery. He gave her a generous pension. Letourneur once gave him a bad mark. He made him Prefect of the Loire, then counsel to the Court of Accountings. Clarke had spied on him for the Directory. He made him a marshal and a duke. Soult tried to become King of Portugal. Napoleon winked at the betrayal.

To be sure he was a high-strung individual, over-burdened with worries and responsibilities. He lost balance once in a while. Well known are his outbursts with Talleyrand, his scenes with Fouché, the kick he is supposed, on uncertain grounds, to have applied to Volney's posterior. But such episodes were few and his wrath was of brief duration. "You think I am angry," he said to the Abbé de Pradt, after a loud-voiced altercation with that gentleman. "Well, feel my pulse!" He repented of his violent moments, calmed down, admitted his mistakes, and strove to repair hurts with some positive favor or some delicate word. He wrote to Decrès, his naval minister: "I am distressed that you should have lost your temper with me. But once the flurry is past, there is nothing left. I hope you will have no bitter memories of our quarrel." Marks of a real sensitiveness were observable in Napoleon at all times. "All that I know of him," writes the Duchess d'Abrantes, "indicates that he was a great soul forgiving and forgetful. . . . It was useless for him to try to be vindictive. His good nature always got the better of him." "Don't imagine," he said one day, "that I am not as tender-hearted as anybody else. I am quite a good fellow at bottom. But when I was still a mere boy I set out to deaden the string of sentiment in my make-up. Touch it now and it yields no sound." That was not true, in spite of the boast. But as a man exercising power Napoleon feared sentimental weaknesses. The example of Louis XVI was always present to his mind. "When a king is known for his kind heart," he wrote to Joseph, "it means that he is a failure."

Whenever possible he was merciful and considerate. He tried to save Cadoudal. He pardoned the Prince of

Hatzfeld. He commuted the sentence of Saint-Simon, who had been arrested in Spain while fighting against France. Some brutal remarks dropped on occasion from his lips. Looking at a battlefield he once said: "One night in Paris will square accounts for all this." On the other hand he expressed shocked emotions at the horrors of war, even after brilliant victories. After each battle he inspected the field to make sure that the wounded had all been cared for. Whenever he came upon a wounded man he talked to him and saw personally to his comfort. He was especially distressed at the sufferings that forced war contributions caused to exhausted populations. At Verona he cried, in Bourrienne's presence: "Bleed the rich? Well, perhaps—it's tough, but it's war! But bleed the poor? That is outrageous!" And he returned to the poor the contributions that had been exacted of them.

He had a tender affection for the men who endured hardships with him, especially the plain soldiers. "A hundred times," says Maret, "I have seen him walk about at night among the bivouacs, stopping at one fire or another to chat, to ask what was boiling in a pot, to laugh till his sides would shake at the witty answers he sometimes received. He liked the jokes and strange expressions of the soldiers and could repeat them with all their zest and flavor." Their embarrassments and absurdities delighted and disarmed him.

Captain Coignet relates that while he was still a grenadier the Emperor ruled that members of the Guard should have to know how to swim and he established classes in that art. Coignet was called before him.

"You know how to swim?"

"No, Sire."

"Why not?"

"I am not afraid of going under fire—I am afraid to go into the water."

"So you are not afraid of fire! Well, we can excuse you from the water."

He was simple and unexacting with his servants, showing them all the pleasanter side of his nature, perhaps because with them he did not have to be guarded in the words he used or in the demeanor he adopted. His doormen, messengers, valets he often scolded and on occasion even shook one by the collar; but he took an interest in them and in their families and overlooked little slips. "His bad humor was never of long duration," writes Aly, his last mameluke. "If he happened to be in the wrong, it was not long before he would come and give a tweak of the ear or a slap on the back to the person on whom his wrath had fallen. Then, after a few words relating to the subject of the outbreak, he would lavish such agreeable epithets as 'my son,' 'my boy,' 'my child.' "

Simplicity and easiness of manner were characteristic of him all his life long. They were conspicuous in his private tastes and pleasures. His amusements were, of course, infrequent and brief. He ate soberly and rapidly—he was not a bon viveur. He had no liking for social life. His main relaxation was reading. He read much and rapidly. When he had finished a novel, a geography, a history, he would throw it either into the fire or through the door of his coach. He read, moreover, from the standpoint of a man of the literary profession. All his life long, from the *Souper de Beaucaire* down to the memoirs he dictated at St. Helena, he was possessed by a hunger for expressing himself. He wrote most of his bulletins and proclamations personally. The official newspaper of the Empire was the *Moniteur*. For it he wrote long articles, unsigned, expressing his views on current events. His thinking was animated and rapid, his style forceful, interesting. He had a great gift for the striking phrase, for imagery, for rhetorical flashes. Had he not become a general and then head of a state, he would surely have been a writer. For that matter he was one. A history of French letters could never be called complete unless a place were found in it for the writings of Napoleon.

In his private habits and tastes he was decidedly middle-class, in fact "tight." However, he considered magnificence indispensable to the prestige of his throne and insisted on being surrounded by it. "Parsimonious in his personal expenditures," writes Caulaincourt, "he was sumptuous in everything pertaining to the dignity of the crown." He also thought that public sumptuousness was a contribution to the support of the nation's industries.

He had no artistic ideas of his own. He judged works of art primarily by the reputations they had won in the world at large. He gathered them into the state museums because he thought it was a sovereign's duty to do so, viewing that sort of patronage, moreover, as another guarantee of his glory, as another personal achievement. Of music, on the other hand, he was actually fond, especially Italian music. He organized concerts frequently. He would listen to Mme. Grassini, a soprano, by the hour. He often hummed tunes himself, always off key.

Beyond any doubt, however, his favorite aesthetic enjoyment was the theater. In his young days he spent most of his evenings at the Français, the Feydeau or the Opera. He liked tragedy better than comedy, viewing the latter as somehow beneath him. For that matter, the whole Revolutionary era gave its preference to the buskin. Corneille was his favorite dramatist and he was always keen for hearing, or even for reciting, that poet's declamations. He found something nobly exhilarating in them, something that seemed to echo or reflect the grandeur that he was fain to attribute to his own work and era. "If Corneille were living today," he once said at Saint-Cloud, "I would make a prince of him." Sincere words! Among the most deeply felt that he ever uttered!

This idea of grandeur he took very seriously, in that respect, as we have seen, showing himself to be a man of the South and an Italian in particular. He set out in earnest to revive all the splendor of the old régime. The Emperor and the Empress each had their households, their services of honor, their ladies and gentlemen of honor, their chamberlains, officers, pages. Starting with his grand dignitaries and officers of the crown, who remained more essentially political than decorative, he soon went on and created a full-fledged imperial nobility, cutting it out of whole cloth. He thought of it as replacing the old nobility. Like the latter it would be hereditary but based upon achievement.

In March, 1806, he created twenty-one duchies, bestowing them on his leading marshals and on selected ministers. Lefebvre became Duke of Dantzig, Kellermann, Duke of Valmy, Ney, Duke of Elchingen and later Prince of the Moskva, Davout, Duke of Auerstädt and then Prince of Eckmühl, Masséna, Duke of Rivoli, Augereau, Duke of Castiglione, Savary, Duke of Rovigo. Among civilians Cambacérès became Prince of Parma, Talleyrand, Prince of Benevento, Maret, Duke of Bassano, Lebrun, Duke of Piacenza, Régnier, Duke of Massa. More numerous still were the counts, barons and chevaliers of the Empire, who were selected from among the prefects, the leading magistrates and the higher clergy. All such people were further blessed with perquisites and prerogatives, dotations, landed endowments, entailed properties.

That this horde of new nobles, this regiment of great soldiers decorated with names of victories, should create a decided newly-rich atmosphere about the court was only to be expected. Most of them came from the people, got their schooling in the camps and had no other sort of education or upbringing. At any rate they were novices to social life proper. Murat's father was a tavern-keeper, Ney's a cooper, Junot's a fuel dealer. Masséna had been a cabin-boy on a ship and Lannes a house-painter. The recognition of such men was all to the credit of the Revolution and the Empire, but their manners and their language were hardly those to lend brilliance to a court society. Their wives were often of origins just as humble. Mme. Lefebvre, famous as Mme. Sans-Gêne, had been a washerwoman before becoming a marshaless and a duchess. Many of her new associates were in the same boat. "Have all my colonels chamber-maids for sisters?" cried Napoleon one day. Some of the women, to be sure, came from higher social levels. Junot, Augereau, Lannes and Rapp married into banking or commercial circles. But the majority of Napoleon's associates had climbed so high at such dizzy speeds that they found themselves in an utterly strange world. The Imperial Court often gave evidence of an uncouthness that provoked no end of mirth among hangovers from the old society.

Napoleon had a sort of melting pot very definitely in mind. His own nobility rubbed elbows with great names from the old days. Even under the Consulate he began to lure aristocrats by offers of posts, titles and other favors. He had a deep respect for the great families of the past. "They belong to France, to history," he declared. "I am the guardian of French glory. I shall not let them perish." Expressing his full thought to Caulaincourt one day he said: "If we are to end the Revolution, we must make a blend of all opinions and use men of the most opposite views." For that matter not a few among the young men of the great families thrilled at the epic of imperial France. Some of them, such as Ségur or Fézensac, tossed prejudices of caste aside and enlisted under the tricolor. Others entered the Council of State, the diplomatic service, the prefectures. Young France was with Napoleon almost to the last man. The old folk surrendered less readily.

All the same, on the proclamation of the Empire, offers of distinguished positions brought the bulk of the old aristocracy to the Tuileries. Napoleon could count a Brigode, a Périgord, a Croy, a Mercy-Argenteau, among his chamberlains. A Mme. de La Rochefoucauld was lady-in-waiting to Josephine. Mmes. d'Arberg, de Bouillé, de Chevreuse, de Montalivet, de Montmorency-Matignon, de Mortemart, de Turenne, de Vintimille, were ladies of the palace. Josephine's almoner was a Rohan.

The movement gained momentum as the years went by. Some of the converts, in order to avoid the sarcasms of the bitter-enders, pretended that Napoleon had compelled them to do as they were doing. No one believed them. "Vanity," wrote Mme. de Chateaubriand, "caused more defections than fear." Others, bending backwards in a praiseworthy loyalty to their old princes, could only regret their inability to serve the new leader. "If only he were a Bourbon!" cried the Comte de Damas. "What a joy it would have been for me to devote my life to deserving a citation from him in the army!" In 1808 Napoleon had an impression that the fusing process was lagging. He therefore sent commissions as second-lieutenants to numbers of young men in the faubourg Saint-Germain. Over the protests of their families they set out for their regiments, none too happily. On their first furloughs, writes Frenilly, they returned home "drunk with glory, eager for war, enthusiastic for the Empire."

The reconciled nobles often received new imperial titles, to become the subject of gibes from the hold-outs, who dubbed them "rebuilt counts." Such antagonisms, these rivalries between the old nobility and people with imperial titles, were to subsist to the very end in Napoleon's court. The Emperor thought that intermarriage might be a solution, and ordered his prefects to draw up lists of marriageable girls. The proposal met with nation-wide laughter. Now, said the quips, things had come to a "conscription of—girls." The idea was not a bad one, perhaps, but in this work of re-splicing the new France to what remained of the France of old what Napoleon really needed was time, and time was not to be given him. "What a pity," he exclaimed one day, "that I am not my own grandson!"

The imperial court was governed by a strict, an over-strict etiquette. It had not served long enough. It had not been polished by generations of experience. Napoleon supervised court life, as he did everything else, in minutest detail. Audiences, presentations, dinners, spectacles, balls, hunts—nothing was left to chance. Hand-kissing was re-established along with imperial levees and bedtimes. Only certain dignitaries had access to certain rooms. Armchairs were for sovereigns, chairs for princesses, stools for duchesses. Folding doors opened wide only before Imperial Highnesses. Display at court functions was dazzling, far surpassing anything that Versailles had known of old. At great receptions the chandeliers of the Tuileries looked down on throngs of men in gay uniforms or highly colored costumes, and women in silk and velvet gowns, low-cut with gold or silver dog collars that blazed with gems. For a "coquetry of glory" the Emperor appeared at these sumptuous assemblies in the uniform of the chasseurs of the Guard, a green coat with red collar and red stripes. To be sure, he embellished that modest outfit with vest and breeches of white cashmere, silk stockings and buckled shoes. But the more simply he dressed himself, the more insistent he was that others should be magnificent, in order, perhaps, to sharpen the contrast.

They were dreary affairs, these court functions. His entourage had neither the grace nor the ease of the court of Louis XVI. It lacked naturalness and also self-confidence and security. All the people there seemed to feel that the power they held depended on the outcome of a battle, that the structure within which they were moving was magnificent but that a whirlwind might pick it up on the following morning and bury them under its rubbish. Josephine had a keen taste for society and a great superficial charm. Nevertheless she seemed stiff and out of place at such gatherings, especially when the Emperor was present. He wanted to be a genial host and have people enjoy his parties. But he was too much of a soldier. His brusque exterior, his stern manner of speaking, froze the men and women who stood in lines to either hand as he went by, masking chilled hearts under a forced gaiety. Napoleon had never been and was never to be a society man. That, perhaps, was what did him most harm in the minds of his contemporaries, what enabled his opponents to draw the most cruel pictures of him. His one-sided education, his ever obvious distaste for wasting time, made him inadaptable to a drawing-room. He did not know how to talk to women. He was always treating them inconsiderately and in such ways as to earn sharp retorts, which for that matter he never took in ill part.

The Duchess de Fleury was a returned exile with a reputation for many love affairs.

"Well, madame," Napoleon said to her, "are you still fond of the men?"

"Of course, Sire, when they are not boors."

Mme. de Chevreuse had become a lady of the palace. She did not like the Emperor and made no secret of it. Noted for her sharp tongue, she never gave ground before Napoleon and was always snaring him into a game of repartee at which she had no equal. Sometimes he would leave her with the remark: "I can see that I have overcome the aversion that Mme. de Chevreuse has for me." But he never really thought so, nor did anybody else.

One evening he was complimenting her on the gown she was wearing—he pretended, for one of his manias, to have a keen eye for the well-dressed woman. As he talked on, the duchess, unresponsive, assumed one of her little attitudes that led her friends to expect something.

"That green dress becomes you wonderfully," said Napoleon. "You make a striking picture. What a pity, though, that you are red-headed."

Mme. de Chevreuse was slow in coming back, but finally, looking the Emperor icily in the eye, she answered:

"Red-headed, Sire? Really, can I be that? No gentleman ever told me so before!"

Napoleon shrugged his shoulders and turned away. After all—what did it matter? A pretty woman too well-born might treat him as an upstart. But he knew what he was, what he was doing, his real worth; and if he had every reason to doubt the good will of those patricians who were accepting his largess, he could take comfort in the profound respect, the awe-struck devotion of those who really saw him at work—his soldiers, to begin with.

Beyond the court, in Paris, in the provinces, a society gradually formed again, something very different, to tell the truth, from the society that the Terror had sent to the guillotine. The Directory had seen a whirlwind of pleasures, a madness in debauchery. Now there came a definite reaction in morals. The Civil Code restored the

framework of the family, religion recovered the ground
it had lost, education became better and more general.
Everywhere, under an impulse deriving from above,
ideas of duty, of discipline, of devotion to the public
welfare, came to the fore. So in the moral as in the political field a revolution had been worked within the space
of a few years. The charm, the gaiety, the wit, the care-
free, delicate sentiment of the eighteenth century almost
completely disappeared. Life became more practical and
more serious. Not that there was any less social life.
Quite to the contrary! All winter long, over all Paris,
whether it was wartime or time of peace, the doors of
the mansions swung wide, drawing-rooms were brightly
lighted, the streets were crowded with carriages. Balls,
concerts, dinners with a great display of silver, banquets
with ruinous menus, were the order of the day. Napoleon's sisters (especially Pauline), Hortense, Cambacérès,
Talleyrand, Berthier, Fouché, the ambassadors, vied with
each other in ingenuity and splendor. Never in Paris
had so much money been spent on gowns, jewels, candles,
violins.

Some of the salons of the old régime, as notably that
of the Princess of Vaudémont, and one survival from
the old days, the salon of Mme. de Montesson, the mor-
ganatic widow of the Duc d'Orléans, entertained the
generals, ministers and high officials of the Empire. However, in the full midst of Paris, there was one island,
one shoal of solid rock, against which Napoleon's advances, threats, police raids beat in vain, and it was to
hold out in defiance against the omnipotent master to
the very end—five or six hundred people at the most,
but people who by their names, their connections, their

character, majestically represented the France that was no more and stood resolved to ignore the unwashed or half-washed society that foregathered about the Emperor. Such was what now came to be called "the faubourg Saint-Germain."

Though they had been recalled from exile by the First Consul and repossessed of such portions of their lands and castles as were not held by new owners, these counts and marquises of long standing thought they were in no sense bound to be grateful. Having sulked for Bonaparte, they continued sulking for Napoleon, waging against him and his entourage a hide-searing warfare of epigram and satire. They ridiculed these "cubs of lackeys and kitchen scullions," these "anointed mongrels," these more or less reformed terrorists, who were peopling the antechambers of the Tuileries.

The drawing-rooms of the La Rochefoucauld-Doudeauvilles, of the Montmorencys, the Polignacs, the Coignys, the Durases, the Aiguillons, the Fitz-Jameses, the Damases, were hermetically sealed against anyone not of the bluest blood who had not been tested and tried. Those circles maintained the atmosphere of Versailles as Versailles had been before the Revolution. Émigrés at home, they remained jealously loyal to their princes and to the manners, the language, the ideas of long ago. For them nothing whatever had happened in the world since 1789.

Though he would never confess as much, the Emperor was not strong enough of mind to ignore this impotent but irritating opposition. It made its way under his skin and he was well aware that all his power would be powerless against it. He kept a sharp eye on it, carefully reading each morning the reports which Fouché compiled from the information that well-placed spies transmitted to him. The Duke of Ótranto embroidered and embellished these reports as he saw fit. He feared the consequences to himself and his Jacobin colleagues of any complete reconciliation between the old régime and the new. Angered at times, Napoleon would chastise too pungent an epigram, too scathing a pamphlet, by sending the guilty author to mourn the old monarchy at a safe range from Paris.

That was the case with Mme. de Staël and Mme. Récamier. Napoleon has been sharply criticized for his policy towards these two women, and he was in fact too severe with the inoffensive Juliette, who sinned only in remaining steadfastly loyal to her old friendships. The case of Mme. de Staël is not quite so simple. Necker's daughter, international by birth, marriage and background, had begun by admiring Bonaparte and had even dreamed of becoming his inspiration. Rebuffed, she became his enemy and incited and gathered about her all the scattered animosities that she could find. Napoleon rightly judged that that superior but erratic intelligence, to which all the adversaries of France were burning incense, might become the center and driving force of a political opposition that had so far not found a leader. For that matter he did nothing very terrible to her. He forbade her Paris, obliging her to live in her beautiful château at Coppet, where she kept open house to intrigue and ran a declamation bureau against the Empire throughout his whole reign. She openly prayed for his defeat and that took a deal of courage. She was a man in skirts. The Emperor frankly detested her and scolded

Fouché for dealing so leniently with her. Mme. de Staël looked forward to his downfall and kept predicting it. "That woman is just a crow," said Napoleon.

As for the fate of the arts under this despot of glory, it must be said that Napoleon loved and patronized artists, showering orders on David, Gros, Gérard, Isabey, Prud'hon, Vernet, Canova. But he did all that, really, in the same spirit with which he fostered the silk industry at Lyons or personally bought works by Gobelin or sets of Sèvres china—because he was interested in everything French and thought of himself as in all respects the responsible promoter of the nation's prosperity.

Those painters and sculptors were, like their epoch, inclined towards the austere and the grandiose. The air that people breathed under Napoleon was heroic. Art sought its examples in Greek and Roman antiquity. Decoration itself had the same inspiration—stiff-backed chairs, draperies sprinkled with palm leaves and crowns, furniture on severe lines, jewels overladen with warlike miniatures. Napoleon took the greatest personal interest in architecture, but that was because that art lends itself to the expression of wealth and power. Like the Caesars with whom he had so much in common, he was a great builder, but tended to prefer the imposing, the magniloquent, to the simply beautiful. He had no flair for the delicate, the graceful, the restrained. His taste was linear and colossal. Among all the monuments for which he approved plans the Arch of Triumph at the Étoile is the one that most fully expresses him.

Literature languished under his reign. Shut up within stereotyped themes and language it strove in vain to disguise its poverty under rhetorical trappings. The theater, like the novel, like poetry, like the hazy treatises on history written at the time, was conventional and stupid. Napoleon could not help looking back with envy upon the age of the Great King. "I wish above all else in the world that I could have a chance to reward a fine tragedy." That was a constant complaint with him. But who was to write one? Not Raynouard, the author of *The Templars;* not Arnault, the author of *The Venetians.* Népomucène Lemercier wrote a *Philip Augustus* and an *Agamemnon,* Luce de Lancival a *Hector.* Ducis translated and adapted Shakespeare. Marie-Joseph Chénier had some good lines and here and there an eloquent scene, but on the whole his plays were a bore. Among a host of flat and colorless rhymsters the best was still Delille. The orators were flowery and rambling, in the style of Fontanes. Bernardin de Saint-Pierre finally managed to die. There were only two writers of the first rank and both were hostile to Napoleon—Chateaubriand and Mme. de Staël.

The latter exercised an influence upon a number of the talents of the period, notably upon Benjamin Constant, a writer of some profundity and a subtle orator. Constant was of the type of the liberal who is richer in learning than in will-power. After belonging to the Tribunat, he declared himself against the Empire. During the Hundred Days he became its adviser and, as it were, its constitutional prompter.

Between Chateaubriand and Napoleon there was less a conflict of ideas than a rivalry in glory. Chateaubriand detested the Corsican for monopolizing the footlights all the time. Otherwise he admired while envying him.

Deep down he was sensitive to the extraordinary appeal of Napoleon's personality and, profoundly French himself, he could not help rejoicing in the glory the man brought to France. More than that, he was under obligations to Napoleon, for the Emperor helped very appreciably to make him what he became by organizing a state publicity around *The Genius of Christianity*. Napoleon thought at that time that he could annex Chateaubriand and he tried to make a diplomat of him. The death of the Duc d'Enghien spoiled everything. Chateaubriand resigned. Retiring to his agreeable home in the Vallée aux Loups he was not disturbed for his opposition to the Empire. The Emperor was always thinking that he might be won back. He sensed the greatness of the man and knew that Chateaubriand's support would lend moral prestige to his régime. Salon intrigues prevented the proud "Enchanter" from ever going over to Napoleon. Barred from playing any political rôle the author of the *Martyrs* and the *Itinerary* contented himself with serving as a slogan for the faubourg Saint-Germain. Napoleon bore Chateaubriand no grudge for the startling article in the *Mercure de France* in which he wrote: "Vainly doth Nero prosper. Tacitus is already born in the Empire . . . and already a just Providence hath delivered to an obscure babe the glory of the master of the world." Napoleon, in fact, was shocked when the French Academy submitted to him a list of nominees for a prize that he had offered without mentioning the name of Chateaubriand. He tore up the list, which a too servile minister had countersigned.

The Emperor's attitude towards his political opponents gives perhaps the best key to his character. It was difficult for him to distinguish between his private and his public personalities. More often they tended to be one and the same. Napoleon was wholly absorbed in the task that he had set for himself. The imperial tunic was part of his flesh. Certainly he had moments of relaxation, of slackening, moments when he was free to manifest the ordinary feelings of men. His errors in conduct, his mistakes in judgment, show well enough that he was of our common clay. But there was in him a spirit of domination that was present in everything, controlled everything. As his dizzy life carried him onward he departed more and more from the common rule. A crushing thunderbolt was needed to restore his normal balance and give back to that superhuman soul, while still enhancing its grandeur, enough weaknesses, and sufficiently touching ones, to bring out all the humanness that lurked in it.

CHAPTER XXII

The Continental Blockade

On the Emperor's return the France that had been so restless was swept with a wave of confidence and joy. The peace long yearned for at last reigned on the Continent. Prussia had, one might say, evaporated, and the Russian alliance looked like a stable guarantee of the Empire of Napoleon. England seemed permanently isolated. Doubtless she too would soon be coming to terms.

Napoleon applied himself to domestic affairs with a will. He was happy, he said, "to change the general's harness for the administrator's." He had to retouch his ministry. Talleyrand insisted on becoming a grand dignitary. He therefore named him Vice-Grand Elector and Grand Chamberlain, with enormous emoluments. However, he deprived him of the portfolio of Foreign Relations, considering it unwise that one department head should be allowed to acquire too great a superiority over his colleagues and so be tempted to play the prime minister. In this rôle Napoleon intended to have no one but himself.

Talleyrand was disappointed at abandoning a place so influential. He proceeded secretly to detach himself from the Emperor's interests and without once forgetting to display the greatest admiration and respect for him, to go on from intrigue to intrigue and finally to complete treason.

Foreign Relations were given to Champagny, a good subordinate in whom the Emperor would never find anything more than an errand boy. So too, in raising Berthier to a Vice-Constableship, Napoleon withdrew from him the portfolio of War and gave it to Clarke. Portalis combined eminence as a lawyer with the talents of a most able diplomat. His death left the Ministry of Worship vacant. Napoleon filled it with Bigot de Préameneu, too servile a person to be of any real use. Cretet replaced Champagny in the Ministry of the Interior. Though Fouché was acquiring too great an influence in the Senate, the skill with which he had suppressed two Royalist uprisings in the west during the Emperor's absence increased Napoleon's confidence in him. He was to be preponderant in the new ministry.

Discerning observers might have noticed a considerable change in the Emperor's attitude at this time. His power was at the zenith, yet he seemed bent on strengthening it further and further, so putting himself beyond attack from anybody. He showed himself more jealous of his prerogatives than ever before. However, the moment he was at home again, he set to work with new zest and with his usual unfailing meticulousness to give a fresh impetus to public works, to agriculture, industry and commerce.

The problem now was to strengthen the economic defenses of the country against the consequences of the Continental Blockade. The enforcement of that policy was

the inflexible pivot of all the Emperor's acts—it was his
fixed idea. So far in his career he had shown a rare
proportioning of imagination to a sense of realities. He
lost that balance just at this point, giving the advantage
to his imagination. He failed to distinguish between what
was possible and what was impossible and not always
did he choose the appropriate means. Determined to
crush the adversary, and wholly under the sway of that
resolve, he underestimated the adversary's powers of
resistance and overestimated his own capacities (the
defect is common in exceptionally fortunate men). Lured
on and on by his illusion he was to rush head down into
a whole quagmire of abuses, encroachments, annexations,
wars, and issue from it five years later only for a final
plunge to ruin.

At Tilsit, Czar Alexander had undertaken—in good
faith it would seem—to join the blockade, but Russian
opinion was not with him in regard to that policy. The
closest intimates of the Czar were friendly to England.
Alexander, however, made the promised gesture towards
mediation in London. Canning and Castlereagh had inherited the spirit of Pitt. Not only did they rebuff him.
They answered Napoleon's Berlin decree by a brutal act
of violence that was designed to intimidate any country
that might be thinking of deferring to the decree of the
Emperor of the French. On August 16, 1807, a British
fleet appeared before Copenhagen and summoned Den-
mark to break relations with Napoleon and to hand over
its fleet as a pledge. The Danish cabinet courageously
refused and for five days, in consequence, Copenhagen
was cannonaded with red hot shot. The city was destroyed
and finally capitulated (September 7). The Danish ships

were transferred as prizes of war to English harbors.

Instead of intimidating the friends of France this high-handed and barbaric act aroused intense indignation on the Continent. Alexander gave King George's ambassador his passports and tried to bring Sweden into the Franco-Russian orbit. As a precautionary measure Napoleon had already sent Brune to occupy Swedish Pomerania. Gradually the enormous mechanism of the blockade was organized and extended. The Danes, outraged, signed what amounted to an alliance with France. Austria closed Trieste and Fiume to English goods and some weeks later broke off relations with England. Prussia, trembling, submissive, had already preceded Austria down that road.

The British ministry did not falter on that account. Other countries refused to join Napoleon's blockade. They had to be forced to, because the system was absolute. A hole in it anywhere would make it a failure. Portugal was at that time governed by a regent who more or less represented England. Portuguese harbors were still open to English vessels. Napoleon threatened in vain. "If Portugal does not do as I wish," he said to Count de Lima, the Portuguese envoy at Fontainebleau, "the House of Braganza will be off that throne within two months."

The Spanish Bourbons, thinking to gain a point, were ready to support French intervention in Portugal. Napoleon therefore ordered Junot to cross the Pyrenees. The Braganzas were frightened and hastened to send the English ambassador home. It was too late. The Emperor had declared war. Some days later a treaty was signed at Fontainebleau with the court at Madrid. Spanish troops would join Junot's army. Portugal was to be partitioned and its territory distributed between Napoleon, the Spanish Prime Minister, Godoÿ, and the Queen-Infanta of Etruria, whose states in Italy would pass, in compensation, to France (October 27, 1807).

Junot's army was badly equipped, badly trained and handled worse still. On its way across Spain the conduct of the soldiers astonished the Spanish people and angered them with France. The force crossed the Portuguese frontier in November and arrived at Abrantes in very bad condition. Hunger, cold and exposure to tremendous snow-storms had worn it out. It had pillaged and plundered all along its line of march. It advanced upon Lisbon down the valley of the Tagus wading knee-deep through rainwater and mud. An article in the *Moniteur,* which Napoleon had himself dictated, announced the dethronement of the Braganzas in advance: "The Prince Regent of Portugal is losing his throne . . . because of his refusal to seize goods of English origin in Lisbon. . . . The fall of the House of Braganza is one more proof of the destruction that awaits anyone who stands by the English."

The Portuguese government had no conception of the condition Junot's troops were in. As they drew near the Braganzas put all their treasure aboard ship and sailed for Brazil. Junot entered Lisbon two days later, November 30. He was supported by 1500 ragged grenadiers who had not a field piece and not a cartridge. The slightest resistance would have destroyed his army.

The Emperor was in Italy when he learned of the fall of Lisbon. Insignificant as it may have been it strengthened him in an impression that nothing in Europe could stand in his way. He had come to Milan to settle affairs in Italy on the spot. Eugene reported on his administration as viceroy and received due praise for the wise and orderly government he had provided. Napoleon was dissatisfied, on the other hand, with the Queen of Etruria, who had made no effort to expel the English. He deprived her of her kingdom, therefore, and annexed it to the Empire as the Grand Duchy of Tuscany, henceforward to be an appanage of Elisa Bacciochi.

Going on to Venice the Emperor was received magnificently. The city had prospered under French rule and seemed to have no longings for the age-old freedom it had lost. Looking out over the Adriatic from the lagoons Napoleon experienced a return of his haunting dreams of the East—an indelible imprint that Egypt had left upon him. How about partitioning the Ottoman Empire? However, the thought had to give way to more immediate preoccupations. Elisa and Joseph came to see him in the city of the doges. During the two years that he had sat on the throne in Naples Joseph had failed to give the slightest indication of fitness to serve as head of a state. He had left everything to favorites in order to devote himself to frivolous pleasures. English products were landing helter-skelter on his coasts, thence to make their way over all Italy. Napoleon scolded. Joseph bowed and promised to do better. Back in Milan again Napoleon learned that in reprisal for the blockade London had forbidden neutral ships to touch at Continental ports without first paying duties on British soil. Napoleon answered with the Decrees of Milan which declared that any vessel obeying the English Order in Council was by that fact denationalized and to be treated as an enemy ship (December 16, 1807).

But what none of the great powers in Europe had dared to do—stand up against Napoleon—a pontiff unarmed, but strong in the sense of his spiritual mission, at this moment essayed with noble courage. He refused to bar the English from his territory. A sovereign of peace he claimed the right to observe strict neutrality in temporal struggles. "What is Pius VII thinking of?" cried Napoleon. "Of putting my thrones under the interdict? Of excommunicating me? Does he think my peoples will drop their muskets and strangle me on that account? Men, to be sure, have preached this disgraceful doctrine of the popes—raving lunatics born for the world's misfortune! On that basis all the Pope would have to do would be to shave my pate and lock me up in some monastery! Does he think the world is living in the brutishness and ignorance of the ninth century? Is he mistaking me for Louis the Débonnaire?"

Cardinal Fesch had been serving as ambassador in Rome, pouring oil on the fire by his stupidity and haughtiness. Napoleon recalled him. He had already seized Civitavecchia as a first step towards breaking the Pope's resistance. He now sent Le Marois to occupy Ancona and the territories of the Holy See on the Adriatic. He further demanded that Pius VII subscribe to a pledge that had the ring rather of vassalage than of alliance: All enemies of the Empire were to be expelled from the pontifical domains.

The Pope made no answer. He took personal responsibility for all his acts: "It will be seen that they are dealing with me and me alone. If my authority is to be overridden by force, I alone shall be the victim of the oppression. I shall be the one to feel the heel of the soldiers of France." Napoleon forthwith directed General Miollis to take possession of Rome. Miollis did so on the 2nd of February, 1808, the French troops entering the Eternal City and marching on Castel Sant'Angelo. Of this episode Napoleon wrote to Caulaincourt, his ambassador to the Czar: "My troops have entered Rome. There need be no talk about it, but if the matter does come up, point out that the Pope is head of my country's religion and that it is only proper that I should make sure of the way in which that spiritual function is exercised. This is not a territorial annexation. It is a precaution."

Miollis met no opposition. His orders were strict and severe: He was to brook no slightest rebellion. However, the Roman populace made no move. Miollis established meticulous policing, organized a government for the territory and incorporated the papal troops with his own army. The Pope had taken refuge in the Quirinal and considered himself a prisoner there. Short of funds he was soon obliged—one of the ironies of history—to pawn the tiara that Napoleon had given him as a present at the time of the Anointment. But he cried aloud through his representatives in all the courts abroad, and his voice, overreaching the peaks of power, struck down into the depths of the peoples who were Catholic at heart. Christendom so came to detach itself from Napoleon at the critical moment in the curve of his destiny, the moment when he embarked on the least defensible of all his policies and the one that was to be most ruinous in its consequences—the conquest of Spain.

CHAPTER XXIII

Baylén

NAPOLEON WAS TO BLAME HIMSELF FOR IT ALWAYS, AND he was right in doing so. He was led into the venture by the necessity of extending the blockade farther and farther afield, but to some small extent also, as we shall see, by a distorted feeling of megalomaniac pride born of the flatteries of Talleyrand. The Emperor was somehow losing that keen perception of realities that had served him so long and so marvelously. Once launched on the bootless enterprise, he dared not draw back for fear of losing prestige. So for year after year he was to squander the best of his strength upon it. The war with Spain was the real cause of the decline of the Empire: Napoleon was to perish in it.

For months he had been gazing at Madrid. Spain seemed to be a country in full decadence which had taken to its bed to die in the gorgeous robes of its history. It was ruled by a disgraceful family that could deserve no shred of pity.

Charles IV was a grotesque idiot, a sodden tippler. Maria Luisa of Parma was a woman with the face of a ghoul who lived entirely under the sway of a lover, Manuel Godoÿ, a sometime member of her bodyguard, whom she had wangled into the prime ministry and made Prince of La Paz. The heir apparent, Ferdinand, Prince of the Asturias, was a coward and a hypocrite, greedy for money, hating his parents and Godoÿ and just as cordially detested by them. Disgusting scenes were the order of the day in that family of degenerates. The queen wanted to disinherit her eldest son in favor of one of his younger brothers. Ferdinand rebelled and opened his father's eyes to the real rôle that Godoÿ was playing in the royal family. Meantime his party, managed by a priest, the Canon Escoïquiz, formerly his governor, was organizing a rebellion designed to force Charles IV to abdicate.

Ferdinand was counting on assistance from Napoleon. He had written him asking for imperial patronage and soliciting the favor of becoming a member of the Bonaparte family by some marriage or other. The whole intrigue came to light. Enraged, the queen obtained an order for Ferdinand's arrest, and Charles IV in his turn begged Napoleon to come to his aid against this monstrous, unnatural son whom he had resolved to deprive of the succession.

In the face of this twin appeal Napoleon hesitated. The Bourbons of Spain were in his hands in any event. He was inclined on the whole to interfere. He had nothing but contempt for Godoÿ, who had deserted him before Jena and then come around again but only in fear. French troops were virtually in control in Spain as a result of the expedition to Portugal. Since Charles and Ferdinand were both incompetent to sit on a throne it looked like a fine chance to bring Spain into the imperial system and close one more channel of seepage to British trade.

Napoleon could not have been worse informed by his intelligence agents, among them the inept Beauharnais, brother to Josephine's first husband. They gave him a wholly false picture of the Spanish people—a mixture of various races that had been fused and ennobled by the heroic Reconquest, by an ardent religious faith and by a strict monarchical tradition. That rugged, sober people, cherishing traditions of an almost barbaric chivalry, could never have been brought to accept a foreign yoke. Napoleon knew nothing of all that. He heard talk only of poverty, wretchedness, bad government. He thought that his name alone would rally the empire of Charles V and Philip II to the imperial eagle. On returning to Paris he took the matter up with Talleyrand. Talleyrand was afraid of the Bourbons and was ready to have done with them in Europe. He urged the Emperor to follow the example of Louis XIV and seat a prince of his own blood on the throne in Madrid.

New developments supervened to postpone decision. Ferdinand suddenly sought his father's forgiveness, betrayed his accomplices and obtained a surface pardon. In those circumstances Napoleon thought of marrying him to his young niece, "Lolotte," daughter to Lucien. This project of a so to say private settlement came to naught. Unwilling to sacrifice Charlotte, the Emperor intercepted her letters to learn her real attitude. Having assured himself of her dislike of Ferdinand and the whole Spanish tribe, he sent her home to Italy. By that time he had made up his mind to interfere in Spain. He reinforced the troops beyond the Pryenees and placed them under the command of Murat.

The Spanish sovereigns took refuge at Aranjuez and for a moment thought of imitating the Braganzas and sailing off to their possessions in the New World. Nothing would have pleased Napoleon more. In leaving the ground free they would have been playing into his hand. But on a rumor that their rulers were about to flee, the Madrid populace turned out into the streets in riot, and the uprising spread to Aranjuez. On the night of the 17th-18th of March, a mob entered Godoÿ's palace and pillaged it. He hid in his garret to avoid being lynched. It was useless for Charles IV to strip him of his offices and dignities. The rioters demanded the head of the unworthy favorite. Hunger obliged the wretch after thirty-six hours to issue from his hiding place. He was saved from being torn to pieces only on a promise by the Prince of the Asturias that he would be tried and punished according to law.

Charles IV was overwhelmed by these outbreaks, and fearing for his own life, resolved to abdicate, naming his son king under the title of Ferdinand VII. Murat was already advancing on Madrid. He hurried his march. The accession of Ferdinand was spoiling his own plans, for he had been thinking of the Spanish throne for himself, by grace of the Emperor. He refused to recognize Ferdinand, entered Madrid on March 23rd in splendid array, and persuaded Charles IV to rescind his abdication.

On receiving news of these happenings Napoleon had the impression that he could force his arbitration on both the father and son and, once he had them under his personal influence, oblige them peaceably to cede their rights to him. He sent Savary to Spain to request Ferdinand to proceed to France and state his case. He himself set out with Josephine for Bayonne in order to meet the young prince halfway.

Ferdinand started out in all confidence, in company with Escoïquiz and Savary. But at Vittoria he began to have his doubts. He halted. Napoleon lost patience. From the castle at Marracq, where he had set up his establishment, he sent Ferdinand a peremptory order. The prince did not dare refuse. On April 20th he crossed the frontier and arrived at Bayonne. But the departure of the Prince of the Asturias had filled the old couple with new fears and alarms. Was the Emperor turning against them? They hurried to France in their turn, taking Godoÿ with them—Murat had rescued the favorite from his plight.

Bayonne welcomed the party with royal honors. Charles IV threw himself in tears into Napoleon's arms. In the Emperor's presence he assailed his son violently:

"You have covered my white hairs with shame and bitterness. . . . Leave my presence! May I never set eyes on you again!"

A few days later, entirely in Napoleon's hands, he declared himself the sole legitimate King of Spain and named Murat his lieutenant general.

So "the tragedy," to use Napoleon's expression, "advanced towards its last act."

But he had been reckoning without the Spanish people. On May 2nd Madrid rose, to prevent the departure of Ferdinand's brother and his sister, the Infanta Maria Luisa, whom Napoleon had also summoned to Bayonne.

Such of the French as were cut off were massacred. Murat shot the revolt down ruthlessly and when order was restored assumed full powers.

When reports of the insurrection arrived Napoleon frightened the poor king with an outburst that was very largely put on. Charles IV accused his son of fomenting the Madrid revolt and struck at him with his cane, while the queen rebuked the youth for his cowardice and treachery. A coward in truth, he proceeded to sign away his crown. On the same day (May 5) Charles IV abdicated in favor of "his friend, the great Napoleon," charging him to settle the matter of the throne as he should see fit and stipulating only that Spain should remain an independent country with Catholicism as the privileged form of worship. In compensation the Emperor gave him the palace of Compiègne and a civil list of seven millions and a half. Ferdinand and the other royal children were sent to Valençay to be guests of Talleyrand. "Your mission this time is not a little honorable," wrote Napoleon to his Vice-Grand Elector, with his tongue in his cheek. "You are to receive three distinguished guests in your house. Entertainment of this sort is strictly in the French tradition and is moreover consonant with your rank."

He proceeded to offer Spain to Joseph, who would be replaced at Naples by Murat. A promotion of kings, very much like a promotion of army officers! Joseph could do nothing but pack up and start for Bayonne. There a junta of dummies proclaimed him "Sovereign of Spain and the Indies" under a constitution that had been outlined by the Emperor. On the 9th of July he crossed the Pyrenees to take his seat on a throne that was already as hot as an overheated griddle.

A short military occupation would be enough to "pocket Spain." So thought the Emperor. A few commonsense reforms in administration and in the courts would win the intelligent Spaniards. More and better food and a less onerous government would win the Spanish masses. So again thought the Emperor—until a few weeks' time had shown him that he was thinking altogether amiss.

Murat was at loose ends in Madrid. He was going to be a king in Naples, to be sure, but that seemed paltry business as compared with the prospects he had been coddling. He flared wroth against the Emperor. Disappointment, helped perhaps by the hot weather, made him ill. Joseph was expected at any moment. Madrid recognized his election as king, but revolts broke out in a number of towns. A revolutionary junta formed at Seville and then moved to Cadiz, taking the pompous title of "Supreme Junta of Spain and the Indies." It called on all Spaniards to save the independence of their country, and the Spaniards had too red a blood and too impulsive a national temperament not to heed such a call. They rushed to arms without distinctions of class, costume or trade—monks and peasants, brigands and caballeros, all as one man. The Asturias rose, and Old Castile and Leon followed suit. The revolt broke out in Galicia on May 30, the birthday of the Prince of the Asturias, to cries of "Long live Ferdinand!" Catalonia and then Aragon took fire. At Valencia a furious populace exterminated a force of three hundred French soldiers who had taken refuge in the citadel. The Cadiz

Junta appealed to England for help and England began forthwith to fit out an expeditionary army.

The French were fairly strong—80,000 men, but they were largely raw recruits, and they had to fight an unheard-of war, a war of surprises never ending and without quarter. In that rough and rugged country not a rock, not a bush, not a road, that did not shelter its ambush. Small bands of men, the *guerrilleros,* harassed, decimated, exhausted the French columns. The sick and wounded were finished off with barbaric refinements. "All along the road," writes Sergeant Lavaux, "we found murdered soldiers. Some were half burned, others had their arms and legs cut off, others were nailed to trees or hung up by the legs." The French paid back in kind. The same soldier naïvely confesses: "We had orders to burn and kill everything and everybody in the first village that should fire on us, sparing not even babes in cradles. . . . For six consecutive weeks, day in and day out, we did nothing but pillage and burn." Unhappy Spain had become hell itself. The hatred of the priests was inflamed by the violence that Napoleon had done to the Pope. They promised palms of martyrdom to defenders of the faith. Napoleon was pictured as the anti-Christ. The war became a crusade. "Is it a sin to kill a Frenchman?" asked a new catechism. "No," it answered. "One earns heaven by killing one of those heretic dogs."

Far away in France Napoleon had no sense of the intensity of the Spanish reaction to his policy. He did know that there was a rebellion in Spain and that it must be subdued without delay. He sent reinforcements on reinforcements to his brother, who had lost heart on his first ride to Madrid and was sending back complaints against the soldiers. "Try to be patient," Napoleon answered. "I will not leave you without anything that you may need. But do not become the accuser of my soldiers. To their devotion both you and I owe all that we are. They are dealing with brigands who are cutting their throats and who have to be repressed by terror. Try to win the affection of the Spaniards but do not discourage the army. It would be an irreparable mistake."

Bessières won a victory at Medina del Rio Seco, July 14, 1808. That enabled Joseph to get through to his capital, where he was received by silent, sullen crowds. Napoleon thought the victory presaged better things, especially since Lassalle had taken Valladolid, Duhesme was besieging Gerona, Moncey was marching on Valencia, and Verdier was before Saragossa, held off by the heroic Palafox.

However, the insurgents were best organized in Andalusia, where they had more ample resources and even little armies with generals—Generals Castaños, Reding, La Peña. General Dupont stormed Cordoba by main force. He sacked the town, but then, instead of going on to Seville, as Napoleon had ordered, he fell back upon Andujar and then back again upon Baylén, at the entrance to the passes across the Sierra Morena.

There Dupont lost his head. Cut off from his subordinates he thought he was surrounded by Spaniards. He fought the attackers off for six hours under a scorching sun. Then two of his regiments, made up of Swiss troops, deserted. Wounded himself he feared lest his whole force of six thousand men would be put to the sword. He therefore asked for a truce, and on the 22nd of July he

JOSEPH BONAPARTE, KING OF SPAIN
From the Portrait by Gérard

capitulated. To aggravate the circumstances he included in the surrender the divisions of Vedel and Dufour, which might easily have escaped. At least he obtained the honors of war. But the Seville Junta violated the word that had been given and refused to ratify the terms. The prisoners, after odious treatment, were sent to rot, partly on Cabrera, one of the Balearic islands, partly on scows in the harbor of Cadiz. Hardly one of them ever returned to France.

All Spain thrilled. Her patriot militias had forced an army of French veterans to surrender in the open field! Heroes of Austerlitz, Jena and Friedland had filed, stripped of their arms and with lowered heads, through jeering lines of improvised *guerrilleros!* But the effects of Baylén did not stop there. Panic spread among the French generals. They retreated everywhere.[1] Bessières evacuated Galicia. The siege of Saragossa was raised. Joseph, ill advised by Savary, fled Madrid after ten days on the throne. The bulk of the French army was now north of the Ebro. What had set out to be a military promenade had ended in a complete disaster.

Having learned a little something Joseph wrote to the Emperor, sadly: "It will take two hundred thousand Frenchmen to conquer Spain and a hundred thousand guillotines to uphold the prince who is sentenced to reign over the country. No, Sire, one cannot imagine what this people is like. Each house will become a fortress

---

1 [The trait was characteristic of the new conscript armies of the Republic and the Empire. Irresistible on the offensive the French of this era could not retreat short of a débâcle. So Italy had been lost in '99; so the line of the Nienen was to be lost after Moscow and the Rhine after Leipzig. So it was to be as the Old Guard wavered at Waterloo. Napoleon in person checked incipient stampedes at Lodi and Arcola; Macdonald another after Sacile in the Wagram campaign.—A. L.]

and each man has the will of the majority. I will emphasize but one point as an example: Not one Spaniard will be on my side if this conquest is carried through. We shall not find one guide, one spy."

Soon Portugal also was lost. During his command at Lisbon Junot had done nothing but have a good time. England landed an army there under Wellesley, the future Duke of Wellington. An insurrection broke out at Oporto and soon spread all over the country. Taken by surprise Junot marched on Wellesley's red-coats. He was beaten at Vimiero. Despairing of a successful defense in the face of an enraged population, and having been long without news from France, he signed an agreement at Cintra on August 30th, whereby Portugal was to be evacuated and his army transported to France. An English fleet in fact landed his men on the shores of Saintonge and Brittany some days later. He had not lost as much as Dupont had lost at Baylén, but for the second time a French army had capitulated. Napoleon's prestige was shaken. Europe served him with notice of that by a restless stirring on all hands.

CHAPTER XXIV

Erfurt

NAPOLEON WAS AT BORDEAUX WHEN HE HEARD OF THE Baylén affair. His rage knew no bounds. "Since the world has been the world," he exclaimed, "nothing quite so inept or so cowardly has ever been heard of!" He ordered Dupont's arrest the moment the general's feet should touch French soil.

He began by trying to instill a little energy into Joseph, who was begging to be excused in Spain and allowed to return to Naples. Give up the Peninsula? cried Napoleon. Never! He would go there himself, and his presence would set everything in order! "What do I care about a few rebels?" he stormed. "I will finish them off with my dragoons. I will find the Pillars of Hercules in Spain, but no such limits to my power!"

Could he have meant that? Could he really have been so far wrong? He seemed, at any rate, to stand ready to throw all the resources of the Empire into the enterprise, if necessary. "Spain will be reconquered by autumn," he said to Joseph. And he sent him Ney.

But before crossing the Pyrenees in person he had to make sure of his rear in Europe. Everywhere signs of hostility were reappearing. The peoples were in motion.

249

He had to attend to them and without a moment's delay.

In spite of the obsequious exterior she manifested, Prussia was following the lead of a patriotic minister, Baron Stein, and making a whole series of social, civil and military reforms which were to amount to a complete reconstruction of the nation. An act of imprudence ruined Stein. He wrote to Wittgenstein after Baylén that what was going on in Spain should serve as an example to the other peoples whom Napoleon was oppressing. The letter was intercepted and Napoleon demanded Stein's dismissal. Frederick William could only accede. Shortly afterwards Stein's brother was forced to sign an agreement reducing the Prussian army to 42,000 men. In compensation, to be sure, French forces were to evacuate the country. In order to find new divisions for Spain Napoleon was obliged to regroup his armies and bring them closer to the Rhine.

Austria had always been sorry that she had not fallen upon Napoleon after Eylau. She was outraged at the abolition of the Pope's temporal power and at his confinement to the Quirinal, where he was sitting without a staff of ministers and without a court. The shady doings at Bayonne had been the last straw. Did the Corsican think himself the master of the universe? Soon he would be selling out the old crowns! Could the Hapsburgs be sure even of themselves?

"We shall die if necessary," declared the Archduke Charles melodramatically, for those were romantic days, "but with arms in our hands."

The Archduke could feel himself entitled to say a word. Austria owed her military reorganization to him. He had developed a sort of militia which doubled the

nation's military strength and brought it to nearly 700,-
000 men. Great fortifications were being built in all parts
of the country. Napoleon was not deceived. He could see
plainly enough that Vienna was preparing for war. However, he wanted to gain time. On August 15, 1808, he
tried to frighten Metternich, the Austrian ambassador:
"Austria is arming rather heavily. Who is attacking that
you should be so concerned for your safety? . . . Remember—the next war with Austria will be to the death!
Either you will come to Paris or I will smash the monarchy completely. But do you know what is to come of
all this? The Emperor Alexander will send you word
that he would like to have you stop this arming. And
you will stop!"

Metternich protested that the intentions of his master
were pacific and Napoleon pretended to believe him. It
seemed more than ever urgent to him, however, to
strengthen his alliance with Russia. He could not turn
to Spain until he and the Czar were in agreement as
to the maintenance of the status quo in Europe.

The idea of another interview between the two Emperors had long been under discussion. Alexander himself was eager for one. He had lived strictly up to his
undertakings at Tilsit in spite of the growing hostility
of his household and the plaints that were audible everywhere in Russia as to the Continental Blockade. He had
stuck to the alliance because he expected great things
to come of it, not only in Finland but at the expense
of the Turks. Napoleon had at first shrunk from giving
the Czar those satisfactions and Alexander had grown
very uneasy over his postponements and tergiversations
in the matter of action in the East. Caulaincourt had

replaced Savary at St. Petersburg late in 1807. He had unwisely gone so far towards letting himself be "be-witched" by the Czar that Napoleon was soon to be twitting him for being more Russian than French. He was put to it to calm Alexander's impatience. But then England's resolve to push the war to the bitter end in-clined Napoleon to let the Czar have his way. He went back to the plan he had toyed with in Egypt. Unable to win the seas, he would threaten the English in their pos-sessions in India with the help of the Russians. He gave form to that dream in a famous letter, which he wrote to the Czar, February 2, 1808: "If an army of 50,000 men, Russians and French, with perhaps a few Austrians, should march by way of Constantinople upon Asia, it would not have reached the Euphrates before England would be trembling and falling to her knees on the Con-tinent. I am ready in Dalmatia. Your Majesty is ready on the Danube. A month after we agreed to start, our army would be on the Bosporus. The move would make itself felt in India and England would come to terms."

The Czar was delighted. "Ah, the great man!" he cried in Caulaincourt's presence, as he read Napoleon's letter. "There he is back at the Treaty of Tilsit! Tell him that I am devoted to him for life, that my em-pire, my armies, everything, are at his disposal."

And so far so good. But when one came down to de-tails complications began to arise. The Czar wanted to break up the Turkish empire and insisted on the point, but just there the question of Constantinople came up and blocked everything. Caulaincourt and Rumiant-zov could not reach any agreement in their talks. Time went by. Napoleon was engrossed with the Spanish business. Alexander squared accounts for the delay by invading Finland. In August Napoleon again proposed a talk, but by that time he had dropped the dream of the East. The important question then had become the defense of the Empire and the checkmating of Spain. The Czar was none the less ready for the interview. He knew how badly Napoleon needed him and he set out to take as much advantage as possible of so favorable a juncture.

The meeting was fixed by common accord for Erfurt at the end of September. Napoleon thought of dazzling everybody with the spectacle of his power. Buttressed by the Russian alliance his Empire should seem unshakeable and in a sense above reverses. He despatched a force of troops under Oudinot to occupy the town. In order to surround himself with a display that would satisfy his instinct for the theatrical, he invited his German vassals to join him at the conference. The Grand Duke of Baden and the kings of Saxony, Bavaria, Württemberg and Westphalia accepted. The losers in the last wars, in other words the Emperor of Austria and the King of Prussia, sent representatives—Baron von Vincent, for Vienna, Count von der Goltz for Berlin. In addition to his ordinary following Napoleon took along with him the leading actors of the Comédie Française, Talma, and Mlles. Bourgoing, Raucourt and Duchesnois.

The two sovereigns met on September 27 in the outskirts of Erfurt. They embraced with every show of affection, then remounted their horses and, chatting like old pals, rode into the flag-draped town side by side, while bells rang and cannon boomed. Talleyrand, Cau-

laincourt, Berthier, Lannes, Duroc, served as the immediate escort of the imperial pair.

That evening Napoleon and Alexander attended a
performance of *Cinna* by Talma. Then, for two weeks,
entertainment followed on entertainment in one dizzy
round. Erfurt literally overflowed with sovereigns, ministers, ambassadors. "Princes and visitors are flocking
here from all directions," the Emperor wrote to Cambacérès, "and things continue to develop to our common satisfaction." The various crowned heads met each
other at brilliant dinners, military reviews, hunts, balls,
and each evening, in a din of rolling drums, the two
Emperors led a regiment of kings into a lighted hall
to listen to plays by Corneille, Racine or Voltaire. One
evening Talma was doing *Oedipe,* and he came to a line
that read:

"The friendship of a great man is a gift of the gods."

The fascinated audience saw the Czar turn towards
Napoleon and shake his hand warmly as he whispered:

"I am realizing the truth of that more and more every
day!"

The Emperors made a visit to Weimar where Duke
Charles Augustus entertained them magnificently. At a
dinner confined to representatives of the older reign-
ing houses in Europe Napoleon chatted interestingly
of his early beginnings: "When I was a lieutenant in
the artillery . . ." All those kings hung slavishly on his
every word and smile. What a piquant contrast! . . .
Goethe and Wieland were admitted, for a glimpse of
the "hero of the age." With Wieland the Emperor discussed Tacitus and the larger problems of religion. He
congratulated the author of *Werther* on his writings,

talked letters and invited him to pay him a visit in Paris: "You are a man, Monsieur Goethe!" he said. Both writers received the star of the Legion.

All these sideshows did not detract from interest in the main performance. Napoleon had outlined to Talleyrand in advance just what he expected to gain at Erfurt: "We are going to Erfurt. I want to come away with my hands free to do what I choose in Spain. I want Austria to be frightened into keeping quiet. I do not care to be involved in any definite way as regards matters in the East." He was particularly concerned not to be tied regarding Constantinople.

Alexander too had come to realize the dangers of any common action in the East. He was afraid that he might be reduced in the end to pulling the chestnuts out of the fire for this too powerful crony of his. He seems really to have had Moldavia and Wallachia in mind, territories that were already occupied in part by his troops. He was less interested in promises for the future than in immediate stakes. Napoleon had no difficulty in accepting the Czar's views. They were altogether harmonious with his own. The Czar could feel free to take the Danube provinces. The larger projects could wait—did they not have all the future before them? In return he asked Alexandria to intimidate Austria and halt her in her preparations for war.

The Czar would have accepted beyond any doubt had it not been for a base and sordid treason on the part of Talleyrand. The Grand Chamberlain had decided that things were going badly in Spain and that the imperial régime was due to collapse sooner or later. He wanted to make his own future secure whatever the outcome for the Emperor might be, even were it to the detriment of France.

Chatting with Alexander at a party one evening he advised him to resist Napoleon's demands and "not allow himself to be lured into steps that would involve threat or offense to Austria." A paragon of cynicism, Talleyrand was already in Austria's pay! Six months before Erfurt he had informed Metternich of the plan to break up the Turkish empire.

The day after that the Prince of Benevento called on the Czar again. "Sire," he said, "what are you doing here? It is for you to save Europe, and you can do that only by holding Napoleon in leash. The French people is civilized and its sovereign is not. The sovereign of Russia is civilized and his people is not. The sovereign of Russia should therefore be the ally of the French people. The Rhine, the Alps, the Pyrenees are conquests of France. All the rest is a conquest of the Emperor. France has no interest in it."

This talk reversed Alexander's attitude completely. Though Talleyrand was no longer minister Europe still regarded him as the chief spokesman of French diplomacy. For a man of his experience to talk in such language and in a manner so obviously hostile to Napoleon was enough to turn the Czar's thinking in quite new directions, and notably in the direction of a future in which Napoleon would have no part.

The atmosphere changed at once. Alexander had seemed inclined at first to keep Austria quiet. He now began to hedge, to parry, to make no answer at all. He was thinking of mortgaging the future as regarded Austria and secretly informed Emperor Francis of his friendly intentions: "No one has a right to interfere with the measures a foreign sovereign judges best," he declared to Baron von Vincent. He did advise caution, however.

Far from suspecting the cause of Alexander's change, Napoleon was astounded and finally lost his temper at the Czar's reticence.

"Your Czar is as stubborn as a mule," he remarked angrily to Caulaincourt. "He plays deaf when he doesn't want to hear."

Tired of arguing Napoleon finally let himself go. He threw his hat to the floor angrily and stamped on it in the presence of the impassive Russian.

"You are violent," said the latter coldly. "For my part I am stubborn. Bad temper has no effect on me. Let's chat, let's consider—otherwise I shall go home."

Eventually Alexander pretended to yield, at least as a matter of politeness. A German who had become half Slav, he liked to conceal his thoughts, disguise his real feelings. He seemed to accept joyfully a plan that Napoleon broached of striking a family alliance between the two courts. For a long time the French Emperor had been facing the necessity of divorcing Josephine. He now suggested that with her out of the way he might marry the Grand Duchess Catherine, Alexander's sister. The Czar mentioned a number of difficulties, among them the probable opposition of the Czarina-mother. He vowed that he would do his best to overcome that obstacle.

However, the moment he returned home, he was to affiance his sister to the Grand Duke of Oldenburg, who was an insignificant cripple but a prince at any rate, and above all not a Bonaparte.

The two ministers, Champagny and Rumiantzov, had great difficulty in finding a text that exactly fitted the Franco-Russian accord. In its final form it declared that the Czar and the Emperor would publicly offer peace to England on the basis of the Continental status quo. France would keep her conquests and Joseph would be recognized as King of Spain. Russia would keep Finland, Moldavia and Wallachia. The integrity of the Turkish empire would be guaranteed. If Austria opposed Russia's annexation of the Danube provinces, Napoleon would support Russia. If, on the other hand, Austria broke with France, Russia would join forces with the latter. On a plea by the Czar Napoleon consented to reduce the Prussian war indemnity by twenty millions. The treaty was to remain secret. It was signed on October 12, 1808.

It was not the perfect understanding that Napoleon had dreamed of, but at least, he thought it could hold the young Emperor for some time still and keep Europe guessing. He had imagined he could charm Alexander as he had done at Tilsit. Instead the Czar had drawn away. Talleyrand's warning was working in his mind. His politeness, his gracious language, were masks to conceal deeper designs. He would bide his time and meanwhile collect dividends that were due. His attitude could then change to fit circumstances as they developed.

When the two men separated two days after the hat episode, their friendship was for public consumption only. Napoleon turned away thoughtful and at heart worried. His fortune looked brilliant enough to the eye, but a storm was gathering. He had probably gained a few months' time. He would have to use them to finish Spain. By spring, he could be sure, he would have Austria on his hands.

CHAPTER XXV

Somo Sierra

WILLING TO LEAVE NOTHING TO CHANCE, HE PLANNED his campaign with the usual carefulness. The troops withdawn from Germany plus 80,000 freshly drafted men gave him a force of 200,000. Joseph and Marshal Jourdan had established headquarters at Vittoria. Napoleon arrived there on November 5.

There was not a moment to lose. Recent weeks had rendered the situation of the French still more perilous. Elated by their successes and with their guerilla bands now armed and provisioned by the British, the Spaniards were engaged in a turning movement that was designed to cut off Joseph and force his surrender. Napoleon's presence as usual roused enthusiasm among the French. More than that they were now led by the best generals of the Empire, Lannes, Victor, Soult, Ney, Lefebvre, Mortier. The forward march began.

Within a fortnight three major defeats had disorganized the Spaniards. Soult beat them at Burgos on November 10; Victor and Lefebvre at Espinosa de los Monteros on November 11; Lannes at Tudela on November 23. Thereupon Napoleon marched on Madrid. General San Juan tried to stop him at the pass of Somo

Sierra. An overwhelming charge of the Polish light-horse annihilated the Spanish army. On December 2nd Napoleon was before Madrid. The authorities had taken flight. The city was in the hands of the mobs. It made a show of resistance and then surrendered. Napoleon disdained to enter. Striking the pose of an angry conqueror he declared that unless the Spanish people "asked Joseph back again," he would dismember the country; and then at once, with an idea that he could rally mass opinion to his brother, he abolished the Inquisition, feudal taxes, inland customs' duties, and replaced the chaotic Spanish legal system with the Code.

It was like talking to deaf-mutes. The Spanish people would have nothing of reforms that emanated from the detested foreigner. On December 19th, therefore, Saint-Cyr occupied Barcelona and the siege of Saragossa was resumed. Palafox was still holding out there. The struggle was to last for four months, heroic, merciless. In the face of famine, pestilence, sufferings untold, the Spanish seemed to grow more spirited and undaunted from day to day. Exhorted by their priests they beat off every attack. Lannes was finally sent to end the matter. He wrote back: "What a war! They are wonderful people—or shall we say lunatics?—and one has to kill them! To win a victory breaks your heart!" The town could be taken only by destroying it, reducing one house after the other.

From Madrid Napoleon had been thinking of an advance upon Lisbon. The English were now in his way. Canning had scornfully rebuffed the pleas for peace that had been sent by France and Russia. Not content with helping the Spaniards with supplies, arms, munitions, money, England had also sent a fresh army under command of Sir John Moore (Wellesley had been removed because of the too favorable terms he had accorded to Junot). With 30,000 men Moore advanced into Old Castile. By mid-December he was between Salamanca and Valladolid, threatening Soult. Napoleon sent Ney to attend to him and himself set out with the Guard and a powerful assortment of artillery.

Winter lay heavy and deep upon the mountains, but again the French army scaled the passes of the Guadarrama—an exhausting march, now through snow and slush, now over glare ice or in deep mud. Old veterans themselves began to complain, accusing their Emperor of carrying ambition too far. Marching in their midst Napoleon pretended not to hear. He chatted with them as usual, jesting, encouraging. At last he could feel his claws tightening upon an army of Englishmen, and he had resolved to give them the lesson of their lives.

Moore, however, had seen Soult and Ney closing in upon him and decided to retreat. With the French Emperor hot upon his heels he fled towards La Coruña to take ship. The retreat of the red-coats became a rout. Apart from a miracle they would all have been lost.

But the miracle happened. On New Year's Day, 1809, Napoleon was on the road to Astorga when news reached him from France, bad news, so bad that he thought it best to change his plans entirely. Austria was about to move. The flaccid attitude of the Czar was encouraging her to attempt revenge at a time when Napoleon seemed to be lost in Spain with the flower of his army. That was not all or the worst. Loyal and trustworthy agents in France sent word that Fouché and Talleyrand had

MARSHAL NEY
From the Portrait by Meymer

worked up an intrigue, a serious one. Foreseeing Napoleon's death on a battlefield as more than likely, they were grooming a successor of their choice. Napoleon could not dream of remaining in Spain. He sent Soult to follow the English in his place. For that matter he thought that the more serious part of the work in Spain had been done. The *guerrilleros* had gone into hiding. The provincial governments were one by one submitting. Joseph was in a position to re-enter Madrid as a pacifying king.

Dreams! Dreams, ever fresh, ever rosy! They were part of Napoleon's genius. They enabled him never to collapse under burdens ever heavier. He did not foresee, or at least chose not to foresee, that with him gone the great military machine that he had set in motion with all the resourcefulness of his strategic science would at once cease to function like a body deprived of its soul; that Soult would move too slowly and allow the English to regain the seashore and re-embark; that Joseph was a playboy king who would straightway lose the few Spanish sympathies that had been won and then start to quarreling bitterly with the French generals, who were already squabbling among themselves; that the guerrilla would at once be resumed with doubled fury, reducing the best French regiments to skeletons of their original selves; that England would return with a stronger army into a devastated country, flaming with hatred, which had become the cancer of the Empire; that that army would be commanded by Wellington, ironical, persistent, cool, who, with a dash of luck, would eventually show himself to be the only adversary Napoleon had so far met who was at all worthy of comparison with him.

The Emperor lingered for ten days in Valladolid, re-grouping his forces to make surer of winning. He appointed Soult and Ney as joint leaders-in-chief. On the 17th of January he leapt into the saddle and galloped away towards Bayonne. Behind him lay war, veiled by a deceptive screening. Before him loomed war, another war, a war he had not wanted and had done everything to avoid, a war that was to create for the Empire the most dangerous situation that had so far confronted it—the historic "Crisis of 1809."

Napoleon alighted from a post-chaise in the courtyard of the Tuileries during the night of January 22. He proceeded without losing a second to "settle this Talleyrand business." He got Cambacérès out of bed. The Prince of Parma strove vainly to calm his wrath. Conspiracy between the Grand Chamberlain and Fouché was only too certain.

The two men had long been hostile to each other. Now they were walking hand in hand. The Empire presented a glittering exterior, but eyes as discerning as theirs could not fail to see the cracks and the weaknesses in the imperial edifice. Wars every year recurring were constantly exposing their chief to the chance bullet of an enemy soldier or to the dagger of an assassin. And he had no heir, no real heir, that is, for his brothers could not possibly replace him as leader of a government that was basically military in character. Joseph had behaved like a pitiable idiot in Spain. There was the half-mad Louis who was lining up Holland against France. There was the insignificant Jerome who was disgracing himself with his follies in his Westphalian kingdom. They succeed Napoleon? Fouché and Talleyrand were hard-headed men, without ideals and without scruples. But they saw broadly and far ahead. They saw things as they were and they shrugged their shoulders. Only a great soldier, with his gold braid tarnished by many victories in battle, would have the prestige required for filling Napoleon's shoes. A Bourbon restoration seemed impossible to the unfrocked bishop and the worried regicide. What would that lead to except ruin and chastisement for them? The only man in sight seemed to be Murat.

But this speculating on the eventuality of his death, this settling such questions without once consulting him, looked like nothing less than a crime to Napoleon. The widely bruited accord between the two so recent cronies was not only a threat of dire things to come. It was an actual attack on the chief's prestige at a critical moment. It was a blow struck at sound public morale, which it could not fail to bewilder. Napoleon was resolved to hit back with a vigor that would set an example.

He was less angry at Fouché than at Talleyrand. He did not yet know of the latter's treason at Erfurt. He did know of despicable pilferings of public monies on the part of this grand dignitary whom he had stuffed with millions. He also knew that ever since the Prince of Benevento had been replaced at the Ministry of Foreign Relations he had been ridiculing imperial policies, condemning Napoleon's attitude towards the Pope and pretending to disapprove of the war in Spain though, whatever he might be saying now, he had strongly urged it in the first place. Talleyrand, therefore, was the man for Napoleon to smite.

First he sent for Fouché. The scene was violent. The Minister of Police was imperturbably cool and defended himself adroitly. That he was worried over the outlook for the future he did not deny. He had hoped that Napoleon would establish a firmer underpinning for the dynasty by divorcing Josephine and making a new marriage that would produce a male child. There could be no question of his own loyalty or devotion. For that matter it was all to his personal interest to stick to the glorious master whom France had chosen.

Fouché pleaded his case so well that Napoleon cooled off. He was well aware of the services the man had rendered him in tracking down Bourbon agents and in handling dissident priests and even old friends on the republican Left. He knew also that Fouché's talents would be indispensable now that another campaign was in the offing. He accepted the minister's explanation. He needed him too badly.

But the next morning, the morning of the 23rd, the Emperor called a council of ministers at the Tuileries. His address was a stinging rebuke to the group as a whole for allowing public confidence to be shaken during his absence. Conditions on Exchange were bad. The Legislative Body was giving itself independent airs. The drawing-rooms in the faubourg Saint-Germain were cackling. The wildest rumors were going around, unchallenged. The Emperor's face grew redder and redder as he talked.

Finally he walked over towards the Prince of Benevento, who stood leaning with his back against the fireplace, an amused smile on his face. The Emperor assailed him:

"You, sir, are asserting that you had nothing to do with the death of the Duc d'Enghien. Do you forget that you advised me in writing to have him shot? You pretend not to approve of the war in Spain. Do you forget that you advised me in your letters to go back to the policy of Louis XIV?"

Then, finally, he came to charges that were as dishonoring as they were true:

"You are a thief, you are a coward, you are a man without faith. You do not believe in God—you betray everybody—there is nothing sacred in your eyes—you would sell out your father. . . . You deserve my breaking you as I might a glass. I have the power to break you, only I despise you too much. Why have I not had you hanged to the iron gates at the Carrousel? But, look out —there is still time! Do you know what you are—you are a silk stocking filled with ——!"

Talleyrand did not answer a word. The Emperor adjourned the terrified ministers and stormed out of the room. When he was gone Talleyrand remarked:

"What a pity that a man so great should be such a boor!"

Napoleon removed him from his post as Grand Chamberlain, but an incomprehensible weakness for the man prevented his going further. By all that he was and represented the aristocratic Prince of Benevento still overawed the genius who had risen from the Corsican middle classes. Napoleon's failure to punish him was one more mistake. Talleyrand was the sort of man who had to be put out of the way if one did not want him to wreak his vengeance. He was to go on appearing at court as though nothing had happened, and soon the Emperor would be consulting him again officially, finding him at hand and well knowing his competence. Later on, in his capacity as Vice-Grand Elector, Talleyrand was to sit on the Council of the Regency. But under a deferential exterior he was never to cease intriguing against the Emperor and, placed by the course of events in a controlling position in the moment of defeat, he was to become the chief artisan of Napoleon's downfall.

CHAPTER XXVI

Essling and Wagram

The Emperor still thought that he could at least postpone war. He solemnly warned Austria in a declaration that he made in public before the assembled diplomatic corps:

"Really, it would look as though Vienna sat on the banks of the river Lethe and not on the Danube. The people there seem to learn nothing from experience. They want another lesson? Well, they will get it, and this time it will be terrible. . . . I was busy on a battlefield that England had chosen. Austria saved the English in 1805 when I was about to cross the Strait of Calais. She saves them again this time when I was chasing them into La Coruña. But she is going to pay for this new trick and through the nose. Either she will disarm at once or she will have a war that will destroy her."

Austria, unfortunately, was not in a position to heed the warning. For her it was then or never. Her preparations were complete. She had an army of five hundred thousand men, what with first line troops and reserves. They were all well equipped and well organized. She could further figure that the best French regiments were immobilized in Spain; that England would be there to supply such funds as she should require; that a new spirit was stirring in the German peoples, who were weary of the military occupation and were thinking of Napoleon as their oppressor. Last of all she could rely on the Czar's good will. Going farther in the direction of the hints he had dropped at Erfurt, Alexander was begging the Emperor Francis "to be firmly persuaded of the interest he, Alexander, had in preserving the integrity of Austrian territory."

Knowing that Austria was ready Napoleon hastily reorganized and strengthened his forces. He raised 80,000 men from the old classes and drafted the same number from the class of 1810. With the veterans he had left in Germany under Davout and auxiliaries supplied by the Rhine Federation, he could count on 300,000 men for the campaign, 200,000 of them French. Large as it was, it was, alas, far from being the Grand Army that had camped at Boulogne. That force had been tested at Austerlitz, decimated at Eylau, and was now giving its last gasps in Spain. The proud, unflinching, thoroughly trustworthy *grognards* had been professional soldiers, hardened in the wars of the Republic. Now it was an army of young men torn straight from their firesides, rapidly trained, with no direct experience of war, courageous enough, but possessing neither the endurance nor the tradition of army pride of the old veterans. The imperial Guard itself had been almost entirely rebuilt. It now knew distinctions between an Old Guard and a Young. Among Napoleon's closest lieutenants many were to miss rollcall this time. Still present were Bernadotte, Berthier, Davout, Masséna, Lannes and Augereau. But Murat, the marvelous cavalry officer, was on a throne in Naples. Ney, "brave among the brave," was in Spain with Soult, Mortier, Jourdan and Victor. In the military balance in Europe a great change was apparent. The pre-eminence of France was by no means so evident. Napoleon was not unaware of the fact, as his attitude revealed. In spite of his tireless activity, he seemed worried, less sure of himself. He sent Berthier away to Germany to take command. He himself had to linger in Paris, where his presence seemed absolutely necessary. Police reports were showing a steady change for the worse in public opinion. Talk was ironical, bitter, sarcastic. The ground was giving way under the Emperor's feet.

On March 2nd, Metternich, the Austrian ambassador, informed Champagny that in view of the movements of the French army his master considered it indispensable to mobilize. Talleyrand's successor replied that France did not want a war but that, since Austria was beginning one, Austria would have to bear the consequences. Napoleon proceeded to rush his last arrangements.

The Austrians were too quick for him. Without a declaration of war the Archduke Charles crossed the Inn on April 10th and invaded Bavarian territory. Before him lay the two armies of Masséna and Davout, with Berthier in supreme command. As a whole they seemed to form a motley and fairly vulnerable line, since the main French corps were separated by Bavarian and Württemberg contingents. The Archduke Charles shrewdly figured that he could break through the German section of the French line and then deal with the French marshals separately, destroying Davout at Ratisbon and Masséna at Augsburg.

He was reckoning without Napoleon. The latter left

Paris on the 13th in his traveling coach, without an escort, without military attendants, without a staff. On the 17th he was at Donauwerth and at once took charge of operations. Berthier was an excellent major general but a miserable generalissimo. Left to himself he never knew what to do next.

Napoleon ordered Masséna to make a forced march on Landshut and Davout to drive down the Danube upon Abensberg. So the two armies, which were too far apart, would come together to stop the advance of Charles. The first shock occurred on the 20th of April at Abensberg, Lannes coming off with the honors of the day. The Austrians were thrown back upon Landshut and there they were again beaten on the 21st and hurled across the Isar. The day following Napoleon turned north and joined Davout at Eckmühl. A battle lasting seven hours occurred, ending in a splendid charge by Nansouty's cuirassiers. The three days of fighting had cost the Archduke sixty thousand men and 100 guns. He decided to retire across the Danube into Bohemia to reorganize. The road to Vienna again lay open.

The French pursued the retreating Austrians to Ratisbon and entered that town, which offered virtually no resistance. Napoleon, however, ventured too near the skirmish line and was struck in the ankle by a bullet, suffering an inconsequential wound. "I am touched," he said, without showing much interest. The doctors cut his boot free and dressed the wound. The news spread rapidly through the lines and was naturally enlarged upon. Napoleon remounted his horse and rode along the front to reassure his soldiers and congratulate them.

The Bavarian campaign lasted five days. It was a model

for rapidity, precision and restraint. Napoleon did not try for a finishing victory. He wanted to fight a few battles and hold the Austrians under control. That would season his raw recruits, bring them together under fire, limber up their organization and make them ready for more decisive engagements.

News from other theaters meantime was not so good. The Archduke John had defeated Prince Eugene at Sacile, and Napoleon had to send Macdonald to halt a débâcle and reorganize things. The Tyrol was in full insurrection. Andreas Hofer, a tavern-keeper, had organized bands of mountaineers, driven out the Bavarians and even forced a French corps to capitulate at Innsbruck. A general uprising was brewing in Germany. Major Schill had started a sniping war that was costing the French dearly. The soldiers under his command had been allowed to desert from the Prussian regular army. In Poland, finally, the Austrians under the Archduke Ferdinand had taken Warsaw. According to the treaty signed at Erfurt the Czar should promptly have invaded Galicia. Instead he did not stir.

Bringing all these notes together at Ratisbon, Napoleon decided not to follow the Archduke into Bohemia but to make for Vienna. After a bloody battle at Edelsberg he arrived before the capital on May 10th. The Archduke had neglected to put the city in a state of defense. It capitulated almost immediately and Napoleon was again in headquarters at Schönbrunn (May 12, 1809).

The Austrians were massed on the broad plain called the Marschfeld on the left bank of the Danube, behind Lobau island. There they were awaiting the arrival of the Archduke John, the victor at Sacile, who was retreating past Laibach and Klagenfurt before an Italian army reorganized by Macdonald. Lefebvre had pacified the Tyrol. The Poles had recovered and were driving through Galicia upon Cracow. Napoleon figured on beating Charles before the latter received the reinforcements from Italy. The restlessness in Europe required an immediate decision.

He gained a foothold on Lobau island and, on the day of Pentecost, May 21, two army corps, under Masséna and Lannes, crossed the narrow branch of the Danube to the north of the island and occupied the villages of Aspern and Essling. That was a venturesome move, because the bulk of the French army still had to cross the river before it could engage the Austrians. With great difficulty a pontoon bridge was thrown across the south, the main, branch of the river, which was a mile and a quarter wide at that point. Its normally swift current had been much strengthened by recent rains. The bridge gave way for a first time, and Charles profited by the mishap to attack the French at Aspern and Essling where they stood cut off from their bases. In spite of the enormous disparity in numbers, the battle was not decisive, owing to the doggedness of the two French marshals. Having failed to take the French positions by evening the Archduke suspended fire.

The French army continued its crossing all night long. At daybreak the Emperor found himself at its head on the edge of the Marschfeld. He ordered the attack and for a time it looked as though it had succeeded. Lannes broke the Austrian center. But just then the great bridge across the Danube broke again, owing in part to the still rising flood, in part to burning floats that the Austrians sent down the river. The reserves failed to come up and, what was worse, the flow of munitions stopped. Since Napoleon was unable to send reinforcements, Lannes was finally obliged to retire. Thereupon the Austrians counter-attacked, thinking to sweep the French into the Danube. The fight lasted eleven hours. Essling was lost and taken nine times.

The sun was just setting when Lannes fell. He was riding from regiment to regiment encouraging his soldiers when a cannonball smashed his two knees. As he was being carried to Lobau island on a stretcher made of boughs Napoleon caught sight of him. He ran to his side and embraced him:

"Lannes—do you know who I am?"

"Yes, Sire," murmured the great soldier, who was soon to die. "You are losing your best friend. But save yourself—and save the army!"

Save the army! Yes, it had come to that! Napoleon could see that soon he would have nothing but bare bayonets to match against the artillery and musket fire of the enemy. He retired from the front lines, where he had been exposing himself all day long, and, contrary to his custom, called a council of the marshals. Some were for withdrawing beyond the wide branch of the Danube and reorganizing the army under Vienna. Napoleon was against that. The battle had been costly, he said, but it had not been a defeat. It would look like one if the French went too far back. He proposed withdrawing to Lobau island, wait there for reinforcements from France and Italy, build better bridges and begin the fight over again at the same point under better conditions. Masséna and Davout agreed with him.

Masséna took charge of the retreat to Lobau island. It went off in good order. Not a wounded man was left behind and not a gun. Had he pushed his advantage the Archduke might have won an overwhelming victory. Instead he let the opportunity slip.

It was a serious setback for Napoleon just the same. He had lost fewer men than the Archduke but his imprudence in crossing the Danube with his rear uncertain had almost led to a disaster of the first order. Austria made haste to broadcast her victory to all Europe and all Europe rejoiced. Nationalisms lifted their heads everywhere. Italy stirred under the preaching of her clergy. Germany boiled with patriotic enthusiasm. Jerome was for a moment threatened at Cassel. Prussia notified Vienna that she would resume war on the next Austrian victory. Alexander of Russia cooled more and more towards France. He now said he would fulfill his obligations as an ally only if Napoleon gave him the assurance that "he would not remake Poland." Unless the Emperor could win a victory very soon, an undebatable victory, he would have all the peoples of Europe upon his hands.

He prepared to win a victory. As the dangers thickened and magnified he kept perfectly cool. "The kings," he said, "have made a rendez-vous on my grave, but they seem to be in no great hurry to gather there." The confidence his troops had in him was unshaken. Also, as things turned out, Charles failed to attack him then and there, as he should have done, when the French army was disorganized. A good tactician, the Archduke never had a genial inspiration.

The engineers and naval experts in Napoleon's Guard soon had a broad strong bridge built on piles to connect Lobau island with the mainland. A sturdy row of spilings protected it upstream and broke the current. Lobau island itself became a powerful fortified camp, sheltering enormous supplies of food, ammunition and livestock. Napoleon personally designed a series of portable bridges that could be thrown at the last moment across the smaller arm of the Danube. He came every day from Schönbrunn, inspected the works, encouraged the soldiers, shared their lives. June passed that way. Meantime the snipers in Germany were suppressed, and on Napoleon's insistence Major Schill was shot at Stralsund by a Prussian firing squad. The Poles would have seized all Galicia but for the ill-will of the Russians, who, either of their own accord or on orders from their leaders, fraternized with the Austrians. On the whole, therefore, the situation of the belligerents remained unchanged.

But now suddenly Napoleon received an unexpected reinforcement. Acting under Macdonald's tutelage Prince Eugene had driven the Archduke John into Hungary and beaten him at Raab (June 14th). He now effected his junction with the Emperor. Early in July Napoleon was ready to resume the offensive against the Archduke Charles, who had established himself on the Marschfeld with his left on the outskirts of Wagram.

The heat was stifling, but on the night of the 4th-5th, under cover of a hail storm, the French crossed the narrower branch of the Danube at four points not far from the village of Engersdorf. The Austrians made no move. During the forenoon Napoleon's whole army advanced into the plain in battle formation till it had spread out, fan-shaped, between Aspern and Neusiedeln. The Archduke's troops were deployed in lines exactly parallel to the French and so were somewhat more thinly arrayed in view of their eccentric location.

In the afternoon Napoleon directed a sharp attack on the high ground at Wagram with the corps of Bernadotte, Macdonald and Oudinot. The French were about to pierce the Austrian line when two columns belonging to Macdonald attacked Bernadotte's Saxons by mistake. The disorder resulting spoiled the maneuver. As a symptom the incident was significant. Napoleon's army was now made up of too disparate elements, and his lines were getting to be too long, in view of the numbers engaged, for him to handle them with the speed and precision that had featured his battles of yore.

Night fell. The troops bivouacked where they stood, supping on hardtack and brandy. Napoleon conferred with his lieutenants around a fire that was kept ablaze with dry hay. He had not slept a wink for three days. Firing was resumed at four in the morning, the Austrians opening a heavy drive on Masséna on the French left, with the idea of cutting Napoleon off from the river. Masséna had to give ground and in the center Bernadotte's Saxons wavered. Napoleon joined the two marshals and stiffened them, meantime concentrating all the Guard's artillery, Macdonald's corps and Nansouty's cavalry in the center. The Austrians had thought the victory theirs but suddenly the hundred heavy pieces commanded by Drouot began to mow them down. Macdonald counter-attacked and drove the Austrians before him. Masséna also resumed the offensive. On the right

Davout stormed the high lands at Neusiedeln and Oudinot captured the town of Wagram.

"The battle is won!" cried Napoleon, as he took in the situation with his glass from the top of a knoll. In fact the Austrian line was off balance on a ten mile front. At three o'clock, fearing that his left would be turned and his line of retreat into Moldavia cut, the Archduke ordered a general retirement. He had suffered heavy losses. All the same there was no rout. His army fell back in good order in the direction of Prague (July 6, 1809).

Brilliant as the victory was, Wagram was not Austerlitz. Napoleon won and in view of Essling he was satisfied. But he was not situated, as he had hoped to be, in such a position as to be able to strike a death blow at the Hapsburg monarchy. The Spanish frying-pan was sputtering. The attitude of the Russians was more than disquieting.

"It's not much of an alliance I have there," he remarked to Savary.

Accordingly when his marshals showed their eagerness to press the campaign, he answered:

"Enough blood has been shed. Let us have peace."

An offer of peace in fact came, delivered by Prince Lichtenstein after one last engagement at Znaim. A truce was signed on July 11th and Napoleon went back to Schönbrunn to await the conclusion of negotiations.

CHAPTER XXVII

The Pope Arrested

In the castle of the Austrian emperors, as formerly in the barn in Poland, Napoleon plunged into public business again, striving to ward off the dangers that had gathered about him during those critical months and were undermining his power.

First there was the matter of the Pope. The conflict with the Holy See had been odiously aggravated by the zeal of Jacobin subordinates. Seeming also to lose, in his growing exasperation, the restraint that in days gone by had lent wings to his genius as a statesman, Napoleon forgot all about the much that he owed to the pontiff personally—all about the Concordat and the Anointment—and decided, after Ratisbon, to annex the Papal States to the Empire (May 17, 1809). So the new Charlemagne stripped the Pope of the temporal power which the Charlemagne of old had recognized. He left him just the Vatican and an annual income of two millions.

Pius VII countered by excommunicating Napoleon. The Emperor had ordered Murat to brook no sort of resistance on the Pope's part: "If he starts preaching revolt, arrest him." Miollis, with Radet, a colonel of the gendarmerie, executed the instructions to the last letter on the day of Wagram. Radet and his men forced their way into the Quirinal at three o'clock in the morning, entering through the windows. Pius VII received them unflinchingly, gowned in his pontifical vestments. On his refusal to recognize the imperial decree, Radet informed him that he was to be taken away from Rome.

"This then," commented the Pope quietly, "is the reward I get for my many favors to the Emperor. Perhaps I have been guilty in that respect in the Lord's sight and He is punishing me thus."

Radet escorted him, with his Secretary of State, Cardinal Pacca, into a closed carriage. The carriage door, further, was locked with a padlock. On all-day drives, maintained in spite of his fatigue and the fact that he was suffering from a fever, Pius was taken first to Florence, then to Genoa, then on to Alessandria. Since neither Elisa nor Pauline was eager to assume the responsibility of keeping him, he was finally driven to Grenoble. There he was treated with consideration but strictly as a captive.

When Napoleon learned of what had happened, he was filled with angry regret. "I am sorry they arrested him. It's a foolish piece of business." But it was his own fault. He had not qualified his orders properly. Now he could see that it was too late to change them. However he ordered that the Pope be transferred to Savona, provided with an honorable household and enabled "to receive the homage of the public." Meantime the Cardinals, the heads of the Orders, the Roman Chancellery and the pontifical archives were to be "shipped" to Paris. He intended eventually to set up the Pope there. Dizzily whirling in the vertigo that had laid hold on him, he was now resolved that the successor of Peter, the spiritual leader of Europe, should reside at his court as his temporal subordinate, under his immediate control. The powers were by now numb to any shock from the diabolical Corsican. They said nothing. But affections had gradually been turning away from Napoleon everywhere, even in France. The movement was accentuated by all these doings. Napoleon's glory had long sufficed to veil his despotism under a brilliancy that could readily dazzle. Now the magic touch was gone. He had lost his power over people who, laymen or clergy as they might be, still placed the spirit above interests and the law above force.

After the Emperor's departure from the Spanish peninsula, his lieutenants got along fairly well for a time. Soult won at Oporto (March 29, 1809). Master of Portugal, he began plotting to set himself up as king. Victor won at Medellín and Sebastiani at Ciudad Real. That enabled Joseph to sit a little tighter on his throne. But meantime the best soldiers of France were falling by the thousands in insignificant ambuscades—those "old mustaches" who had seen Italy and the camp at Boulogne and whom Napoleon had missed so much at Essling and Wagram.

Soon all north Spain rose at a call from General La Romana. Ney was threatened in Galicia. Wellesley, again in command of the English in Spain, landed by surprise at Oporto with heavy reinforcements and forced Soult to evacuate Portugal, carrying his dreams of royalty with him. Discipline was breaking down in the French rank and file. Operations were too small and too numerous, offering too little inspiration and too many temptations to crime. Joseph was striking attitudes as a divine right absolutist and presuming to govern in Spanish style. He ordered the marshals about like a potentate. They scoffed at him and meantime were hating each other cordially. To bring order into such chaos Napoleon finally assigned the supreme command to Soult. It was in vain. Wellesley caught Victor in a bad fix at Talavera (July 28). In spite of that Victor would have cleaned up had not Joseph, everlastingly timid, everlastingly stupid, ordered a retreat. With the exception of Madrid and a few towns that were strongly held, Spain defied France to rule her.

The English were encouraged by these gains and—Napoleon having his hands full with Austria—thought of repeating them in other areas on a more sonorous note. On July 29th they occupied Walcheren island, at the mouth of the Scheldt and laid siege to the fortress of Flushing. By an adroit maneuver Admiral Missiessy got the French fleet out and took it to Antwerp. But that town itself was directly threatened.

Paris was informed by telegraph of the debarkation and Cambacérès called a council of ministers. Fouché was the only person capable of taking any initiative. At that moment he was holding the two portfolios of the Police and the Interior. He was for mobilizing a heavy force of the National Guard and putting Bernadotte in command. That marshal had been sent home to Paris after Wagram. Cambacérès refused, fearing that to show too much independence of action might anger the Emperor. They finally decided to send word to Napoleon and stop at that, merely despatching a few battalions to reinforce Louis, King of Holland, and defend Antwerp. Fouché, however, took the bit in his teeth and on his own responsibility ordered twenty prefects in the northeast to mobilize the National Guard. Napoleon did not disapprove—on the contrary. But, he pointed out, Flushing was hardly tenable in the first place. Malaria was endemic and epidemic in the Belgian marshlands. That disease could be counted on to drive the enemy out. Let the English occupy the fortress and they would soon be withdrawing of themselves. Things turned out exactly as he foresaw. The English hospitals grew overcrowded and their last regiments were soon en route for England. Napoleon was tickled. The defeat of the English in "the most serious attack the English had ever tried against him" came in very handy for the delicate negotiations he was conducting with Austria from Schönbrunn.

Metternich and Champagny were not able to come to any agreement after the Znaim truce. Napoleon had originally intended to dethrone the Hapsburgs and reorganize Austrian territories into three separate states. He had now given up that idea and was halting at territorial cessions and money indemnities. His demands were so harsh that the Austrians refused to consider them. Napoleon was in a hurry to get back to France in order to turn in earnest to the Spanish matter. He was also aware that the Austrians were still quite powerful in the field. He therefore reduced his expectations little by little. After much bickering and haggling an accord was finally reached.

The Treaty of Vienna, signed on October 14th, none the less reflected the magnitude of Austria's disaster—she ceded Illyria and part of Galicia, paid an indemnity

LOUIS BONAPARTE, KING OF HOLLAND
From the Portrait by Hodges

of 85,000,000, and undertook to reduce her armaments by one-half. It was far from reflecting Napoleon's statesmanship at its best. To put the matter bluntly it was a stupid treaty, a brutal treaty, which was a mere abuse of victory, a mere venting of spite, and could never be anything more than a truce. Its only possible fruitage could be more hatred, not more peace. It expanded a French empire that was already grotesquely unwieldy. It upset the balance in Europe and the balance in France.

Nevertheless, Napoleon had been given a warning as to the character of the fatal trend into which his megalomania had been drawing him ever since the interview at Tilsit. Two days before the treaty was signed he was reviewing the Guard at Schönbrunn when a young man elbowed his way up to him as though to hand him a petition. Arrested and searched, the boy was found to be carrying a long knife. He said that he was a student, named Stapps, that he was the son of a Protestant clergyman, that he had intended to kill the Emperor. Napoleon questioned him personally, Rapp acting as interpreter:

"Why did you want to kill me?"

"Because you are responsible for the unhappiness of my country."

"Did I ever do you any harm?"

"You have harmed everybody who is a German."

"Who induced you to attempt this crime?"

"Nobody. I was firmly convinced that in killing you I would be doing a great service to my country and to Europe. That was why I got the knife."

"You are either crazy or sick," said Napoleon, trying to find an excuse for pardoning the boy.

"I am neither."

Napoleon sent for Corvisart. The doctor decided that in fact the young man was in perfect health. The matter of a pardon came up.

"I don't want a pardon," exclaimed Stapps. "I am sorry I did not succeed."

"But after all—if I pardon you, you will change your mind?"

"I will kill you just the same, if I get a chance."

Stapps died before a firing squad crying "Long live freedom!"

CHAPTER XXVIII

Marie Louise

IT WAS AT SCHÖNBRUNN, BEFORE HIS RETURN TO FRANCE, that Napoleon decided on an important step: to divorce Josephine. He had had no particular complaint to make against her of late. Ever since the Consulate Josephine had mended her ways, and, apart from her extravagance, her huge debts, her jealousy, which had occasionally gathered a cloud between them, they had been very happy. The Empress was a pretty woman who wore her clothes exquisitely. She was a marvelous hostess at receptions, public and private. Bent on pleasing him in every way she was, as the Emperor said himself, "the delight of his interior" (so he always called his private apartments). After thirteen years of married life she still held the love, and had won the sincere good will, of the dictator.

It broke Napoleon's heart to end such a passionate relation, yet an evident public interest compelled him to do so. He had to have a direct heir. Fouché was ever harping on the point, urging him to proclaim a divorce. In his cynicism the minister even went to Josephine and begged her to make the first move herself. Napoleon rebuked him for doing that on a number of occasions. All the same he could not help realizing that Fouché was right, that as long as he was without a son, "France was just an annuity based on his life span," and that, however popular Josephine might be, a second marriage on his part would satisfy a public demand.

Marie Walewska had been his mistress since the campaign in Poland and she had joined him at Vienna after Wagram. Her announcement of pregnancy made up his mind. He was sure now, after having long been in doubt —he was able to have children. In order to avoid any chance of a weakening on his part, as it were in order to burn his vessels behind him, he sent word from Schönbrunn to his architect at Fontainebleau, whither he intended to return from Germany, ordering him to build a wall between his rooms and those of the Empress. Fouché made haste to start the gossip going in Paris.

All through the month of November most distressing scenes occurred between the Emperor and the Empress, first at Fontainebleau, then at the Tuileries. "Polity has no heart," exclaimed Napoleon, "it has nothing but head." After long resistance Josephine gave in. Napoleon plated her retreat with gold. She would retain her title as Empress, her honors, her household, an income of three millions, a town house, a number of country estates, in a word all the sumptuous luxury and display to which, probably, she was even more attached than to her status as Napoleon's wife.

The divorce ceremony took place on December 15th in the Emperor's study. The whole family was present in formal assembly. Cambacérès had drawn up the text of the reciprocal declarations, but both the principals made revisions that added a simpler, more human note:

"I have lost hope," declared Napoleon, "of having children of my marriage with the Empress Josephine. That is what impels me to sacrifice the tenderest affections of my heart, to consider nothing but the welfare of France. . . . No sacrifice is above my courage when I have been shown that it is to the advantage of France. . . ."

Josephine tried to read her statement but her voice broke. Regnault de Saint Jean d'Angély, Minister of the Imperial Household, came to the rescue and finished for her:

"I owe everything to the Emperor's kindness. It was his hand that crowned me, and on the throne I have received naught but evidences of affection and love from the French people. I think I am doing honor to those sentiments in consenting to the dissolution of a marriage that has now become an obstacle to the welfare of France."

The next day the Senate legalized the divorce by a senatus-consultum, or resolution, Prince Eugene delivering a well worded and very touching speech on the occasion. Josephine retired to Malmaison while Napoleon went to hide his grief, sincere and very acute, at Trianon. The religious union was dissolved on January 12th, 1810, by the Official of Paris, the open conflict with the Pope making the latter's personal examination of the case impossible.

Public opinion and the army viewed the separation with sorrow. Many criticized sharply. Josephine, it was felt, had shared Napoleon's lot during his early days and during his ascent to power. In throwing her away he was bidding farewell to happiness and perhaps to good luck.

Who was to replace the lady who had stepped down from the throne? A Russian grand duchess? An Austrian archduchess? A Saxon princess? Napoleon seemed to have only to choose. At first he was inclined towards Russia, and Caulaincourt was directed to ask the Czar for the hand of his youngest sister, Anne. Wagram had tended to warm Alexander somewhat towards France, but he was personally averse to becoming brother-in-law to "Bonaparte." The Czarina-mother was vociferously opposed to the project, describing it as "disgraceful." Without giving a definite refusal, the Czar decided to allow matters to drift along. Napoleon, unfortunately, was in a hurry. Judging the Saxon alliance too paltry, as devoid of diplomatic significance, he turned to Austria and asked for the hand of Marie Louise, the Emperor's eldest daughter. Metternich had secretly proposed the match in advance.

This alliance was regarded with disfavor by many of Napoleon's entourage. Murat and Cambacérès, for instance, were against it. But Talleyrand, the Beauharnais family, Fouché himself, were for it. For his own part, Napoleon was delighted. Imagine! A little Corsican squire entering an imperial family eight hundred years old! It was a new anointment for the Caesar of fortune that he had been but yesterday, in fact a much more impressive anointment than the first. Such a marriage was not only a flattery to his pride, which at that moment was touching zenith. It offered, he thought, definite diplomatic advantages. As regarded Europe it would solder him to the lines of the ancient kings. In France it would

splice him to the legitimate monarchical tradition, Marie
Louise being a niece of Marie Antoinette. In coming
to share his throne she would be giving him not only
heirs but ancestors.

Another thought was also working in Napoleon's mind.
His situation in Europe had become very difficult since
his adventure in Spain and his spoliation of the Papacy.
If the princes were kowtowing and toadying, the peoples
were now hostile. England was not disarming. Prussia
was skulking about watching for her chance. The Czar
was no longer "enchanted." To balance so many declared or potential enemies the French empire needed
support on the Continent. Who was better able to supply it than Austria? The Wagram campaign had enabled
him to perceive how many vital forces the Hapsburg
monarchy still could rely on. After disasters in the field,
overwhelming disasters, Francis I had enjoyed triumphal acclamation on returning to Vienna. The fact had
deeply impressed Napoleon. Returning to an idea of
Louis XV, which in the day of that king had been called
the principle of "reversing alliances," he judged that
an understanding with Austria, based on family interests, might be a very good way to extend and consolidate
peace.

Overtures from the Tuileries were received with great
fussiness of assent in Vienna. Francis and Metternich
hoped the marriage would enable them to obtain attenuations in the terms of the last treaty. The proposed
future bride was the only one to express alarm. She
had been brought up to fear and hate "the Corsican,"
who had done little else but thrash her father and rob
the Austrian empire of territories. She had clapped

her hands over Essling and wept over Wagram. On learning of Napoleon's divorce she had written: "I pity the unhappy princess he finally chooses." However, petted by the family, lectured by Metternich, calmed as to her religious scruples by the Nuncio, she finally submitted, a new Iphigenia, to the sacrifice required of her.

At eighteen Marie Louise was an overgrown child. She was not as stupid as has been asserted, and she was much better educated than has been admitted. She knew five languages. She could write, paint and play the piano. For the rest she was without character and without will power, following the moment's pressure. Tall, slender rather than not, with a prominent bosom high set, she had blue eyes that were inclined to protrude, sensuous lips, a fine complexion, silky hair, well molded joints. In a word, she was thoroughly Austrian, thoroughly Hapsburgian and every inch an archduchess. Those traits of race and family delighted Napoleon as he studied her portrait.

He made haste to dispatch magnificent presents to Vienna, and those attentions touched Marie Louise without altogether dispelling her terrors. As she bade farewell to her family at Saint Pölten, whence she was to take the road to France, her sobbing was so violent and so long continued that no end of encouragements, fondlings, embraces, were required to persuade her to go on with her program. Napoleon had no conception of this state of mind on her part. Everything was carefully hidden from the French ambassadors and, if they did divine something of what was going on, they held their peace. Caroline Bonaparte, the Queen of Naples, went to Branau to meet Marie Louise, and thereafter at each change of horses sent Napoleon little notes about the journey which were calculated to flatter his male's vanity and illusions. He almost came to believe that he had made a long range conquest of his imperial bride's heart.

He rode out along the Champagne highway to intercept her and met her train of carriages at Courcelles. It was raining in torrents. Tossing proprieties to the wind he rushed to her carriage. Her equerry recognized him and with the cry, "The Emperor!", threw open the door. In an instant Napoleon's arms were about her.

With the first excitements of the encounter over, the Emperor's solicitous attentions agreeably astonished the archduchess. She tamed quickly, finding that his pictures had failed to do him justice. They were to stop for the night at Compiègne, where appropriate festivities had been planned by the authorities. Napoleon brushed them aside without ceremony, showed Marie Louise to her quarters and, for another disregard of convention, refused to leave her that night.

The next morning, while he was dressing, he asked Constant, his valet, whether any comment had been made in regard to his upsetting of the program. Lying diplomatically the valet shook his head. Then one of his friends came in, probably Duroc. Napoleon's face beamed broadly, and tweaking Duroc's ear he said, gaily:

"Marry a German girl, old man! They are the best women in the world. They are sweet, they are good-natured, and they have everything to learn. They are as fresh as roses."

He dressed with great care and returned to the bride's apartments. After a long wait he ordered breakfast for two to be served at her bedside. It was noon, but she had not yet arisen.

The official wedding took place five days later, April 2, in the Square Room in the Louvre, which had been redecorated to serve as a chapel. Napoleon was dressed in white satin, with many jewels, the Regent diamond being sewed to his plumed cap. Marie Louise was gowned in crimson and moved with difficulty under her heavy robes, her crown weighted down with gems, and a ponderous train which the Queens of Spain, Holland and Westphalia supported as ladies of honor, with no great signs of beatitude. The imperial couple this time received the nuptial benediction from Cardinal Fesch.

THE MARRIAGE PROCESSION OF NAPOLEON AND MARIE-LOUISE

From the Painting by Garnier

CHAPTER XXIX

The King of Rome

A REAL HONEYMOON FOLLOWED AND IT WAS TO BE A long one. Napoleon showered his wife with thousands of delicate attentions. Marie Louise was altogether happy now and said to Metternich: "Everybody thinks I am afraid of the Emperor. Really he is afraid of me." Fear was not quite the word. He gave her a very tender affection that had an understratum of awe. He remodeled his life during those first months that he might be entirely at her service. Normally so methodical, he refused audiences; a hard worker, he deferred pressing chores; indifferent to the table, he prolonged his meals; sensitive to drafts, he lived with the windows wide open. He did everything he could think of to please her. She, for her part, became sincerely attached to him and towards the end of the year wrote to her father: "I cannot thank God enough for having granted me this great happiness, nor you, my dear papa, for not having yielded to my prayers at Ofen."

She was already pregnant. With the marvelous confidence which he always showed and which seemed to do sheer violence to Fortune, Napoleon did not doubt that the child was to be a son. He established the unborn heir's household and selected his governess—one of the most highly esteemed ladies of the court, Mme. de Montesquiou, wife of the Grand Chamberlain, Talleyrand's successor. The delivery took place on March 20, 1811, just after five in the morning, and not without danger both to mother and child, the infant presenting itself in wrong position.

One hundred and one guns announced the happy event to Paris, and all France rejoiced that the problem of succession had at last been settled. The young prince received the title of "King of Rome," a magnificent name, laden with the whole history of Europe and binding the young French empire to the tradition of the ancient empire of the West. The baptism did not take place till over two months later—June 9th. The ceremony, in Notre Dame, was the most gorgeous for display that the Empire was to know.

At that moment Napoleon really touched the peak of his power. The birth of a son closed the era of the adventurer. He could now murmur the words that a poet was to put upon his lips: "The future, the future! The future is now mine!" Never, in fact, had fortune so blessed a human being. Everything had come out well, even his imprudences, even his blunders. Everything trembled before his frown. He was the visible master of the European world.

The French Empire comprised 132 departments. To get a firmer hold on Spain, Napoleon had incorporated Catalonia, Aragon and Navarre with France (February 8, 1810), Joseph protesting in vain. Louis Bonaparte had become too Dutch to enforce the blockade properly. Napoleon therefore annexed Holland on July 9th. Still in

enforcement of the blockade he annexed the Grand
Duchy of Oldenburg and the Hanseatic cities, Bremen,
Hamburg and Lübeck, on December 13th. France at
that moment stretched from the Ebro to the Elbe, from
Brittany to the Garigliano and to Zara. Including the
vassal kingdoms the great empire spread from the Strait
of Gibraltar to the Vistula and to Sicily.

Charlemargne had been outdone. King of Italy, Mediator of Switzerland, Protector of the Rhine Federation,
overlord of the Kings of Spain, Naples, Westphalia,
Bavaria, Saxony and Württemberg, Napoleon ruled 80,-
000,000 human beings. He had ceased to be a merely
French monarch. He was lord of Europe. France still
remained the axis and the basis of his power, but he
was thinking of molding the whole Continent into a
federation of states of which he would be sovereign, with
his capital as the capital of Europe. The Pope would
have a palace in Paris opposite the Emperor's, and the
vassal kings would be required to reside there for a certain length of time each year. The omnipotence of the
Rome of the Caesars was to come to life again with
France as its pivot.

Built up in less than ten years' time this amazing
edifice was one to dazzle and overawe the plain man.
But discerning eyes could already see the cracks in the
foundation and predict that it would collapse at the first
fairly severe blow. The only person who believed in the
permanency of the Empire was the Emperor himself.
Once and for all he had committed himself to his star,
to his genius, to the spell he exercised over France. But
around him many were doubting and, with an eye to

the morrow, trying to work out safe and well-lined retreats from the inevitable storm.

In France itself a general atmosphere of uneasiness and apprehension had replaced the confidence and the enthusiasms of the early days. The people were tired of war. The draft, hungrier and hungrier, was eating up too many children, too many futures. It was being avoided in more and more frequent cases by desertion or mutilation. By the end of 1810 the authorities had taken note of 160,000 delinquents. The departments were overrun with platoons of soldiers who were sent to root out such men and arrest them. France was coming to look like the Vendée of Revolutionary times. Agriculture was undermanned and getting along from hand to mouth. Food shortage was the normal case. Industry, trade, foreign commerce, shipping, were paralyzed by the blockade. In spite of state orders and subsidies they had fallen anew into the depression from which the Consulate had rescued them. Salt, tobacco, and beverages were heavily taxed under a system of so-called "combined duties." Finance, milked dry, was hostile. The bourgeoisie had again lost the political importance for which it had made the Revolution. It was therefore tired of glory and longed for liberty again. Paris suffered and complained. It complained in voices so shrill that in March, 1812, Napoleon moved his court to Saint-Cloud to avoid the unfriendly demonstrations that now greeted his every appearance on the streets.

This growing disaffection cannot be ascribed solely to the material fatigue of a country that had been overstrained and was wearing out. It was even more largely due to a deep-seated withdrawal of sentiment, to the hurts that had been done to faith. Part of Napoleon's power had sprung from the peace that he had brought in the domain of religion. Now he had broken that peace —an error of the heart and therefore unforgivable. The mistreatment that had been inflicted on the Holy Father and such cardinals as stood faithful to him had cost the Emperor the support of all Catholics. Vainly did he strive to win them back by calling a national council. On the whole the French clergy retreated behind the authority of the Pope, who, uncomplaining, without anger, continued in his prison at Savona to be the spiritual leader of the Catholic world.

From the time of his second marriage Napoleon became more autocratic than ever. He would tolerate no independent views, taking the slightest criticism in ill part and no longer asking for a word of advice. "Follow the orders I have given you to the letter in this matter," he wrote to Berthier. "I alone know what should be done." From 1811 on Napoleon had, with the exception of Cambacérès, no men of distinguished talents and statesmanlike views about him. More and more, in order "to keep the shop running," he had to attend to everything himself, be everywhere at all times. Now the Empire had become too unwieldy for that, the volume of business too vast and too complex. The despot could tolerate nothing but errand boys anywhere. He had made sovereigns of his relatives and thrust them upon Europe, but he treated them as so many corporals. Let them make a show of resistance and he stood ready to crush them. "You are a subject," he wrote to Elisa. "Like all other French subjects you are obliged to obey orders from the ministries. A warrant issued by the

Minister of Police would be enough to send you to jail."
So he talked to Murat. More cautious language he used
only to his elder brother, Joseph.

A veritable restoration followed the archduchess into
the Tuileries. The most distinguished names in France
came and crowded about the niece of Marie Antoinette:
the Praslins, the Muns, the Turennes, the Henins, the
Brancases, the Noailleses, the Haussonvilles. Now willingly, now sullenly, the faubourg Saint-Germain, the old
aristocracy, began to man the offices of the imperial monarchy and to people the court, the army staffs, the higher
posts in the state. With a few honorable exceptions the
old nobles now rallied to the exacting taskmaster who
knew them to be, as he said, "better qualified to serve,"
or—to express his real thought—less likely to debate his
orders. To them he began to reserve favors, honors,
emoluments.

The Emperor never categorically repudiated the Revolution from which he had issued and to which he owed
his throne. He did become mistrustful of it, gradually
dispensing with the old revolutionaries who had at one
time formed the backbone of the imperial bureaucracy.
Fouché was disgraced on a charge that he had undertaken unauthorized negotiations with England. Really
it was because, in spite of his title now as Duke of
Ótranto, he still represented the Jacobin tradition. His
dismissal was fraught with the most far-reaching consequences. Better than anything else it was symptomatic
of the progressive enwrapping of the military dictatorship in the cocoon of absolute monarchy. Napoleon replaced that master detective, Fouché, with the inept
Savary. Savary proved unable to supply the Emperor

with trustworthy information at times when public opinion was either restive or bewildered. He punched brutally and stupidly in situations that required adroit fingering.

The colossus was weak abroad as well as at home. The vassal kings chewed at their bits, fretting. The allies of the Empire were allies only because they dared not be open enemies. Austria was disgruntled at the loss of her provinces and vexed at the subordinate rôle that she was now playing in Europe. She panhandled favors from the Emperor but meantime negotiated day and night with the Czar. Alexander had been angered by the dethronement of the Duke of Oldenburg, now his brother-in-law, but the elevation of a French marshal, Bernadotte, to the status of heir apparent to the throne of Sweden disgusted him. He always had reason to fear that Napoleon would one day reconstitute Poland. The blockade was turning out to the disadvantage of Russia, and he ignored it in a decree of December 31, 1810, which allowed British goods to enter Russian territories under neutral flags. Alexander had thrown up powerful fortifications beyond the Niemen and he virtually mobilized his army, one corps at a time. He never dropped his double-faced procedure, however. Not a day went by that he did not send some friendly note to Paris.

Prussia continued apparently prostrate, but she was reorganizing on the sly. Scharnhorst overrode the prohibition of Prussia's ever having more than 42,000 men by instituting the "krumper" system, whereby all the young men in the country went through a series of two months' periods of military training. Excellent materials for a great national army were so being prepared for a future war that every day grew closer at hand.[1]

But the real sore, the running sore that gnawed deeper and deeper, was Spain. Spain kept devouring men by the regiment. Napoleon sent Masséna there "to get things over." The "old lion of Rivoli" did win a victory at Ciudad Rodrigo, but then Wellington brought him to a halt before the impregnable lines of Torres Vedras, which covered Lisbon. In spite of another brilliant success at Fuentes de Oñoro, Masséna was left in the lurch by the jealous Soult and compelled to retreat. Napoleon removed Masséna from command and for a time seemed to be thinking of getting out of the hole in Spain by restoring the crown to Ferdinand. He finally rejected the idea as likely to seem a concession to England and so to shake his prestige.

For the great adversary, the bulldog that would never lose its grip, still continued to defy the conqueror from the depths of the sheltering sea of which he had not been able to gain control. England was ruined. Her business was at a standstill, her people starving. She wavered for a moment in December, 1810, then she stiffened. That was to be the end. She would never hesitate again. In his effort to reduce her, Napoleon could annex one territory after the other and force his onerous will upon state after state on the Continent. It was all in vain. England fought doggedly on, untiring in her support of resistance, ever ready to finance an attack. Napoleon could not now have abandoned the blockade even had he wanted to. Actually he thought that by carrying it

[1] A "krumper" was a member of the "awkward squad."

farther and farther and enforcing it better and better, he could finally bring the enemy to her knees. Unfortunately that policy failed. The peoples whom it compelled him to oppress were to rise at the first sign he gave of weakening. He had conquered the Europe of the kings. He could not conquer the Europe of the peoples. The blockade that did not destroy England was to destroy Napoleon.

The Czar had always been a lukewarm friend to Napoleon. Gradually, under the influence of the people about him, but especially for reasons of policy, he became an enemy. There had been no overt break but Napoleon could have no doubts left by the early days of 1812.

The alliance with France had never been ratified by the Muscovite nobility. The imperial court, from the Czarina-mother down to the humblest chamberlain, detested "Bonaparte." The nation itself shared those sentiments. The principal market for Russian raw materials was England. The blockade paralyzed Russian trade. Alexander had joined it only because he saw a chance of dividing Europe up with Napoleon. Now he had been allowed to take Finland from Sweden and the Danubian provinces from Turkey, but Napoleon stubbornly refused to agree on Constantinople. The Grand Duchy of Warsaw was another thorn in the side of the Russian empire. Personal considerations figured too. The domineering attitude of Napoleon hurt the Czar's vanity by relegating him at the very best to second place.

He continued altogether lavish in flatteries to Paris, but following Talleyrand's hint Alexander edged away from the French alliance. During the campaign of 1809 his troops fraternized with the Austrians and killed no one that was not Polish. Clandestinely opening his states to British products, he laid prohibitive duties on French goods. At the same time he reinforced his army along the Polish frontier and opened negotiations with Vienna, Berlin and Stockholm with a view to an eventual coalition. He maintained an espionage service in Paris. An agent of his, one Tchernitchef, procured secret information belonging to the French general staff through treasonable complicities.

The Czar answered Napoleon's repeated complaints on this matter with carefully worded denials, but took advantage of the opportunity to demand compensation for the Grand Duke of Oldenburg for the abusive encroachment on the part of France that had recently dethroned that sovereign. Napoleon did not take the trouble to answer. He could not believe a war with Alexander possible. He could not, because he would not. He thought that a frank discussion would clear up all misunderstandings. For that matter his representative in St. Petersburg, Caulaincourt, was misleading him, deliberately or otherwise. Napoleon recalled him, as on too friendly terms with the Czar in Russia and with Talleyrand at home, but without dismissing him from his service altogether. Caulaincourt's successor, Lauriston, hardly kept him any better informed.

However, his mistrust aroused, Napoleon set out to strike alliances which, if worse came to worst, would display a front well calculated to discourage Russia. He replaced Champagny with Maret, a person of whom he felt absolutely sure, in order to conduct this diplomatic campaign. He opened negotiations with Austria and Prussia, with Sweden and Turkey.

The latter two did not respond favorably. The Emperor had forbidden Bernadotte to conquer Norway. The marshal had never ceased to hate Napoleon in spite of the many benefactions he had received and frequent forgiveness for acts bordering closely on treason. He was already in collusion with England and Russia. The Sultan could hardly forget that at one time Napoleon had made plans that called for nothing less than a dismemberment of the Ottoman Empire. Very properly, therefore, he rebuffed the French offer of friendship and preferred to deal directly with the Czar. That was a sound move, for, in order to have his hands free in the west, Alexander restored Moldavia and Wallachia to Turkey.

In case of hostilities Prussian territory would have to be used by Napoleon for transit and as a base. Prussia was in no condition to resist his demands, which amounted to orders, and so, willing or unwilling, signed a treaty of alliance, February 24, 1812. She agreed to furnish an auxiliary corps in exchange for a promise of an eventual expansion of her frontiers which would in part compensate for past losses. Austria, for her part, tried to sell her support as dearly as possible. In exchange for a relatively small contribution of men, Napoleon offered to compensate her, in case of war, at the expense of Russia and in Illyria. Metternich took the pledge on March 14th after long hesitations; but, as Prussia had already done, he took pains to inform Alexander that Austria had been forced to enter the alliance and that she would treat Russia with all the consideration possible.

Further to overawe the Czar Napoleon massed imposing forces in Germany. Berthier and the members of the general staff crossed the Rhine towards the end of February. Not counting the Austrian army that had been sent into Galicia, Napoleon's force totaled 423,000 men, of whom a scant half were French. The Rhine Federation and Poland furnished 120,000. The rest were a motley gathering from all the countries of Europe—Italians, Dutch, Swiss, Croatians, Spaniards, Portuguese, Danes. These foreigners were sprinkled about among the eight French corps and blended more or less well with them. The imperial Guard, or rather Guards, Young and Old, was an army all by itself. Its artillery comprised not less than 1150 pieces, heavy and light. The generals, with the exception of Murat, Davout and Ney, were second line talents—Eugene, Oudinot, Gouvion-Saint-Cyr, Mortier, Lefebvre, Reynier. The reserve corps were entrusted to Victor and Augereau.

The generals were all jealous of each other and tricked each other as occasion offered. Davout insulted Berthier at Marienburg, and thereafter Berthier did all he could to undermine the Emperor's confidence in Davout. The fact was that the marshals were now all wealthy men. They wanted to retire from arms, settle down in their mansions and on their country estates and enjoy their incomes and their fortunes. "I see clearly, gentlemen," Napoleon remarked at Danzig, "that you don't like the idea of fighting any longer." They did not gainsay him. They were tired in fact, and they showed their nervousness and disinclination. If their experience had increased their eye had lost its quick discernment. Their leader, moreover, had by now come to tolerate no initiative except his own. Apart from some exceptional flash, they were henceforth to be mere agents of execution and not always good ones.

The army that had thus been brought together to fight Russia was the most formidable assemblage of men that modern times had seen in the field. It was the Great Army, but in cohesion, endurance, enthusiasm, it was far from being the Grand Army of 1805. Napoleon himself had become a husband, a father, an absolute monarch. He was no longer the soldier, twin brother to the lightning bolt, who had once known how to rape Victory when she withheld her favors. He was still the consummate strategist. He still had the same skill, the same clear intuition in battle. But he was not as strong physically and he could not think quite so fast. The task of carrying Europe on his shoulders had aged him prematurely. He had taken on weight, a great deal of weight. His health had long been iron-bound. It now played him false at times. He had a bladder trouble; and a sluggish liver complaint, which was common to all the Bonapartes, lent a golden, yellowish glint to his complexion. At times he had violent cramps in the stomach, and often a deep-seated cough. His energy, his thinking, showed the effects of this physical decline.

To be sure, it was only now and then—he was forty-three! The stuff in him was still sound at bottom. But the overstrained life he had been forced to lead had burned his candle at both ends. He had had premonitions of the change at Austerlitz. "One has only a certain length of time for war," he there remarked. "I shall be good for six years more. After that I shall have to stop too." The war with Russia coincided with these developments. Sudden attacks of inertia on his part, an incapacity for daring that was quite new in him, were to play a very important rôle in that campaign. After it Napoleon's curve turned rapidly downward. The eagle's wings still could flap mightily, but the eagle itself was tired. Short of wind, it could hold itself only with an effort at altitudes which seemed to have become too great and to which it had soared too rapidly.

CHAPTER XXX

Borodinò

O<small>N</small> A<small>PRIL</small> 25, 1812, N<small>APOLEON</small> <small>RECEIVED</small> <small>FROM</small> K<small>UR</small>-akin, the Russian ambassador, what was virtually an ultimatum. Alexander demanded the complete evacuation of German territories east of the Elbe. There were no compliments this time. The Czar had finished his preparations and had joined his staff at Vilna. Bernadotte and the English were sure to co-operate.

Napoleon sent Narbonne to the Czar to make one last effort at an amicable settlement. He had no great confidence in the move. He knew that war held the floor and that the talking would henceforth be done by cannon. He set out from Paris on May 9th, leaving Cambacérès in charge. Marie Louise was with him. The Emperor of Austria, the King of Prussia, all the German princes, were waiting at Dresden, and they paid him fawning adulation. Marie Louise displayed her jewels with childish glee before her relatives and laughed at their cries of amused jealousy.

Meantime Napoleon's ponderous military machine was advancing to the Niemen. It took a month to get there —a first and very serious loss of time. What with one delay or another, Napoleon himself did not cross the river till June 24th. He had waited for the last of his troops to reach the other side. As he rode down to the river bank at Kowno a rabbit was frightened out of a thicket and ran between his horse's legs. The horse reared without warning and the Emperor was thrown. A voice that no one identified called out:

"A bad omen! A Roman would go home."

Napoleon smiled and remounted.

That same day he addressed a proclamation to his soldiers. It strongly contrasts in tone with the burning exhortations of Italy and Egypt:

"Soldiers: Russia is in the clutch of her fate and her destiny must be fulfilled. Does she think that we have deteriorated, that we are no longer the soldiers of Austerlitz? She gives us a choice between dishonor and war. Our choice cannot be doubtful."

Such rhetoric was appreciated in those days. It was welcomed with enthusiastic cheers by men who had been swept together from homes all over Europe which few of them were ever to see again. They, for their part, did not dream of any such fate. For fifteen years Napoleon had been unconquerable. Whenever he appeared on a battlefield victory had come running to meet him. What could an effeminate Czar with a staff of parade-ground generals do against that god of war? However big the Russian empire might be it was going to be conquered. Then victory would bring the great, the final peace which everyone was hoping for, and the Emperor would be able to bestow everlasting happiness upon a reposing, united Europe.

To meet Napoleon's vast force, which could be followed in case of need by reserves that he had left in barracks in Germany, Alexander had three armies. The first of 110,000 men and 560 guns was operating in the Dvina region under the command of the Minister of War, Barclay de Tolly. The second of 37,000 men and 200 guns was stationed at Wolkowysk under the command of Bagration. The third of 42,000 men was at Lodz. A court intrigue had momentarily eliminated the two best Russian generals, Benningsen and Kutusov. Forces, therefore, were very unequal and it looked like an easy victory for Napoleon.

But Alexander had other assets—weather, climate, vast distances. National sentiment too was with him. He had proclaimed a holy war and mysterious and inexhaustible Russia had rallied to his call. The obedient Russian peasant was to burn his villages and his crops before the invading host that advanced in three parallel columns, leaving nothing but a desert for it to feed on. Bernadotte had suggested the general lines of Russian strategy. It was to retreat and retreat before the French army, always avoiding battle, luring the enemy deeper and deeper into a hostile country where, eventually, he would be buried in snow and destroyed by cold and hunger.

Napoleon understood the maneuver and sensed its dangers. He well knew how Charles XII of Sweden had fared in Russia. He was astonished and then alarmed at finding no resistance before him—at the most, now and then, on the horizon, a squadron of Cossacks, who fled at the first approach of the imperial battalions. Impatient, sometimes, he would gallop ahead at all the speed his horse could endure and then come back after an hour or two, having found nothing but solitude and silence. Now and again he would hear something like a booming gun. He would straighten up, his eyes glittering with joy. Then it would prove to have been only a distant clap of thunder rumbling through a muggy stormy air.

Five days of marching brought the French to Vilna, which had been left without defense. Napoleon set up a provisional government there. In order not to open an unbridgeable gulf between himself and Alexander he refused to unite Lithuania and Poland. That was a grave blunder. It deprived him of the precious aid that Polish patriotism would have brought him.

To the delegates of the Warsaw Diet who pleaded with him he replied:

"I have many interests to reconcile, many duties to fulfill. . . . I have guaranteed the Emperor of Austria that I will leave his territories intact. I cannot sanction any movement that would tend to disturb him in his possession of such Polish provinces as he now holds. . . . I will reward your devotion in any way I can under the circumstances."

Meaningless words! And they dampened the ardor of a generous, passionate people. Napoleon may have been wise in refusing to irritate Austria. He was wrong in sacrificing Poland to his hopes of a reconciliation with Alexander. But, alas, those hopes were all the more precious to him in that now he was beginning to see more clearly the difficulties of his enterprise. His army was already wearing out, melting away. The weather was torturing—extreme heat followed by pouring rains. Fever and dysentery were spreading among the troops. Provisioning was bad. Numbers of soldiers, especially the non-French elements, were throwing down their arms and deserting. Others had turned bandits and were following the track of the army at long range. Horses were dying by the scores.

Could Napoleon see stalking in the dusk before him the shade of the adventuresome Swede whom the steppes had swallowed up a century earlier? At Vilna he received General Balakov, the Russian Minister of Police, who had come to French headquarters ostensibly to propose an amicable settlement but really to look around as a spy. The Czar, he said, was not the aggressor. He was still disposed to treat, but on condition that the French army evacuate Russian and German soil immediately. The Emperor could not consider such a proposition. It would be confessing defeat. It would destroy his Empire.

He tried to persuade Balakov that the Czar was foolish in going on with the campaign. Alexander himself was a uniform, not a military man. His generals were all dolts—all except Kutusov. The Russians were sure to be beaten and chased across the Dnieper. No one wanted peace more than he, but he would consent to peace only if Russia undertook to help him wholeheartedly against England.

He kept Balakov for dinner and questioned him in a familiar chat about the Russian court and army—and about Moscow.

"Why are there so many churches?"

"Because our people are very devout."

"Nonsense! Nobody believes nowadays. Which is the best road to Moscow?"

"All roads lead to Rome, Sire. Take the one you like best. Charles XII went by way of Poltawa."

Certain now as to Alexander's intentions Napoleon could see that he had not a moment to lose. However, he lingered for three more weeks at Vilna, a delay that was seriously to compromise his plans. It is explainable only in part. The Emperor did need to overhaul his army and reorganize the supply system. Meantime he sent Davout after Bagration, who was somewhere in the neighborhood of Minsk, and ordered Jerome to support the marshal. The young King of Westphalia knew not the first thing about warfare and spoiled the maneuver by sheer indifference. Bagration escaped the net that had been thrown about him. Napoleon gave his brother a dressing-down. Jerome took offense, refused to play any more, and went back to his good times in Westphalia.

Leaving Vilna at last Napoleon started in pursuit of Barclay de Tolly. The Russian sidestepped at Vitebsk (July 28th) and joined Bagration on the Dnieper. Napoleon delayed again at Vitebsk, taking two weeks to rest his troops. The Guard itself had lost a quarter of its numbers. The Italians and Bavarians had been reduced by a half. Berthier, Duroc, Caulaincourt and Daru were for going into barracks at Vitebsk. They thought that any advance in pursuit of the Russians would be dangerous. Napoleon would not listen. He crossed the Dnieper and pointed on Smolensk, ordering Ney and Davout to attack that place on August 17th.

In the Russian camp the party in favor of active resistance had been strengthened by Bagration's accession. Barclay de Tolly offered a furious battle, but then finally drew off, set the town on fire and plunged again into the distances towards the east.

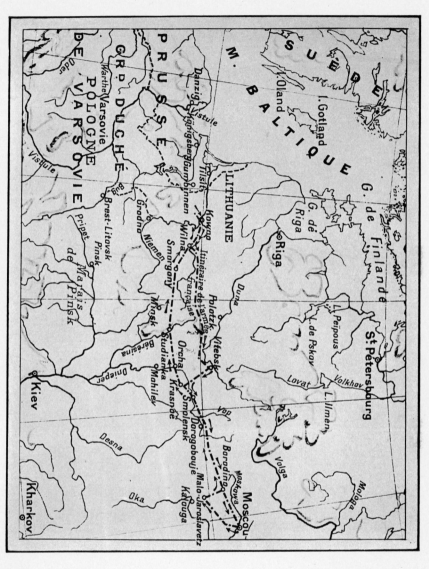

Napoleon for a time considered halting at Smolensk. He could see that the enemy was luring him on and on to unknown distances and into limitless wastes where his army might vanish like a river into sands. But he was within a few days' march of Moscow, the ancient capital of Russia. Its fall would have a great moral effect and doubtless bring Alexander to terms. He was further encouraged to go on by a victory of Schwarzenberg at Gorodoie and another by Saint-Cyr at Polotsk.

"Danger itself drives us on to Moscow," he said to Narbonne. "I have considered all the objections of the wise."

Alas! The army advanced across burned, naked plains that were marked on rare occasion by clumps of birches or firs. As the soldiers trudged along through the mud, vultures—sinister omens—soared above in the sky. That was the road to Moscow! But it was also the road to a battle, the battle so long and so eagerly desired by Napoleon and which he could already see in the offing.

The Russians, in fact, had decided to change tactics in deference to Russian public opinion, which had been aroused by the inglorious retreats of Barclay de Tolly. The Holy City could not be surrendered without a fight! Absolute sovereign that he was Alexander could not ignore the unrest in the Russian masses.

He disliked Kutusov, but he named him commander-in-chief. Barclay de Tolly and Bagration forgot themselves and agreed to fight under the veteran's orders, Benningsen serving as chief of staff. Kutusov was a fat old warhorse with a glass eye, "a Russian through and through." He was not perhaps a great general. He had beaten the Turks and had been beaten at Austerlitz.

Seventy years old and run down beyond his age as the result of his vices, he was a shrewd strategist and he still retained a mental agility that enabled him to take advantage of a chance, to stop when he had had enough, to wait if he felt too weak, to attack if he knew he was the stronger. The Russian public regarded him as its savior, as the one man who might be able to stop Napoleon. Kutusov was by no means so sure himself. Appointed to the chief command just to fight a battle, he considered the battle itself a mistake and said so. However—there were mistakes that one could not help. He was willing to go through with this one and make the best possible job of it.

Just south of Borodinò, a town some seventy miles from Moscow, he entrenched his troops along three hills in a solid net of earthworks. In the center he built what was to be called the Great Redoubt, armed with 27 heavy pieces. He had 120,000 men, with a supporting force of militia and a fine cavalry of Cossacks. Behind this line flowed the Moskva, a tributary of the Volga.

Napoleon arrived on the plain of Borodinò on September 5th. He first carried Swardinò hill in order to have free control of the ground required for deploying his army. It was raining heavily. The French rested, ate and drank, confident, in fine spirits. A mile and a quarter in front of them lay the Russians, who were thinking that the best they could hope for would be to die like brave men. They prayed in front of an image of the Virgin of Kazan, Kutusov himself leading the procession, flag in hand.

On the morning of the 6th the sky cleared and the

sun shone warm. Napoleon worked in his tent, issuing orders.

Colonel Fabvier arrived from Spain with news of Marmont's defeat by Wellington at Arapiles. The Emperor's temper was not ruffled. Victory on the Moskva, he promised, would offset Marmont's mishap. That same morning, Bausset, Napoleon's Prefect of the Palace, came up, bringing a portrait of the King of Rome, by Gérard. Napoleon set the picture up on an improvised easel in front of his tent and showed it to the officers of the Guard and to the soldiers. His son! He was so proud of the boy!

"If he were fifteen years old," he said, "you may be sure that he would be here not merely as a picture!"

A little later he had an opposite whim:

"No—take him away! He's too young to see a battlefield!"

Evening fell upon an absolute silence. The laughing of the French, the praying of the Russians, had come to an end. It was raining again. The two armies slept on the wet ground, the bivouacs stretching away in two long parallel lines through the dark. Napoleon had a bad cold and was suffering from bladder pains. Shaking with chills and fever he drank water incessantly. He did not sleep a wink. He was afraid the Russians would decamp under cover of the night. He kept calling every other moment to ask the time. Rarely had he shown such nervousness and worry. He knew that his troops were worn out by exposure and privations. Would they stand up under the shock? He ordered extra rations of hardtack and rice for the Guard.

Towards morning his aide found him sitting with his head in his hands.

"What is war?" he murmured. "A barbarous business that comes down to being strongest at a given point!"

He talked of the uncertainty of Fortune. Was she betraying him at last? He asked Rapp if he thought they were going to win.

"Of course," the general replied. "But it's going to be bloody!"

At five o'clock Ney sent a messenger asking permission to attack. The Russians had not budged. The Emperor leapt up from his cot, suddenly reassured.

"We have them!" he cried. "Come, boys, let's open the gates to Moscow!"

He mounted his horse and rode to the top of Swardinò hill. There he stationed himself with his staff. He was waiting only for the sun and the first artillery exchanges.

As the sun touched the horizon he called to his officers:

"The sun of Austerlitz!"

It was the same sun as at Austerlitz but it rose behind the Russians and in the eyes of the French. It was a great hindrance to their aim and to their evolutions. Murat galloped along the line of his cavalry in a green velvet cloak embroidered with gold, a plumed hat, yellow boots. The artillery of the Guard was the first to open. The Russians answered. The plain shook. Eugene's troops attacked brilliantly on the left carrying the village of Borodinò and routing the defenders of the Great Redoubt. On the right Davout was wounded. Murat replaced him. With him Ney, magnificent, impetuous, carried the earthwork called the Three Arrows. It was ten o'clock. Victory was already in sight. But Ney and Murat found their men exhausted and called for reinforcements.

Napoleon hesitated. For a long time he paced up and down on the edge of a ravine, dejected, sad. Ney and Murat entreated, urgent. He refused to risk his Guard:

"The situation isn't clear enough. I want to see more definitely. I have to consider the whole checker-board."

In the end he sent just the Friant division.

Ney's rage knew no bounds.

"He's not fighting these wars by himself! He used to be a general! Now he plays Emperor everywhere. He'd better go back to the Tuileries and let us do the fighting for him."

Kutusov profited by the delay, resuming the offensive with all his reserves. Bagration won back the Grand Redoubt. It was a carnage. The earthwork could hardly be seen for the corpses that were piled high about it. Bagration was himself killed. Ney and Murat clung desperately to the Three Arrows. Napoleon then ordered Eugene to take the Great Redoubt at all costs and began beating the stronghold with all his artillery. In a mad charge Murat threw his cavalry in full strength upon it. The infantry followed close behind. The Russian Guard fell back gradually foot by foot. Then Ney came in and turned the retirement into a rout. By three o'clock the whole position was in the hands of the French.

The battle was by that time won. The Russians were in retreat all along the line. On the right Poniatowski began to turn their flank. Had Napoleon sent in the Guard he might have overwhelmed Kutusov and destroyed the whole Russian army. He obstinately refused:

"I am not going to have my Guard destroyed. Two

thousand miles from home one doesn't risk one's last resource!"

The Russian army, still in good order on the whole, was massed along the Moskva, offering a fair target to the artillery.

"Since they haven't had enough," cried Napoleon, "give them some more."

Four hundred guns rained solid shot upon them.

Under a dark sky, in an icy rain and a lashing wind, the ground was one carpet of dead soldiers. For centuries no battle had cost so dearly. Thirty thousand Frenchmen strewed the hillsides and filled the ravines, sixty thousand Russians. And yet the victory had given the Emperor neither prisoners, nor flags, nor guns. He had won a battlefield—and the road to Moscow.

Napoleon realized that. The amount of his losses staggered him—43 general officers killed or wounded! 110 colonels! It was ironical to despatch a communiqué of victory that evening. He was as despondent as he would have been under a defeat. Astonishment and disapproval swept the army. His generals in one voice criticized the way in which he had conducted the battle. "It's a victory of soldiers, not of a general," they cried. "Why the great haste in joining with an enemy when your army is tired and out of breath; and then, when you have him, refuse to finish him off?" Murat averred that he "did not recognize Napoleon that day!" Ney was for an immediate retreat, and Eugene himself, ordinarily so servile, declared that he "could not understand the Emperor's showing such great indecision." The fact was that on that day Napoleon had not been himself—he had been a very sick man.

However, he was well again very soon. The next morning he sent Murat and his cavalry ahead towards Moscow. In order to keep the troops he still had intact, Kutusov had decided not to defend the capital. Rostopchin, the governor of Moscow, was a man of a savage patriotism that was ready to stop at nothing. He ordered the city evacuated of all its inhabitants. Then he opened the prisons and directed the liberated convicts to set fire to the town the moment the French entered. He collected large supplies of combustible materials at appropriate spots for their use. He left Moscow himself on the 14th of September, saving nothing of his private belongings, but taking with him all fire-fighting apparatus. The Russian battalions followed after him. They took up positions some distance away on the Ryazan road.

The French were approaching Moscow at just that moment. They numbered hardly a fourth of the army that had crossed the Niemen three months earlier. However, it was bright, sunny weather and they forgot their suffering in the thought that they were about to enter the wealthiest metropolis of the East. Reaching the crest of the Mount of Salvation they could see the city with its hundreds of vari-colored cupolas and domes spreading out before them like a garden of tulips. "Moscow! Moscow!" The shout rose and rolled in waves along the line of march. The soldiers halted, cheered and clapped their hands in joy.

Napoleon was riding among them. He too seemed radiant. A glimpse of the Kremlin dispelled his anxieties —for one thing he was in better health. The marshals had been sulking since Borodinò. They now crowded

around him in a returning surge of affectionate enthusiasm.

"So there it is!" he said. "The famous town!" And
he added, but to himself: "It's high time!"

He thought that in Moscow he was to lay hands upon
the living heart of the Russian empire. He had even
chosen the words in which he would reply tactfully to
the deputations that would come forth to receive him.
He would rest his troops, wait for reinforcements that
were coming up from Germany and France, and meanwhile think out conditions of peace. With his capital
gone, Alexander could only treat!

Dreams! Dreams that were not to last very long! He
entered streets that were entirely empty, in a silence
that was broken only by the cawing of thousands of
crows. A few beggars approached him to ask for food.
The Russians had left nothing but the corpse of their
city.

Taking quarters in the Kremlin, Napoleon distributed
the army about town, naming Mortier governor.

"No looting!" he enjoined. "You will answer for it
with your lives."

Fires broke out here and there. They were extin-
guished. But during the night of September 15th-16th,
great columns of smoke began to rise. Within a few
hours a strong autumn wind had turned the western
sections of the city into one vast furnace. Wooden
houses, palaces, churches would light up, blaze on high
and then collapse. The Kremlin was just a reef of black
rock beaten upon by a sea of flame.

Napoleon stood at a window and looked out, his forehead pressed against a pane. He could see his prey going up in smoke.

"What a spectacle!" he murmured. "What a thing to do! What a people! They are Scyths—that's all!"

The army bravely did what it could. A few of the incendiaries were captured and shot, but to contend with such a raging inferno was impossible. The air in the town was unbreathable. Wind-driven embers fell on the Kremlin, threatening the powder magazine and the artillery parks. A tower actually caught fire. Napoleon was in danger at any moment of being caught in an explosion. At the urgent entreaty of Berthier, Eugene, Murat, he finally consented to leave the palace of the Czars and ordered his dismayed army to fall back about the city. He himself took quarters in the Petrowskoie castle, three miles away.

CHAPTER XXXI

The Beresina

H E STAYED THERE FOR THREE DAYS. WHEN HE RE-ENTERED the city it was a waste of ruins and ashes. Only two thousand houses and the Kremlin had escaped the conflagration.

Since Moscow had cheated him, Napoleon began considering a march on St. Petersburg. Meantime one thing was certain: He could write a letter to Alexander offering peace.

The Czar could not have signed a peace if he had wanted to. His soldiers and his people were convinced that the French had burned Moscow. They quivered with rage and hatred. Had Alexander weakened then he would have been dethroned, and perhaps worse. But he had no idea of making peace. Deeply hurt in his vanity he wanted nothing but revenge. "Shall we quail when all Europe is gazing at us?" he proclaimed. "Let us set her the example! Let us bless the hand that has chosen us to be the leader of nations in the cause of virtue and liberty!" He reaffirmed his alliance with Sweden and England, entrusted his fleet to English command and forwarded his treasure and his archives to Archangel. Between him and Napoleon there could now be only a war to the death. "One or the other of us," he declared, "must disappear from the world scene."

It was late autumn. A number of alternatives suggested themselves to Napoleon. He could hardly winter in Moscow, so far from his bases and with uncertain means of feeding his troops. His lieutenants opposed a march on Vitebsk to threaten St. Petersburg. The army, they thought, was too tired. To retreat to Poland would be to confess defeat, revive the enemy's hopes and therefore postpone peace. For the rest the Czar's reply to his overtures would soon be coming.

He spent his days as usual working at the Empire's business, reviewing his troops, reorganizing his shattered cavalry, putting the Kremlin in a state of defense. He dated an ordinance reorganizing the Théâtre Français from Moscow—an evidence of his calm frame of mind.

In St. Petersburg Alexander ordered his generals to move upon the Dvina and Dnieper to cut off the French retreat. He now had two new armies at his disposal, Wittgenstein's, made up of troops just recalled from Finland, and Admiral Tchitchakov's, which had just been freed by the treaty he had signed at Bucharest with the Turks. They were sent to support Kutusov, who was in camp near Tarutinò.

Some few reinforcements for the French had come up from Poland, but Napoleon's army was still at less than half strength. On October 13th he called a council of his marshals. He had had no reply from the Czar and the first frosts had appeared. He had to come to some decision. The soldiers were growing restless. "You do not know our climate," Russians had said to them. "A month from now you will be losing your fingernails in our cold." Daru, the commissary general of the army, was for wintering in Moscow. "Yes—but Paris?" Napoleon objected. "Will not France get used to my absence?" The other generals, Davout, Berthier, Mortier, Eugene, were for an immediate departure.

While he was pondering still an attack by Kutusov upon Murat's corps settled matters. Leaving Mortier in the Kremlin with 10,000 men he set out from Moscow on October 19th, followed by an enormous baggage train that lamentably slowed up the march. On the 23rd, at Malo-Yaroslavetz, Kutusov tried a surprise down the new Kaluga road. It proved costly to the French, and to economize his forces and at the urgent entreaty of his lieutenants, Napoleon decided to retreat to Smolensk. Mortier meantime had come along, after blowing up the outer wall of the Kremlin.

Kutusov followed the French at his leisure. When urged to attack he replied:

"Wait till snow comes."

Already, however, his bearded, skin-clothed Kalmucks on little long-haired horses were buzzing around the French rear guard, commanded by Davout, killing stragglers and despoiling provision wagons. The weather was good but the eighteen hour nights were growing cold. The army drooped in spirits as it retraversed the battlefield of Borodinò. Almost no horses were left, and the infantry were obliged to hold off the enemy cavalry with their naked bayonets. Each day as the horses gave out new caissons of munitions were destroyed. The wounded were now being left behind. A long line of Austrian, Dutch, Spanish and Illyrian soldiers followed the army without guns or knapsacks.

At Vyasma Prince Eugene was suddenly attacked by the Russian cavalry and was rescued with great difficulty by Davout. Napoleon now walked, now rode, in a carriage at the head of the line of march and never left it. It was noted that oftentimes he would not speak for hours. At Dorogobuzh the great cold came. Crows were found frozen on the roads. Heavy snows covered the ground with soft layers on which it was hard to walk or with great drifts in which the men often collapsed. Haggard, their uniforms in rags, their faces purple with cold, their mustaches heavy with icicles, their noses often bleeding, the men had now little to eat except the flesh or blood of horses, with perhaps a little flour stirred into water. They slept under the open sky, many of them never waking. In the morning corpses would be found by the hundreds about fires that had died out for lack of wood. Only fifty thousand men still had guns. They never spoke, never shouted, never sang. They trudged along resting their weight on sticks, brushing the driving snow from their eyes. Packs of dogs—or were they wolves?—trouped along beside the black lines of marching men, feeding on the bodies of the soldiers and horses that fell. Stragglers who were captured by the Cossacks were stripped naked and driven at the point of the lance along the roads till they collapsed. And still three days' march from Smolensk!

At the height of the disaster, Napoleon received a courier from Paris. His government had almost been upset by some plot or other. He mentioned the matter only to intimates, with an injunction that they say nothing of it. But the extent to which his power was threatened came forcibly home to him. The Empire was now at the mercy of a whim, a chance happening, a cock-and-bull story.

General Malet had been a soldier under the Republic. Sent to the Conciergerie in 1809 because of a first conspiracy, he had always dreamed of overthrowing Napoleon. He now knew that the Emperor was in Moscow and he thought that a good chance had come. He procured a transfer to a hospital and with the help of a number of individuals whom he misled by false representations, he got hold of some military uniforms and a few muskets. Then he manufactured a number of counterfeit documents, which reported the death of the Emperor, abolished the Empire and set up a new government.

On October 22nd—the Emperor was at Malo-Yaroslavetz at that time—he managed to escape. Putting on a uniform he appeared at the Popincourt barracks as Governor of Paris and bade Colonel Soulier and the 10th legion of the National Guard to follow him. He marched these troops to La Force prison and liberated General Lahorie, sometime chief of staff to Moreau, and General Guibal, both of whom were in prison for old political intrigues. Deceiving them as well, he ordered them to go and arrest the ministers. They took detachments of national guardsmen, seized Savary and the prefect Pasquier, and escorted them to the Conciergerie.

Malet then went for General Hulin, commander of the Fortress of Paris. Hulin offered resistance and Malet shot him dead. Just then he was recognized by an ordinary staff-officer, Laborde, who kept his head and managed to get a word to Malet's men. They arrested their counterfeit leader. An hour later Savary and Pasquier were freed. The movement had begun at six in the morning. It was over by noon.

Cambacérès called a council of ministers that same day. Thoroughly frightened he struck, contrary to his usual habit, immediately and hard. A court martial sat on the 23rd and condemned Malet, Lahorie, Guibal, Soulier, and eight of their aides to death. They were shot at once, none of them, except Malet, having had any idea of what it was all about. "I die," cried Malet, "but I am not the last of the Romans!"

The episode was grotesque—it was laughable—but it was a terrible shock to Paris. Was the Empire so weak, then, that a mere handful of adventurers could all but upset it? Was a mere rumor that the Emperor was dead enough to cause his work to evaporate like so much fog? At his trial the judge-advocate asked Malet who his accomplices were. Malet replied:

"All France, yourself included, if I had succeeded!"

Prophetic words! On the steppe roughened by the corpses of his soldiers the Emperor shivered, and not from cold alone!

A great disappointment came to the "army of ghosts" when it reached Smolensk at last on November 10th. The commissaries had been negligent. No supplies had been collected and the stores were empty. Mutinous mobs of starving soldiers rioted before their closed doors. Napoleon rested but five days there, then he had to rush the retreat. The Russian armies were coming together to cut him off. A series of engagements in fact followed. Eugene lost his artillery and his baggage in crossing the

Vop. Davout had to cut his way through Krasnoi with naked bayonets. In spite of his bravery Ney had to flee at night to avoid capture by Kutusov. On arriving at Orsha the actual army counted a bare 24,000 men.

Napoleon tried to give a shape to the miserable group of skeletons. He put all the horses that were left at the service of the artillery and burned almost all the wagons and bridge equipment. He summoned the corps of Oudinot and Victor, which had suffered less than his own and which had not been able to hold Wittgenstein on the Dvina. Then he resumed his place at the head of the march and pushed on. The army reached Studienka on the banks of the swift Beresina on November 25th.

The river was a mass of floating ice. There Kutusov had counted on destroying the remnant of the French army. "Napoleon's final goal," he proclaimed, "has been unfailingly marked for him by Destiny. The meteor will flicker out in the marshes of the Beresina and in the presence of the whole Russian army." [1]

Napoleon ordered Eblé to throw two bridges across the river. Twice they broke, but Eblé and his men, with devoted heroism, repaired them during the night. "Ignoring the cold," writes Chambray, "they worked with the water up to their armpits. It meant almost certain death for them, but the army looked on. They were sacrificing themselves to save it."

The organized portions of the troops got across the

[1] [Actually Kutusov had been outwitted by Napoleon. The Russian general was waiting in force for the French farther up the river on the road to Vitebsk, where Napoleon had crossed earlier and where the crossing would have been much easier. Napoleon had guessed the maneuver of the Russians and went straight ahead on the road to Vilna.—A. L.]

river in good order on the 27th, but the line of stragglers was suddenly attacked by Cossacks. They rushed for the bridges in a mad panic. "From the great pack of writhing human beings," writes Ségur, "now a dull buzzing sound, now a mighty clamor, rose, a medley of groans and unspeakable imprecations. Many of those who had scrambled ahead were pushed away from the bridge and then tried to climb up its sides, only to be thrown off into the water." The panic was so great that relatively few had managed to cross when Kutusov's advance guard appeared. With his heart in despair Napoleon gave the order to blow up the bridges in order to save the army. So twelve thousand stragglers were either killed by the Russians or made prisoners. The Emperor had escaped total destruction only owing to the devotion of Eblé and Victor, to Oudinot's energy, to Ney's unfailing courage.

He now guided the remnants of his army towards Vilna. The cold was at five above zero. Kutusov followed close on his heels. The rear guard was always fighting the Cossacks. On December 4th the French reached the little town of Smorgoni, some days' march from Vilna.

Calling Murat, Eugene and the marshals into council, Napoleon announced his decision to leave the army in secret and return in all haste to Paris. In his judgment what could be saved of the army had been saved. It was necessary now to save the Empire. That he could do only from the Tuileries. When Europe learned of the disaster it would also have learned of his return. The thought that he had resumed control in France and was preparing new levies with a view to an early revenge

would hold allies faithful and the various enemies
cautious. He did not invite the opinions of his lieutenants. He feared that they might be unfavorable.

For a serious blunder he left the command to Murat
who had shown no initiative whatever since Moscow
and had but one thought—to save his kingdom from a
general collapse which he sensed near. The Emperor
drew up his 29th bulletin, admitting a measure of failure, which he ascribed to the climate, and crowning the
expedition with a halo of glory. Then—it was the 5th of
December—he mounted a sled with Caulaincourt and
escorted by Duroc, Lobau and Lefebvre-Desnouettes,
started off towards France with the horses at a gallop.

His departure was kept hidden from the army for a
time. The men did not learn of it till they got to Vilna.
Napoleon had left no orders. Instead therefore of hanging on at Vilna, which should have formed the pivot of
a line of defense, Murat and Berthier marched on the
moment the horsemen of Platow appeared before the
town, and headed for Kowno. They arrived on December
12th at the place where, six months earlier, the Great
Army, 500,000 strong, had crossed the Niemen. No army
was left now. It was just a disorganized band of starving
fugitives running before the Kalmucks. The wounded,
the last guns, the army cashbox, had been long since
abandoned.

At Gumbinnen Murat denounced the Emperor's ambition in the presence of the officers: "One can't serve
under a lunatic. There is no salvation in his cause." That
cause Murat had already deserted in his heart, and
soon he was to leave for Italy, transferring his phantom

'command to Eugene, who was even less capable than he of exercising it.

When Talleyrand read the 29th bulletin a smile flitted across the features of his death's-head.

"The beginning of the end!" he murmured.

Napoleon reached the Tuileries on the evening
of the 18th and called a council of ministers for the following morning. For the first time he was coming home
in defeat. Deeply as the fact must have touched his pride
it did not soften him. He welcomed with a dark frown
the men who had so badly defended his government
during his absence. He scarcely mentioned the Russian
campaign, affecting to think of it as a mere accident,
which, however, had to be repaired without a moment's
delay. What disturbed him was the Malet business. Why
had his representatives failed to rush to the Empress-
Regent?

"Gentlemen, you took it for granted that I was dead!
But the King of Rome! Your oaths! Your principles!
You make me shudder for the future!"

"Where is the future now?" the others must have been
saying to themselves.

"No one," he insisted, his face a thundercloud,
"thought of my son!"

That son he now intended to make his associate in
the Empire, following the precedent of the Caesars of
Rome and the first Capets. Lacépède, the President of

the Senate, expressed that desire before the senators at Napoleon's order. He thought that by that device he could safeguard the Empire against any surprise—attaching too much importance to mere oaths, as the event proved.

He set to work immediately, bending all his energies to military preparations, the one means available, he thought, for inspiring Europe with fear. He called the class of 1813 and made the cohorts of the National Guard part of the regular army. Adding together the troops he had on reserve in Germany, the remnants of Russia, the reinforcements that would be brought from Italy, and contingents to be supplied by the Rhine Federation, he thought he could have 400,000 men on hand by spring. Then he would take the field against Alexander again, add a new Friedland to a second Eylau, and bring Russia to her knees.

Again his optimism was clouding his sense of realities. If the situation was not hopeless, it was exceedingly dangerous. He was not sufficiently aware of that. Good sense would have counseled him to withdraw from Spain, where Wellington, winning here and losing there, was at least holding Joseph at bay. The old troops from Spain, moreover, would have formed a solid framework for his raw recruits. Napoleon could not bring himself to make that sacrifice. He decided to wait for a time still. After all, he thought, Spain was a side issue. The outcome would be settled in Germany.

General Yorck, commanding Napoleon's force of Prussian auxiliaries, went over to the Russians on December 30th, and all Germany applauded. That country, largely through the work of secret societies, notably the Tugendbund, was now rising against Napoleon from the Vistula to the Rhine. Students, workingmen, businessmen in the towns, began enrolling as volunteers. Fichte, the philosopher, suspended his courses at the university in Berlin. "We shall resume," he declared, "when our country is free, or else we shall have died in an effort to recover our liberty." The Berlin government could not long hold out against such pressure from public opinion. Frederick William still kept sending faithful greetings to Paris, but he was negotiating with the Czar. Stein and Yorck called a meeting of the Estates of Old Prussia at Königsberg, and, acting ostensibly in defiance of their government, voted to organize two reserve armies, the Landwehr and the Landsturm, which would quadruple the strength of the regular troops at the first signal.

Puffed up by a victory which he considered due to his genius, Alexander professed to believe that God had chosen him to purge the Continent of "Bonaparte's" tyranny. His dream was to come true. He was shortly to be the arbiter, the king of kings, in Europe. His religious exaltation fell in harmoniously with his practical aims. Napoleon's fall would win him all Poland, which would be united, but under his scepter. On entering Warsaw he proclaimed: "If the North imitates the inspiring example of Spain the world will soon issue from its mourning, and a Europe that was about to fall prey to the monster will recover its independence and its tranquillity."

He urged England, Prussia and Austria to join forces with him. England was lavish in advances and promises. For a moment she had despaired of running down the quarry. Now she saw herself trumpeting the death in a near future. Prussia agreed out of hand, but Austria made haste slowly. Metternich, now master of Austrian policy, felt himself in no way bound by the fact of Napoleon's marriage to Marie Louise to respect the alliance with France. However he still regarded Napoleon as a dangerous enemy. A shift in luck might leave him a victor who would this time be utterly merciless. "In deference to the future," as he said, he adopted an attitude of expectant mediation. Napoleon was all the more ready to accept these good offices since he was under the spell of "the family alliance." He thought that one successful battle would again bring Europe to his feet.

But France did not rally to his hopes. The draft was becoming more and more burdensome and it discouraged the masses. Napoleon was greeted with catcalls and jeers in the streets of Paris. Soldiers returning from Russia were welcomed with demonstrations of deepest pity. Draft evaders were protected and men who responded to the call were incited to desert. In the newly annexed territories riots broke out and French officials were insulted. Hurrahs for the Cossacks were given under their very noses.

On the whole, nevertheless, the powerful organism of the Empire continued to function. The recruiting depots filled little by little. Napoleon strove to electrify public opinion by fomenting petitions and addresses, by showering lavish pensions on soldiers' families, by money bonuses to veterans. Avoiding increases in taxes, as well as levies on a gold reserve which he had nursed by strenuous economies and piled up in the cellars of the Tuileries, he refilled the public coffers by buying communal properties with state bonds and then selling them to private purchasers. This was a desperate expedient but it enabled him to tide over the crisis of the moment.

He was now aware at last of the great mistake he had made in persecuting the Pope. He had brought Pius VII on from Savona and the pontiff was living in gloomy retirement at Fontainebleau. "Unhappy, ill," wrote Cardinal Pacca, "he takes no more than the bare amount of food required for sustaining life." Napoleon suddenly called on him, embraced him, and offered a new concordat. The Pope accepted it. Was it Divine wisdom? Human weakness? Yes, he would also crown the Empress and her son! Without expressly repudiating the patrimony of St. Peter he agreed to reside at Avignon. Finally he yielded on the question of canonical appointments "in view of the present state of the Church." That was on January 25th, 1813.

Napoleon thought he had successfully closed that running moral sore. But two months later, the "black cardinals" who had returned from exile gathered about Pius VII and hounded him into withdrawing the signature he had affixed to the concordat. Napoleon at once arrested Cardinal di Pietro, the most vociferous of his opponents—and there was the sore open again!

Prussia finally found the courage to make her reversal in policy public. On February 28th Frederick William announced his alliance with Russia. Eugene's wings were uncovered, and, losing the support of Schwarzenberg, who retired into Galicia, he was obliged to evacuate Posen and entrench himself on the Elbe. The French marched out of Berlin through streets that were crowded with joyous cheering mobs, and a Russian army marched in behind them. The King of Saxony alone stood faithful to Napoleon, but he had to seek refuge in Bavaria.

Austria lived up to her promise of mediation and made overtures to London and St. Petersburg. As Metternich had foreseen, they were rebuffed by both England and Russia. He then moved on to "armed mediation," which was a word devised more or less successfully to conceal his hostility to the French. Marie Louise vainly begged her father not to declare against Napoleon. Arming to the limit, Francis waited for the first misstep on the part of France to join the Emperor's enemies. Immediately on his return to Naples Murat opened negotiations with Vienna with a view to preserving his throne. Napoleon had no knowledge of the intrigue but he guessed it. "Your title as king has gone to your head," he wrote Murat. "If you desire to keep it you must deport yourself differently from what you have been doing so far." Between the two dangers Murat did not know what to do. He worried along in a tragic conflict between duty and interest.

Napoleon sent his army, division by division, to the Elbe. Contrary to what he had foreseen he could muster a force of not more than 200,000 men, including the army under Eugene. His troops were mostly French, but they were raw recruits, courageous, with no great physical endurance. The few German auxiliaries Napoleon still had followed him regretfully and were ready to desert at the first opportunity. His main lacks were artillery and horses, the latter especially. The Russians and Prussians had 120,000 men under Wittgenstein and Blücher.

Napoleon arrived at Erfurt on April 25, and at once

339

advanced eastward in a concentric movement upon
Leipzig. On the 30th he won an advance guard action
at Weissenfels, where Bessières was killed, and then, on
May 2nd, a smashing victory at Lützen, which only his
lack of cavalry prevented him from turning into a decisive disaster for the Allies. At Lützen the young French
infantry was called on to display all its heroic mettle.
The enemy fled eastward for over a hundred miles beyond Leipzig with Napoleon in hot pursuit. The Allies
halted at Bautzen, where Napoleon drove them from a
strong position on the Spree, and then again at Würschen
(May 19-22), whence they withdrew behind the Oder.
That was four victories in three weeks. Lack of cavalry
had not permitted him to destroy the foe. Losses, meantime, had been heavy on both sides. "A butchery," said
Napoleon, surveying the field at Bautzen, "and not a
gun captured, not a flag!"

The Allies, for their part, were thunderstruck. They
had been busily cutting up the hide and the lion was
not even dead! With the breath knocked out of them
they needed a truce to gain time and assemble reinforcements. Blackmailed by Austria, ill-counseled by Berthier
and Caulaincourt, over-impressed, perhaps, by a minor
success of Blücher over Maison at Haynau (May 26),
Napoleon committed the fatal mistake of signing the
truce of Preititz (June 8). It suspended hostilities till
July 20th. Meantime a congress would convene at
Prague to discuss peace.

The Emperor was already suspicious that his father-
in-law was betraying him. On June 26, at Dresden, he
had an interview with Metternich at the Marcolini Pal-

ace. He divined the wily diplomat's game and threw his treachery in his face:

"How much has England given you to induce you to play this part against me?" Metternich, livid, sat silent. "I can find a way to die," Napoleon continued, "but I shall not yield an inch of territory. Your sovereigns were born to their thrones. They can let themselves be licked twenty times and still come back. I can't—I am just a successful soldier."

As they separated Metternich bowed and said (or at least boasted afterwards that he said):

"You are lost, Sire!"

The armistice was extended by common agreement to August 20, Napoleon calculating that the added respite would give him time to bring his cavalry on from Spain. The Peninsula had now been definitely lost. Wellington had beaten Jourdan at Vittoria (June 21, 1813). The indolent Joseph had fled. Suchet and Soult stood with their backs to the Pyrenees and could do no more than defend the French frontier. The Prague congress opened therefore under very unfavorable circumstances.

It was little better than a clown performance at best. Caulaincourt, representing the Emperor, was more than ineffective. He allowed it plainly to be seen that what he wanted more than anything else was peace. Metternich had already joined the coalition in secret. He offered Napoleon France, with the Rhine for a frontier, and also Italy. Had Napoleon accepted, Metternich would have gone back on those terms and demanded a withdrawal from Italy and the Low Countries. He had foreseen that Napoleon would refuse and hoped to use the point to rouse French opinion against the "mad ambition" of the

Emperor. Napoleon was badly informed and hesitated, and when he did finally answer, he made the mistake of arguing. On the 10th of August the congress adjourned in his face and Austria declared war the next morning. So card by card Metternich had played the game that he had laid out for himself the day after Wagram.

But during the two months of the truce the situation had completely changed. The Allies now had three armies converging upon Napoleon: 230,000 Austrians under Schwarzenberg, 100,000 Russo-Prussians under Blücher, 160,000 Russo-Swedes under Bernadotte—a half million men in all. Napoleon had been strengthened proportionately. He planned a great drive on Berlin but made a capital mistake and one that was truly astonishing in him. He divided his forces among his lieutenants, sending Oudinot to meet Bernadotte and Macdonald to deal with Blücher.

He himself attacked Schwarzenberg on August 26-27 at Dresden, beat him and drove him in retreat into Bohemia. It was a clean victory and very costly to the Austrians. General Moreau had come back from America to act as military counselor to the coalition. He fell at Dresden, struck down by a French cannonball. However, Vandamme tried to intercept the retreating Austrians but was surrounded and overwhelmed at Kulm (August 29). Oudinot was defeated by Bernadotte at Gross-Beeren, Macdonald on the Katzbach by Blücher. Ney was deserted by his German auxiliaries and thrown back by Bülow along the Berlin road. So the drive on Berlin came to naught, while the plan of campaign of the Allies, which had been suggested by Bernadotte, was carried to completion—to wear the French troops down in scattered battles and then to unite en masse about Napoleon when he had been sufficiently weakened.

His position grew worse from moment to moment. Westphalia was invaded by the enemy cavalry and Jerome fled without giving battle. Bavaria in her turn betrayed and went over to the enemy.

With his back to the wall at Leipzig Napoleon doggedly and courageously held on for four days (October 16-19) against the rising tide of the Allies. The Germans have called that epic struggle the "Battle of the Nations." Ten countries were in fact locked there in a furious hand-to-hand, while two thousand guns roared and thundered. It was the greatest battle the Empire fought. 100,000 dead strewed the battlefield. During the 16th and 17th, Napoleon successfully maintained his positions against the efforts of Schwarzenberg and Blücher. But on the 18th the Saxons and Württembergers deserted to the enemy, opening a wide gap in Napoleon's lines. He patched them up with cavalry charges, but his ammunition ran low. He had lost all hope of winning in any event, and decided to retreat. The retirement was carried out on the 19th across a bridge over the Elster under enemy fire. The subordinate in charge of the bridge, however, blew it up before Macdonald and Poniatowski got their men across. That mishap netted the Allies some 20,000 prisoners.

Napoleon fell back towards the Rhine. Schwarzenberg and Blücher were really too badly broken to offer an effective pursuit. However, on October 30th, the Bavarians, reinforced by an Austrian division, tried to stop Napoleon on the Main at Hanau—a real stab in the back. In a sharp rally the French crushed them and resumed their march. They crossed the bridges at Mainz early in November. Forces in considerable numbers were still occupying fortresses along the Vistula, the Oder and the Elbe. Napoleon tried to get word to them to make their way back to France. He ordered Macdonald, Mortier, Victor and Marmont to hold the Rhine, against which all Europe was soon to be crashing. There was no trace of wavering in him. He assumed that the Allies would not dare to undertake a winter campaign. His one thought, therefore, was to use the few months he supposed he still had at his disposal to mobilize the supreme resources of the nation and save it from invasion.

The Allies placed Schwarzenberg in supreme command and marched on the Rhine. The English had already set the example by crossing the Spanish frontier (November 8, 1813). However, on reaching the banks of the great river Europe halted. It was not that the defenses of the left bank frightened them, or the weary troops, fine soldiers now disheartened, who had been entrusted to Victor, Marmont and Macdonald. The point was that if Napoleon was going to be dethroned, there had to be some agreement as to the way the spoils should be divided. The Czar was posing as a supreme conqueror and talking down to everybody. Proud, haughty, hesitating, he had no very clear ideas as to what was to come of it all. Austria was inclined to recognize the King of Rome under a regency by Marie Louise. Prussia was for dismembering France. England was interested solely in restoring the frontiers of 1789.

Deep down in their hearts the sovereigns were filled with an anxiety they could hardly account for as they prepared to set foot again on French soil. Memories of the great days of the Revolution came back to their minds. What if all France rose to the defense of her territory in one mighty onslaught that would involve them in another Valmy? The plains of Lorraine and Champagne were broad enough to bury armies far larger than theirs! Schwarzenberg himself was doubtful. Pretending to be engaged in a flank movement through Switzerland he was really trying to gain time.

The kings had no idea of the state in which the France that so frightened them found herself. France was tired, tired out. The great machine of imperial bureaucracy was beginning to creak and groan from the disorder in public finances. The masses, bled white by twenty years of war but still loyal to their hero, wanted peace under Napoleon. The middle classes were now threatened in their turn by the drafts and the tax levies that had long been spared them. More selfish than the masses, they wanted peace, peace at any price. The Royalists were buzzing in their drawing-rooms and at their dinner parties. Stealing a march on Talleyrand, Caulincourt, and other high functionaries, they hoped for a restoration.

As Metternich had foreseen, the Emperor was blamed particularly for not having come to terms when he still held the upper hand in Germany, for sacrificing the country to his ambition. The marshals themselves censured him—Ney, Marmont, Macdonald—in no very respectful terms, each according to his temperament and character. Caulaincourt was polite. He had become the intimate confidant of the Emperor and was to remain his negotiator to the end. But he, perhaps, had withdrawn more completely from Napoleon than any of the

others. He had ceased to believe either in the Emperor
or in the Empire. Cambacérès had been the counselor
of the whole reign. He was silent and turned away. He
talked of retiring from public life and developed a sudden interest in religion.

Just then, with the idea of making sure of the few
weeks the Allies needed to resume their march on
France, Metternich repeated the maneuver that had succeeded so well at Prague. He wanted to cast the odium
of prolonging the war upon Napoleon and so have public
opinion with him. His many defeats had taught him the
value of public opinion. Therefore, through Saint-
Agnan, Caulaincourt's brother, he offered Napoleon a
peace that would leave France with her natural boundaries—the Rhine, the Alps, the Pyrenees—in other words,
deprive her not only of the conquests of the Empire
but of the conquests of the Revolution.

Napoleon was slow in answering. What a sacrifice was
asked of him! To those who urged him to accept he
insisted:

"It's easy to talk of peace, but peace is not so easy
to arrange. Europe, really, does not want peace. Do you
think we can hold them off by humiliating ourselves
before them? You are mistaken. The more accommodat-
ing we are, the more exacting they will be. Soon they will
be offering the frontiers of 1790! We have got to fight
once more and fight desperately. Let us win! Then we
can make peace at the earliest possible moment. I will
do everything possible to bring it about, you may be
sure."

That was far-sighted. However, yielding to the pressure of those about him, he asked for another congress,

and, through Caulaincourt, declared that he was ready
to treat "on the principles of Frankfurt." That was December 1st. His reply had hardly come when Metternich
served notice that the Allies withdrew their proposals.
An insurrection in Holland had driven out the French
and acclaimed the House of Orange. But then also the
Russians, the Prussians and the Royalist exiles who had
gathered at Frankfurt were exerting all their pressure
upon him. A printed communication had been widely
distributed and widely read in France. It asserted that
the kings were carrying on the war "not against the
French nation but against the excessive preponderance
that Napoleon had tried to exercise in Europe." They
would not lay down their arms till a proper balance
had been restored. That maneuver was designed to pro-
voke currents of opinion hostile to the Emperor and
so to hasten his fall. Transparent as it was, it had a
certain success. A session of the Legislative Body that
opened on December 19th marked the change in public
sentiment that had been occasioned by the Allied mani-
festo.

For that matter a real opposition party had of late
been forming in the lower chamber under the inspiration of Benjamin Constant, who was still in exile, and
a Girondin deputy, Laîné, who was already leaning
towards a profitable royalism. The speech from the
throne which the Emperor drew up himself recognized
the seriousness of the situation and appealed to the
French to muster all their energies and stand together.
It expressed an ardent desire for peace, but declared
that the Empire could accept no peace that was not
honorable. Laîné was commissioned by the Chamber to

347

make its reply. He reported on the Frankfurt negotiations in what amounted to a general indictment of imperial policy. He went so far as to praise the Allies "for
trying to confine the French within the limits of their
territory and to repress an ambitious meddlesomeness
that for twenty years past had proved fatal to the peoples of Europe." He went on to condemn the excessive
taxation and "the still more cruel excesses of the system
that had been applied in raising recruits for the French
armies."

The Legislative Body voted the printing of the report
by a large majority. It would have been a courageous
act had it not been addressed to a man in dire distress.
Surprisingly, Napoleon did not arrest Laîné. He might
have claimed a right to do so at a moment when the
enemy cavalry were watering their horses in the Rhine.
He merely adjourned the assembly.

But on January 1, 1814, came a regular reception that
he gave to the office staffs of the Assemblies. He could
not control an impulse to hurl a terrific rebuke at his
critics:

"This is not the moment," he declared, "to demand
a change in the Constitution. You are not representatives of the nation—you are delegates from the departments. I alone represent the people. . . . What is
this throne here? Four boards of gilded wood covered
with velvet? No! This throne is a man, and the man is
I, with my will, my character and my renown! I am the
man who can save France, not you. Dirty linen is washed
at home, not in public! . . . You have tried to bespat-
ter me with mud. But know this: I am a man who is
killed but who is not insulted. . . . If I were to do as

you advise, I would give the enemy more than he asks for. . . . You will have peace in three months or I shall perish!"

He dismissed them, and they withdrew terrified.

Meantime he was passing his nights trying to squeeze from an inert country the men, the cannon and the muskets that would defend it from the foreigner. He threw into the crucible the private savings in gold that he had piled up during the prosperous years. He kept nothing for himself. He was thinking of France while those about him whom he had most favored were thinking only of themselves. He had a burst of his old vigor. Danger had suddenly made him young again. He had never been more alert of mind nor more hardworking. Never had he seemed to be more inspired by an all-absorbing genius. Standing alone against a Continent in arms he still looked so formidable that at times Metternich doubted whether the coalition had not better come to terms.

CHAPTER XXXIII

The Campaign in France

THE MAIN BODY OF THE ALLIES BEGAN TO CROSS THE Rhine on December 21, 1813. Bernadotte invaded Belgium and Blücher Lorraine. Schwarzenberg entered Switzerland by way of Basel, intending thence to turn northward through Burgundy and so cut off Italy from France. The Swiss Federation rescinded the Act of Mediation and declared a fatuous neutrality.

This hurried invasion completely upset Napoleon's calculations. He had figured that the attack would not come till spring, when he would have recovered most of the troops that were scattered about in Germany and Spain and made them the kernel of a new and sound army. So everything was failing him at once! Hastily he ordered the reserve camps to send their men to Paris, and to those forces he added such recruits from the class of 1815 as could be mobilized from the center and west —the little "Marie Louises," boys who were too young and not strong enough for war, but who were to fight with a courage that was to bring tears to the eyes of the old veterans.

Napoleon needed only a few weeks to set everything in order at the Tuileries and be free to assume personal direction of the campaign. He expected that those weeks would be provided by the energy and the resourcefulness of the lieutenants whom he had ordered to halt the Allies, or at least to delay them. Not one of them offered any resistance to the troops of the coalition. Macdonald, Marmont, Victor, retired everywhere without offering battle. More disheartened than their troops they could think of nothing except to retreat and then to retreat. Napoleon vainly concentrated the Old Guard at Langres under Mortier and the Young Guard at Épinal under Ney. They too fell back without firing a shot. Alsace, Lorraine, the Franche-Comté, part of the Champagne, were already lost, and within a month! It did no good for Napoleon to try to rally his armies with an announcement that he would go in person to Châlons-sur-Marne. After a brief halt near Saint-Dizier on January 24th, the marshals retired in virtual rout upon Vitry-le-François.

In that desperate situation Napoleon was the only one not to lose hope. In the diplomatic field he had begun to throw out ballast, partly with the idea of concentrating his forces, partly in order to convince his adversaries that he sincerely intended to give up all claims to preponderance in Europe. He recalled all troops from Spain and restored the Spanish crown to Ferdinand VII. Murat had returned to Naples after Leipzig. From Metternich he had had a promise that he would be left the crown of Naples "if nothing better turned up." The unhappy man had seen in that condition a hint that the crown of Italy would be the reward of his treason. Partly on the advice of Caroline he had made up his mind to accept the bargain, but in order to save his face with Napoleon, he told the latter that he would stand by him only at the price of the Italian crown. The Emperor may have been hurt by such a spectacle of ungrateful cowardice. He was not crushed by it. He considered Italy lost in any event and ordered Eugene to leave Milan and join him in France with all the troops that he could assemble. Finally, to remove one last obstacle, he decided to send the Pope home to Rome from Fontainebleau, where the pontiff was still in residence.

On January 23rd he presented his wife and son to the officers of the National Guard. "Gentlemen," he said, "our territory is invaded. I am about to depart to place myself at the head of my army. If the enemy approaches the capital, I entrust the Empress and the King of Rome to your courage. You will take care of them? You will defend them?"

He was acclaimed in answer as he had been in the best days of the Empire. His confidence revived. Forgetting all old scores and many betrayals, public or secret, he organized a regency for Marie Louise, with Joseph, Cambacérès and Talleyrand acting as her counselors.

Joseph had at last become reconciled, in view of the seriousness of the situation, to being nothing but a French prince. From Talleyrand Napoleon had everything to fear. The Prince of Benevento had been reassured by a note from Louis XVIII as to the position that he might expect to enjoy under the Bourbons. He was no longer opposing their return.

Napoleon spent his last hours in Paris with his wife, holding his son tightly clasped in his arms throughout the prolonged interview. He was never to see either of them again.

Marmont, Ney and the aged Kellermann hastened to

Châlons to meet the Emperor. They had supposed he was coming with an army. He arrived alone. Bringing the remnants of their troops all together he would have to meet Blücher and Schwarzenberg at a disadvantage of one to five. But fortunately the enemy command was divided—nothing was lost, therefore, the Emperor declared. He would so maneuver as to take the enemy armies one after the other. For that matter, reinforcements were coming up. A number of the Spanish divisions were at Bordeaux. Macdonald was coming down through the Ardennes. Augereau could move out from Lyons upon Besançon and embarrass the enemy's line of communications.

Once more the old fire gleamed in his eye and the marshals took heart. As for the soldiers the mere presence of the *Petit Tondu* made new men of them. Under him everything was possible. They now asked for nothing better than to fight.

Napoleon entered Saint-Dizier on the 27th. There he learned that Blücher was trying to effect a junction with Schwarzenberg. He had to prevent that. He marched on Blücher, surprised him at Brienne, January 29th, and in spite of his great inferiority in numbers, thrashed him soundly. The "Marie Louises" did wonders in this their first experience under fire. The Prussian general fell back upon La Rothière and Schwarzenberg hurried to his rescue. With Napoleon between them they thought they might encircle him, but he evaded the pincers and got away without too many losses (February 1).

At Troyes heart-breaking news reached him: Murat had gone over to the Allies!

"Murat!" cried Napoleon. "Murat, joining forces with

the Austrians! Why, with Eugene he might have gone to Vienna! Murat, firing on Frenchmen! The Bernadotte of the South!"

He sat silent for a long time, unutterably weary. Finally he murmured:

"Well, all this is going to end in a Bourbon!"

The rout in Paris was general and complete. Spineless, worthless, the Empress took fright. Joseph and the other two ministers sat inactive. Napoleon tried vainly to rouse them from their stupor by letters that were cool and even enthusiastic. Meantime he was undergoing a veritable bombardment from Berthier, Maret and Caulaincourt, who begged him to treat regardless of conditions.

He did not think that things had come to that pass yet, but he did write to Caulaincourt, who was then at Châtillon, where the Allied plenipotentiaries were in session, giving him new instructions and full powers. It was no question of the principles of Frankfurt now. Europe was demanding that Napoleon restore France to the frontiers of 1791, without having anything to say as to the disposition of the territories he was abandoning. Caulaincourt vainly tried to argue. He was told that the Emperor should answer "yes" or "no."

"Then it's no," Napoleon replied over the protests of his intimates. "Leave France smaller than I found her? Never!"

At that moment of anguish he wrote to Joseph, instructing him, in case the enemy should appear before Paris, to defend the capital to the last ditch after making sure that the Empress and the King of Rome were safe. A father's feeling was crying aloud in his heart.

"Astyanax as a prisoner among the Greeks always seemed to me the saddest figure in history. I would rather see my son murdered and thrown into the Seine than have him in the hands of the Austrians and taken to Vienna" (February 8, 1814).

A ray of light suddenly burst over the grim scene. Blücher and Schwarzenberg made a capital mistake which Napoleon had never dared to dream that they would make. Believing that they were strong enough each alone, they separated, Blücher marching on Paris by way of the Marne valley, Schwarzenberg continuing to harry Napoleon and following the Seine. His idea was to wear Napoleon down still more and then finally to turn and destroy him.

"This puts a new face on things," cried Napoleon, on learning of their decision. "I will beat Blücher tomorrow."

He hurried after him. Blücher was marching along the river with his men imprudently strung out so that his advance guard was at La Ferté-sous-Jouarre while he was still at Étoges with the bulk of his army. Napoleon attacked and destroyed one of his corps at Champaubert on the 10th. On the 11th he began again at Montmirail and on the 14th Blücher himself was beaten at Vauchamps. Hacked to pieces, all but destroyed, the Prussian army fled in rout towards Châlons. 18,000 prisoners, flags, guns! They were hurried to Paris and after weeks of intolerable depression the city thrilled with joy.

The Emperor now turned on Schwarzenberg. Schwarzenberg too, with his very heterogeneous army, was following the river in straggling formation. His advance guard, Platow's Cossacks, had already reached the forest of Fontainebleau. On the 17th Napoleon rallied the retreating forces of Victor and Oudinot, and, transporting the infantry in carts to make better time on the march, he fell upon the Russians at Mormant and cut them to pieces. The next day, still racing, he carried the plateau at Surville, defeated the Württembergers at Montereau, and forced Schwarzenberg to flee in rout across the Aube to Chaumont. Seven victories in eight days! Two of the Allied armies routed and in flight!

Schwarzenberg offered a truce. Dreaming again, Napoleon rejected the proposal. "I am nearer Vienna than the Emperor of Austria is to Paris," he said. And he wrote to Caulaincourt: "France must have her natural frontiers. You are always talking of Bourbons. I should rather see the Bourbons in France under reasonable conditions than submit to the infamous propositions that you keep sending me."

The aging Augereau had lost his courage and initiative as a general. He was not venturing out from Lyons for the drive at the Franche-Comté. The Emperor scolded and encouraged him:

"I have destroyed three armies and saved the capital three times! . . . Come, take the front line under fire! Things mustn't go on as they have been going these last days. We must put on our boots and do as we did in '93!"

He was in such high spirits that when Eugene reported an insignificant success over the Austrians at Roverbella he wrote back canceling the order recalling the Italian forces to France. Abandon Italy, dear Italy, in the moment of victory? In any event, Italy would be a good

356

argument to have in his pocket for the peace negotiations!

That impulsive decision deprived him of reinforcements that might have weighed decisively in the final reckoning which was soon to come.

Napoleon was assuming that the Allies had been shaken by the beatings he had been giving them and might therefore be in a more reasonable frame of mind. He was not mistaken. The coalition was, in fact, traversing a crisis. The invasion with all the horrors and crimes of violence incidental to such things had roused the French peasants against the foreign hordes. "I am in command of a gang of convicts," General Yorck, a Prussian, himself confessed. His "convicts" were cutting down orchards, tearing up vineyards, robbing and burning houses and maltreating non-combatants. Reacting, the peasants had gathered up scythes, pitchforks, old guns, and started a war of their own along Spanish lines, giving and asking no quarter, slaughtering isolated bands of soldiers, killing scouts and sentinels, attacking supply trains. The Allies were losing hundreds of men in this way and the sovereigns were growing uneasy. So the French really wanted Napoleon! There might be a general uprising in his favor!

From that moment the English and the Austrians were inclined to come to terms. Only the Russians and the Prussians held out for a fight to the finish. Napoleon had given up all pretensions to a peace in accord with the principles of Frankfurt, but he still clung to the Rhine frontier. He sent Flahaut to the enemy outposts at Lusigny to make a proposition. Flahaut failed.

On February 23rd the Allies held a grand council of

all the leading generals at Bar-sur-Aube. After some heated exchanges Alexander, still firm in his hatred, managed to secure accord among his associates. Castlereagh, the English prime minister, made the harmony more harmonious still some days later at Chaumont. There he proposed a twenty year alliance, under the terms of which England, Austria, Russia and Prussia each engaged to keep contingents of 150,000 men in the field till the war should have ended by mutual consent. Great Britain would pay an annual subsidy of 6,000,000 pounds sterling. This formula won unanimous adhesion and it was signed on March 1st.

The Treaty of Chaumont made the European entente against France permanent. It was later on to serve as the basis for the Holy Alliance. Caulaincourt was at once informed that Napoleon's proposals could not be considered and that if he desired to treat he could hope to do so on no better terms than the ones that had been handed to his representative at Châtillon.

Blücher managed to scrape a small army together and proceeded to advance on Paris, thinking to take the capital, a virtually unfortified city, and make an entry in advance of the other Allies, which would square many unsettled accounts that he held with the French. Napoleon followed in pursuit. About to be caught between Marmont and Mortier on the Aisne, and Napoleon, who was almost at the Marne, the Prussian turned and retreated (March 2). Had Soissons held he would have been captured. General Moreau, an incompetent, surrendered the city. Blücher was therefore enabled to cross the Aisne.

Reinforced by the corps of Bülow and Wintzingerode

he dug in solidly on the Craonne plateau. Napoleon, on his heels, forced a passage of the Aisne at Berry-au-bac and at ten in the morning on the 7th of March, at a disadvantage of two men to one, began the greatest battle of the campaign. On the left Ney attacked Sacken's Prussians, who were posted on the Heurtebise farm. On the right, Victor attacked Woronzov's Russian infantry, which was occupying the park of the Abbey at Vauclerc. It was a bitter fight. Ney had all but won when his raw recruits suddenly wavered and he hardly managed to rally them. Victor, however, carried the Russian position. Napoleon then sent in the Old Guard at the center. Eighty guns opened on the Russians. Ney resumed the offensive and the enemy infantry recoiled. In a furious charge the French cavalry routed the Russian horse. By nightfall Blücher had lost the heights of Craonne. However, his army, though badly shattered, had not been destroyed. He was able to reorganize and make Laon, a formidable fortress overlooking thirty miles of open plain.

Napoleon tried to storm the place on the 9th. Blücher offered furious resistance. The Semilly and Ardon quarters were taken and retaken. Laon was about to be surrounded by the Young Guard under Charpentier when Marmont, who was supporting the movement, allowed himself to be surprised during the night at Athies, where he was routed by the Russian cavalry. On the 10th Napoleon again attacked, but in spite of prodigies of valor on the part of his men the fortress held. That evening he retired upon Soissons.

He gave only one day's rest to his troops, who sorely needed it, then on the 13th marched upon Rheims and destroyed a Russo-Prussian force commanded by a French émigré, Saint Priest. Rheims lighted up as he entered. However, Oudinot and Macdonald, whom he had left to cover Paris from Schwarzenberg, had been driven back along the Seine between Nogent and Montereau, and the Austrians recaptured Troyes. So, after all his efforts, after an incredible manifestation of will power and genius, Napoleon's situation between the two Allied armies was worse than ever before.

If he had not had to worry about Paris, to protect the place and keep it going! Unfortunately Paris was there! The Empress-Regent was a foreigner and a child. Around her every fear had free play, every intrigue a clear field for maneuvering. In their utter prostration Joseph, Cambacérès and the ministers were unable to execute the simplest order from the Emperor. "I am not being obeyed," wrote Napoleon. "I hear only but's, if's and because's. . . . I have never been so badly served." He was thinking of Talleyrand and ordered him watched.

It was too late. Talleyrand had become too powerful. Caulaincourt had kept him posted on every transaction with the Allies. He held the Senate and the ministries through the friends he had in those bodies. He was one of three in the Council of Regency. He hated Napoleon. In Napoleon's fall he saw his own way to power and, though keeping his tracks well covered, he did what he could to hasten it.

Convinced that Napoleon would sooner or later be forced to abdicate Talleyrand seems first to have worked for a proclamation of the King of Rome as Emperor. In the child's name, and with only Marie Louise to deal with, he could be master. But agents of the Bourbons finally reached him with so much adulation and such rosy promises that he finally turned to a restoration of the old monarchy. On March 10th Baron Vitrolles, a bustling messenger of the Count of Artois, appeared at Allied headquarters at Chaumont. He was the bearer of a note addressed to the Russian minister Nesselrode. The note was in Talleyrand's hand, but not signed by him. It read:

"You are walking on crutches. Use your legs and try to do a thing you can do."

It was a bald demand that the Allies should hasten to Paris. Vitrolles claimed that they would be welcomed enthusiastically by the population, which was openly favoring the Bourbons. The effect on the Allies was electric. So then, they could count on powerful support in the capital, since Talleyrand was leading it! Making no embarrassing promises on the matter of changing dynasties they sent Vitrolles away with words of encouragement. Since Napoleon refused to accept the Châtillon proposals, negotiations were broken off entirely on March 17th.

The Emperor was not disconcerted on that account. It was better to have done with such trafficking, he thought, since the imperial Council in Paris was in such a panic that it would accept any terms no matter how disgraceful. Rather than cling to a throne that had lost its glory he preferred to fall as a soldier. He had settled on a plan which, if successful, would reverse the situation and place the Allies in a bad fix. He figured that Paris could hold out for at least a week, seeing that Marmont and Mortier were blocking the road down the Aisne. He would therefore give up trying to defend the capital and by an unexpected maneuver double on his tracks, make Bar-le-Duc, assemble there the garrisons he had recalled from all the forts between Mainz and Antwerp, cut off the communications of the enemy, fall upon his rear with a large army and crush him just when he thought he had won the victory.

As a first step he thought he ought to worry Schwarzenberg a little and entice him to the southeast, so freeing the approaches to the capital to that extent. Marching upon Arcis-sur-Aube he stumbled into the whole Austrian army. It would doubtless have been the part of prudence to retire and avoid battle, but Schwarzenberg attacked. Fighting 20,000 men to 90,000, Napoleon held the Russians off with great difficulty, Ney, Friant and Sebastiani displaying magnificent bravery and initiative. Napoleon himself rode recklessly about the field as though trying, as some thought, to get himself killed (March 10, 1814).

Arcis-sur-Aube was to be the last battle of the Campaign in France. The next day, considering the odds too unequal, the Emperor crossed the Aube, putting the river between him and Schwarzenberg. Then he marched away for Saint-Dizier—the first move in his diversion towards the east. He seemed to be full of confidence and enthusiasm. He said to Caulaincourt, on the latter's return from the conference that had closed at Châtillon:

"Look at these peasants! They are rising and killing the Cossacks on all hands. They were setting us an example. Let us follow it. You are going to see great things. I shall soon have a hundred thousand men in hand. I'll fall upon the nearest—Blücher or Schwarzenberg as it may be. I'll beat him, then the peasants of Burgundy will finish him off. . . . If I'm mistaken—well, we can die, that's all; but we shall have saved our honor."

Schwarzenberg was for following Napoleon according to the rules of warfare. Blücher was obstinately bent on taking Paris. While the leading generals of the coalition were hesitating they were handed a letter from Napoleon to Marie Louise which had been intercepted. It outlined the maneuver that he at present had in mind. A few moments later another intercepted letter was brought in. It was from Savary to Napoleon, urging him to hurry to Paris, where the unrest had increased on news that the English were in Bordeaux. The letters seemed to have no great effect on Schwarzenberg but the Czar caught fire. Napoleon had given them the chance they were looking for! They should take it and drive at once on Paris! There the Emperor's opponents would open the door!

A brief conference was held on the forenoon of March 14th, the Czar, the King of Prussia, Schwarzenberg and Blücher meeting on a little knoll in the open fields in the neighborhood of Sommepuis. An agreement was soon reached—they would make for Paris.

The drive began the next morning, though a screen of cavalry was sent to Saint-Dizier to follow Napoleon and mislead him. Mortier and Marmont had been holding the Aisne. They had disobeyed the Emperor, however, and were now trying to join him, having imprudently advanced as far as Vitry-le-François. The Allied army encountered them at La Fère-Champenoise and drove them back (March 25). Instead of rushing to Paris, which they now knew to be threatened, the two marshals made a detour by way of Provins. They were to arrive before the capital when the enemy was already there.

CHAPTER XXXIV

Fontainebleau

On the 28th the armies of the coalition appeared in three columns before the city of Paris and deployed in a long arc that reached from Charonne to Clichy. There were no fortifications to stop them—at the most, a few earthworks and stockades. Clarke, the Minister of War, had made no preparations for defense. Nevertheless, from its very situation, Paris could have held out for some time. The hills that surrounded Paris to the northeast offered excellent positions. With the National Guard and the corps of Mortier and Marmont, badly shattered as they were, the first assaults could have been held off till the Emperor returned. All that was needed was heart.

But heart was what the government did not have. The masses were patriotic and actual sight of the enemy now aroused them. Vainly they appealed for arms. Joseph, head of the government through his brother's mental aberration, called a meeting of the Council of Regency to decide on what should be done. Clarke demanded the immediate departure of the Empress and the King of Rome. Those who stood loyal to Napoleon, Boulay de la Meurthe, Champagny, Régnier, Savary, protested aloud. If Marie Louise and her son left Paris the Empire was done for. The Empress, they said, should repair to the Hôtel de Ville and appeal to the people, who would rise as one man to defend her. Talleyrand himself—and against the policy that he was secretly favoring—agreed with that opinion. The Council adopted it.

But at that point Joseph read a letter which Napoleon had written him on the 18th of March, confirming his despatch of February 8th: "If the enemy should advance on Paris in such force as to make resistance impossible, send the Regent, my son, the grand dignitaries and the treasure away from Paris in the direction of the Loire."

Resistance was possible, for some days at least. Besides, circumstances had greatly changed since the Emperor issued the order. Disobedience to the Emperor was now necessary in his own interest. But Joseph and Cambacérès did not have the strength of character required for that. At bottom nothing suited them better than flight. The Council, with terror on their faces, bowed. Departure was decided on.

In leaving the Tuileries Talleyrand said to Savary ironically:

"So this is the end! Well—it was fine play for big stakes! What a fall into history! Anyhow—we'll see what is to come of it."

He knew perfectly well what was to come of it, and for that matter nobody around him doubted either.

The next morning Marie Louise, submissive, went down the steps of the Tuileries. Only the little king protested.

"I don't want to leave my house!" he cried. "I don't want to go away!"

He was picked up and carried.

Ten large wagons, followed by the Coronation Coach which had been filled with harnesses and saddles, went out along the road to Rambouillet. Joseph stayed the rest of the day in Paris, incompetent, useless, in the way.

Cannon were booming along the northeast front of the city. Marmont and Mortier had taken charge of the defense. The former held a toe-hold on the Roumainville plateau. The second took up a position on the plain of Saint-Denis. There they withstood a series of violent assaults. At Vincennes the students in the military institute turned plain cannoneers and fought so stubbornly that they had to be dragged from their guns when Schwarzenberg, towards the end of the day, finally turned Marmont's flank and forced him to run for the city. With his right uncovered Mortier then saw himself obliged to abandon Montmartre, where he had put up a heroic fight. At the Clichy barrier Moncey fought like a lion with a mere handful of the National Guard.

Impatient to get away Joseph had given a free hand to the marshals to open negotiations with the Allied command. Marmont was the first to act. He sent a request for a truce to Schwarzenberg. Nothing but Napoleon's arrival could save Paris. The public was waiting for him, calling for him.

And at last he was coming! Learning on the 27th of the rush of the Allies upon Paris, he abandoned the diversion to the east and, by terrible forced marches, made for the Seine with his army. Since that was slow progress at best he finally left the troops and galloped off, alone save for Berthier and Caulaincourt, towards Troyes. He arrived there on the 29th. On the 30th he was at Sens. Changing from horse to stagecoach or plain wagon—anything that he could find—he ate up the road to Paris. If the city could hold on till the 31st, he sent word to Marmont, the enemy would be caught between two fires and forced the retreat.

But Marmont had been won by Talleyrand. He hurried on from his request for a truce to an offer of capitulation, which the Czar insisted on in exchange for a pledge that Paris would be respected. Marmont signed the surrender during the night of the 30th. The French troops were to retire without molestation and the Allies would enter the city the following morning.

At eleven o'clock that night the Emperor leapt from a miserable wagon at a stagecoach relay called "The Court of France." It was near Juvisy. He saw some horsemen approaching.

"Halt!" he shouted.

The commander of the company drew rein and dismounted. It was General Belliard. He had come from Paris.

Napoleon seized him by an arm and in a voice that was sharp, hoarse, panting, asked:

"Where is the army?"

"Sire, it is following me."

"Where is the enemy?"

"At the gates of Paris."

"Who is holding Paris?"

"Nobody. Paris has been evacuated."

"Evacuated! And my wife, my son, my government— where are they?"

"On the Loire, Sire, following your orders. Marmont and Mortier fought like brave men. The soldiers were wonderful. If we had had a reserve of ten thousand men, or if you had been there, we would have driven them into the Seine."

"What I might have expected!" cried Napoleon beside himself. "Joseph lost me Spain. Now he loses me France! And that jackass of a Clarke! That's what one gets for using men who have neither common sense nor character! When I am not around they do nothing but stupidities! What cowards! They capitulate! . . . Well, we've got to undo the harm that has been done! . . . Caulaincourt—my carriage! Let's get along to Paris!"

Dissuading him Belliard explained that the army had left the city, that the enemy must already be holding the gates. The Emperor did not listen.

Just then Curial came up, leading a corps of infantry. He too asserted that it was too late.

Completely crushed, Napoleon sat down on the roadside and remained there for some moments, his head in his hands. Finally he rose, staggering. All the fatigue of those sleepless days and nights had fallen on him at once. He was overwhelmed.

He went into the posthouse and thoughtfully considered his maps in the light of two candles. The others stood around in anguished silence.

"If I had the army . . ." he murmured. "But it will take three or four days for that!"

Suddenly an idea came to him:

"Caulaincourt—I've got them! But we need to gain time."

He ordered him to go to Paris, see the Czar and pretend to accept the Châtillon program. Caulaincourt could argue—then Napoleon would come up with the troops and surprise the Allies.

Caulaincourt went off towards Paris but with no great enthusiasm. At four o'clock the Emperor received a courier from him, reporting that the capitulation was permanent and that the Allies were making ready for their formal entry.

Napoleon shrugged his shoulders and, resigned at last, took the road towards Fontainebleau.

Caulaincourt had some difficulty in reaching the Czar, who was quartered in the château at Bondy. The Allies, Alexander informed him, did not care to hear another word from Napoleon. Caulaincourt insisted. Finally he was shown the door.

The foreign armies entered Paris on the 31st, at noon, the Czar, the King of Prussia, Schwarzenberg, riding at their head down the boulevards. Some young dandies from the faubourg Saint-Germain, a few ladies wearing white cockades, welcomed them with cries of "Long live the Bourbons! Long live the King!"

Alexander reassured the population by his gracious manners and his attitude of condescending friendliness. The Royalists smothered him with flatteries. Some of them, which were too base, disgusted him:

"Your coming, Sire, has long been awaited and hoped for here."

"For my part I would have come sooner. Blame not me but the bravery of the French troops."

It was suggested that the name of the Austerlitz Bridge be changed.

"No," he answered, with a moderation that had its

touch of insolence. "It's enough that I have ridden over it with my army."

Talleyrand had placed his residence at the Czar's disposal. That brought him closer to the leader of Europe and enabled him to work upon him with his masterly suggestiveness. By then the sometime Bishop of Autun had made up his mind and he stated his views in a first conversation.

Napoleon had been beaten and could not keep the throne. His son could not replace him either—the father's shadow would always hang over him. A republic had to be avoided at all costs. To what limits would it not go? There was only one solution that would be honorable alike to Europe and to France—the return of the Bourbons. The country had forgotten them but they represented a tradition. They were legitimacy in person. Limited by a wise constitution, reconciled with the army, they alone would be capable of setting up a satisfactory and stable social order within a reasonable time.

"The republic," he concluded, "is an impossibility. The Regency and Bernadotte are just intrigues. The Bourbons alone are a principle."

Alexander had not been very favorably inclined to the Bourbon princes. Talleyrand won him over. On the 31st the Allies published a notice which declared that they "would not treat with Napoleon or with any member of the Bonaparte family." The Senate was invited to form a provisional government.

The Senate had been made up of men who were under obligations to Napoleon, men whom he had stuffed with honors and money. Now they stood quite ready to depose him. Always on their faces before someone! It mattered little who it might be! They could think only of their salaries, their titles, their positions. They rushed from one yoke to another. Their submissiveness marked new limits as regarded the extent to which human baseness could go.

On the 1st of April, under Talleyrand's presidency, the Senate named a temporary government made up, first of all, of Talleyrand himself and his friend and accomplice, Dalberg; then of Jaucourt, the Abbé de Montesquiou and General Beurnonville. Ministers were appointed—Dupont, the man who surrendered at Baylén, was placed in charge of the Department of War!

On that same day Caulaincourt made one last effort to see the Czar. What he saw was a block of ice and a few hours later he was ordered to quit Paris.

By the following forenoon, the 2nd, the Senate had screwed up its courage to take the supreme step—to vote the deposition of the Emperor on the alleged ground that "he had violated his oath and encroached upon the rights of the people by raising troops and levying taxes contrarily to the Constitution."

Napoleon was at Fontainebleau. He took the news of these doings calmly. He was thinking of marching on Paris with the troops of Marmont and Mortier and his own army, which was marching up from Troyes.

His marshals had fallen back to Corbeil. They protested. Their one thought was peace. The soldiers, for their part, were eager to fight on—they would go anywhere the Little Corporal chose to lead them. On April 4th he reviewed the Guard and was wildly cheered. But afterwards Ney, Oudinot, Moncey, Lefebvre and Macdonald forced their way into his room. The Emperor

read revolt in their set jaws and glowering faces. He tried
to win them back:

"Look at those brave soldiers! They have no titles or
lands to save. They are thinking only of marching and
dying to rescue France from the hands of the foreigner.
We must follow them. A good strong attack on Paris
and the Allies are done for! What do we need for that?
Just one last effort!"

They turned away, refusing to listen. They insisted
on his abdication.

Ney was the first to demand it, and with a violence
which he made no pretense of controlling:

"It is time to have done with this. You must make
your political testament and abdicate in favor of the
King of Rome."

Napoleon did not lose his temper. He argued:

"My wife? My son? They wouldn't last an hour. You
would get anarchy and, within a fortnight, the Bourbons."

They made no answer but hate was written on their
faces. Napoleon turned to Macdonald. The marshal declared that the idea of a battle in Paris over the bodies
of Frenchmen horrified him. Besides—would the soldiers
obey?

"They might not obey you," Napoleon returned.
"They would me."

"The army will not follow you," Ney commented
harshly. "It will follow its generals."

The Emperor's eyes flashed his indignation. An explosion was imminent.

But then suddenly a great weariness, a boundless dis-

MARIE-LOUISE AND THE KING OF ROME

From the Portrait by Isabey

gust, seemed to come over him. He dismissed the marshals with a nod:

"If you please, gentlemen. I will inform you of anything that I may decide on."

He was left alone with Berthier, Maret, Caulaincourt. A few bitter words escaped him:

"The fools! They don't see that the safety of France, their own safety, lies in me. . . . To me it makes little difference. I am a soldier. I can live without an empire."

He went to a table and began to write—his abdication! It was a conditional abdication in favor of his son. Caulaincourt would deliver it to the Allies. But the Emperor still hoped to take the field again and settle everything with the sword. He called in the marshals and read the document to them in a steady, unaccented voice:

"Whereas the Allied powers have signified that the Emperor Napoleon is the only obstacle to peace in Europe, the Emperor Napoleon, in accord with his oath, hereby declares that he is ready to step down from the throne and to leave France, as well as his life, for the welfare of his country which he regards as inseparable from the rights of his son, the Regency of the Empress and the maintenance of the laws of the Empire."

Happy to be rid of him at last the marshals seized his hands and pressed them with an emotion which may have been sincere but which at any rate was selfish.

"Sire," exclaimed Moncey, "you are saving France."

Napoleon commissioned Caulaincourt, Macdonald and Marmont to deliver his abdication to the Allied sovereigns.

"And yet," he added, "and yet—we could whip them if we wanted to!"

The marshals were terribly worried lest he might fly to action again. They therefore pointed out to Berthier that "the reign of the Emperor being at an end, they alone represented the army," and that "the army was to receive its orders from them alone."

Berthier made no answer. At bottom he was with them. But Lefebvre, the real boor among them all, went so far as to say:

"Does he imagine that with all the titles, properties and lands we have we are going to get ourselves killed for his sake? That too is his fault. He took the knapsacks off our backs too soon."

The baseness of his comrades in danger and glory seemed to make the cowardice of the Senate a paltry matter indeed.

"They have no hearts, no feelings," said Napoleon sadly. "I have been defeated less by fortune than by the selfishness and ingratitude of my brothers in arms."

The most beloved of them all, the friend of his youth, the one he had buried in bounties, was Marmont.

Marmont was in charge of the troops which had evacuated Paris and were now on the Essonne. But he had already signed with Schwarzenberg a secret agreement whereby he guaranteed to march his men to Normandy. At the promptings of Talleyrand and Talleyrand's emissaries that weak and conceited soldier had come to think that such treason would win him the good will of the powers that were to be. But in thus stripping the Emperor of a third of the soldiers on whom he could still count, and not only that, of the confidence of the army, he made any recovery on Napoleon's part impossible. Worse, still, he destroyed the claims of the King of Rome.

Alexander, in fact, was deeply stirred by the address of Napoleon's emissaries and for a moment was inclined to consider the Regency again. But the news that Marmont's corps had gone over to the Allies at the command of subordinate officers changed his frame of mind. It had been assumed that the army was solidly Napoleon's. Since that was not the case and the Allies had no reason to be concerned about any danger of a forlorn hope, why bother with the Bonapartes? Napoleon should therefore make the best of the situation and abdicate unconditionally. On that basis he could expect generous consideration for himself.

His envoys returned with the message. A complete sacrifice was demanded of him. He did not give in at once. He was carefully weighing the chances of an heroic dash. But Marmont's treachery had cut him deeply. Such determination as he still had left was gasping for survival.

"And I treated him like a child of mine!" he said to Caulaincourt on the night of the 5th-6th of April. "I was counting on him! And ambition undid him! The wretch does not realize what is in store for him. His name will be blasted forever! Believe me—I am not thinking of myself now. My career is over."

At the moment he was beyond and above events. He was looking at himself in the perspective of history. As regarded his personal fortunes he asked for nothing:

"A veteran's pension—that will do for me! A soldier doesn't need any great amount of room to die in!"

He did ask for decent provision for his wife and child and means of subsistence for his brothers and sisters. But his chief thought was of France and the army. He begged

Caulaincourt to talk with the Czar and persuade him to get better frontiers for France, to keep the tricolor. . . . Caulaincourt somehow managed to undeceive him. All they cared to have from Napoleon was his final and unconditional abdication.

He sat down and wrote out the document, carefully weighing words. He renounced "for himself and his heirs the thrones of France and Italy, because there was no personal sacrifice, not even the sacrifice of his life, that he was not ready to make in the interest of France."

On the morning of the 6th he sent for the marshals and said to them contemptuously:

"Neither you nor the army will have any more blood to shed. Resign yourselves to living under the Bourbons and serve them faithfully. You wanted a rest. You have it now—enjoy it! But the peace you long for will kill more of you on your soft beds than war would have killed around our campfires."

The Austrians and the Prussians stood out for severe treatment of the Bonapartes. Their disgraceful attempts to exploit the situation to their own advantage were ended at last only by the prestige of the Czar. On the 11th of April Caulaincourt obtained signatures to the so-called Treaty of Fontainebleau, which determined the futures of Napoleon and his relatives.

He himself was to keep the title of Emperor and have sovereignty over the island of Elba with an annual income of 2,000,000 francs. His brothers and sisters would divide an equal amount. Marie Louise and her son would receive the duchies of Parma and Piacenza.

The Emperor was virtually alone at Fontainebleau. His ministers and marshals were engaged in one mad rush for the positions they hoped to occupy under the Bourbons. Cambacérès as well as Savary had forgotten that there was such a man as Napoleon. Berthier had been his right-hand man for years. He went coolly over to Louis XVIII.

In Paris the long-cherished hatred of the Royalists broke out in atrocious quips and placards. It was one general inundation of insults and curses upon the ex-Emperor's name and person. Chateaubriand's famous pamphlet on "Bonaparte and the Bourbons" was far from being the most virulent, but it credited him with not a few vices and crimes. So his unparalleled greatness and glory met their reward in those few days in a verbal lynching party.

No great effort was made to keep such things from Napoleon's knowledge. He sent word to the Empress and his son to come to him. They were sent to Rambouillet where they would be under the direct control of the Allies. Napoleon knew that Marie Louise was a weak soul and that Austria would soon be laying her clutches upon her. He would not see her again, or the boy either! He was at the mercy of his conquerors! They were bent on humiliating him, insulting him, perhaps murdering him. Disgust with humanity overflowed his heart.

"Life is unendurable to me!" he kept repeating to Caulaincourt.

During the retreat from Russia he had procured through Yvan a little bag filled with opium powder. On the night of the 12th-13th, he took out the bag, poured the contents into a glass of water, drank the potion and went to bed, having given Caulaincourt final instructions. But the drug must have deteriorated. At any rate

377

it failed to do more than nauseate him. He was seized with stomach convulsions, got to a window and threw the poison up. He was cared for; he was saved.

"Alas!" he murmured. "Everything has failed me— even death! So I have to live! Why did I not fall at Arcis-sur-Aube?"

And yet, the next morning, he was himself again. His extraordinary vitality had regained the upper hand.

"Who knows what the future is to say?" he exclaimed. "I may see my wife and child again. . . . I will write my story!"

That was characteristic of him. The man of action was born again with each rising sun. In the face of the worst disasters he would dream new dreams. Already he was planning his trip to Elba.

On April 12th the Comte d'Artois, as Lieutenant-general of the Bourbons, took up residence in the Tuileries after listening to a *Te Deum* in Notre Dame. He was welcomed trustfully by the people of Paris. The army generals, with Ney in the lead, crowded round him solicitously.

Meantime the palace at Fontainebleau grew lonelier and lonelier. Macdonald was the only one of the marshals to come and bid Napoleon good-by. The Emperor embraced him and gave him as a remembrance Mourad-bey's sword, which he had taken at Aboukir. Napoleon's valet, Constant, and Roustan, his mameluke, filled their pockets with such valuables as they could find and took to their heels. Drouot, Bertrand, Caulaincourt and Maret still stood by, spending a painful week with the unhappy hero.

The arrival of the Allied commissioners who had been

designated to escort him to Elba was momentarily expected. He therefore hurried his preparations. On the morning of the 20th everything was ready. He ordered the Old Guard to be drawn up in the White Horse Courtyard that he might bid the men farewell. Addressing them he began:

"Soldiers: For twenty years I have never failed to find you with me on the road of honor and glory. You have always deported yourselves bravely and faithfully. Once more during these last days you have given me proofs of your devotion. Our cause was never lost with you. I could have kept on fighting a civil war for three years more, but France would have been only the loser by it. The Allied powers appeared with all Europe leagued against me. Part of the army betrayed me. Factions formed for another government. I have sacrificed all my interests to the good of the country. I am going away. You will serve on with glory and with honor. You will be loyal to your new sovereign. Receive my thanks. I cannot embrace you all. I am going to embrace your leader—and I am going to embrace our flag."

Staggering, haggard, his eyes red with tears, General Petit stepped towards him. Napoleon pressed him to his heart with the flag hanging down between their bodies. Then he kissed the faded silk banner itself with its many bullet holes, and the golden eagle on the tip of the staff. That eagle had been present at all his victories.

The great court shook with suppressed sobs. He straightened up, his eyes unseeing. Then he said a few more words in a voice that was no longer master of itself:

"May this kiss of mine make its way into your hearts.

I shall always follow your futures and the future of France. Do not mourn my fate. I have decided to live in hopes of again being of service to your glory. I shall write of the great things that we have done together. The happiness of this dear country of ours was always my one thought. It will always be. Good-by, comrades!"

He walked away between two lines of soldiers looking neither to right nor left. Then he climbed into a carriage with General Bertrand.

CHAPTER XXXV

Return from Elba

THE JOURNEY LASTED A WEEK. DOWN AS FAR AS THE Bourbonnais Napoleon was greeted everywhere with ovations. He took them quietly. Beyond Moulins cheers for the king began to be heard.

At Avignon he met Augereau, who had disobeyed him, who hated him, and who had just issued a proclamation in which he denounced "the ambition of a man who had sacrificed millions of victims and then had not managed to die like a soldier." Napoleon did not know that. He ran to greet his old comrade and took him in his arms.

In the deep south Royalist mobs were forming and they rioted around his line of carriages with cries of "Death to the tyrant!" At Orgon the crowd was so hostile and so unruly that, for a supreme humiliation, Napoleon had to assume a disguise and put on the hat and cloak of an Austrian commissioner. He was so stirred at these manifestations of hatred that he could not restrain his tears. The *Undaunted* was waiting at Saint-Raphaël. He reached that port on April 28th and went courageously aboard. Six days later he was at Porto Ferraio, his new capital. He debarked immediately upon his little isle, which seemed henceforth destined to imprison the life, the memories, the last dreams of a man who two years earlier had made himself the Emperor of the West.

Talleyrand, in Paris, was certain that he was to be the guardian and mentor of the restored monarchy. At his suggestion and under his control the Senate invited "Louis-Stanislas-Xavier, brother of the late King" to the throne. But it gave him power subject to his acceptance of a constitution which it had cooked up on short notice. To those men, who had lived through the Revolution and the Empire, a constitution seemed essential as guaranteeing their honors, their jobs, their pensions. Louis XVIII was at the time at Hartwell in England. He was in no hurry to return to the country that he had abandoned twenty-three years before. However, an exile so long had had but little effect on his pride as a legitimate prince. The conditions laid down by the Senate irritated him. He sent his brother, the Comte d'Artois, ahead to prepare the ground for his home-coming.

The Comte d'Artois was a light, likeable, narrow-minded individual, one of the men who had witnessed a titanic world convulsion "without learning anything or forgetting anything." He was welcomed with sincere cordiality by Paris and the large towns. They were weary of war and thought of the words "Restoration" and "peace" as synonymous. The Count moved into the Tuileries and began promising everything to everybody without knowing just what would come of so many pledges in the end. Suddenly freed from the strong government of the Empire the country was in disorder, and the royal commissioners who were scouring it hither and thither were adding to the confusion.

The problem of dealing with the military situation fell to Talleyrand, indolent as usual and now far less concerned with defending the interests of the country than with winning the favor of the Allied sovereigns for his own person. On April 23rd, with one stroke of his pen, he surrendered the fifty-three fortresses that France still held beyond her frontiers, without stipulating any compensatory advantage, as for instance a guarantee that French territory would be evacuated. That was a great mistake. To commit it Talleyrand must have been very generously paid. The Comte d'Artois ratified everything with a smile on his face.

On that same day Marie Louise set out from Rambouillet for Vienna, taking her little son with her. At the Austrian capital she was to proceed at once to forget all about Napoleon.

Louis XVIII debarked on the 24th at Calais. Overfat, limping with gout, half an invalid, he was a great disappointment to a public that had grown accustomed long since to a galloping military emperor. All the same he was not without qualities. Like many fat men he had a discerning and unprejudiced intelligence. He had a perfect sense of his dignity and a will to see that his hereditary rights were respected. A descendant of St. Louis he regarded himself as the most important sovereign in the world. However, he was too skeptical to take life very seriously and that attitude led him into moments of apparent weakness. He was always more ready to draw up a letter packed with aptly placed Latin quotations than to read the dull reports which were sent him to keep him posted on the state of affairs in France—

quite a different country, after all, from the one he had left in '89.

He was received at Compiègne by a group of self-conscious, over-awed marshals. There also Talleyrand gracefully bade him welcome. He thought himself enough the master from the very first moment to disregard the Czar's urgent recommendations of caution and brushed disdainfully aside the constitution which the Senate had worked out for him. He replaced it with a "Declaration," dated from Saint-Ouen, in which he promised to "grant a Charter to his people." As ministers he selected Talleyrand and a few mediocrities, an exception among them being Baron Louis, who was to prove a skillful financier. The King did "not want any chaperon." The most important matter in his eyes, as in Talleyrand's, was peace and in a hurry. A treaty was therefore rushed through in Paris on May 30th.

France returned to her frontiers of 1791, plus Philippeville, Marienburg and a section each of Savoy and Nice. On the other hand she gave up the Île de France (Île Maurice, Madagascar) and left it to the Allies to dispose as they saw fit of the vast territories that had been made available by the collapse of the Empire. Talleyrand had the brazenness to declare the Treaty of Paris "a good treaty and a noble one." It was a disastrous treaty, and it proceeded directly from the equally disastrous agreement that Talleyrand had made on April 23rd.

The King had his Charter ready by June 4th and on that day he read it to a joint session of a Chamber of Peers largely made up of Napoleon's senators, reinforced by a bake of appointees from among "the great lords of old" and a Legislative Body which was preserved intact in view of the scant hope of obtaining a more cowardly one through any popular election. The charter, a free gift of the sovereign, established a parliamentary system more or less along English lines. Existing institutions were in substance consolidated and the old purchases of confiscated lands declared irrevocable. In spite of its many omissions and reticences the Charter was quite well received by the public.

Napoleon's old officials went over to the new régime almost to the last man. The Jacobins were allowed to hope that bygones would be bygones. The business classes exulted in the persuasion that this time their day had really come. The nobility and the clergy, on the other hand, were less satisfied. They wanted a complete return to the social life of the old régime. The army was more or less openly hostile. The peasants said nothing. They were uneasy, mistrustful.

The court at the Tuileries now filled and overfilled with gold braid that had either never been on a battle-field or had fought against France. Generals of the Empire were sent home on half pay and in many cases were watched by the police. General Dupont, the "capitulator of Baylén," was named Minister of War as an open challenge to the recent past. He cleaned out the army as best suited his grudges and without regard to services rendered or rights acquired. The government governed from day to day, catch-as-catch-can. Tactless debates took place in the Chamber as to the future of confiscated properties. The people in the country flared with anger. Little by little opinion soured all over France.

Talleyrand was the monarchy's choice to represent

France at the Congress of Vienna, which was grimly resolved to put a new Europe together patch by patch.
His first tactic was to break up the harmony that pre-
vailed among the Allies. As regarded France he displayed
a perfect, not to say excessive, disinterestedness; but he
lost no chance to assert a principle that was dear to the
heart of Louis XVIII—"legitimacy." According to that
theory the territories that had so often changed hands in
the course of the previous quarter century should go
back to the sovereigns who had held them before the
Revolution.

Unfortunately Czar Alexander thought that he had
become king of kings in virtue of his victory over Napoleon and set out to force his views upon the Congress.
As against the principle of legitimacy," the needs of
Europe are the basis of right," he declared. Prussia was
inclined to join him and Talleyrand, therefore, snuggled
closer to Austria and England. At the vast, luxurious,
chaotic Congress an extraordinary thing happened. Talleyrand, the representative of the defeated power, gradually acquired an influence and an importance that no one
could have foreseen. Prussia wanted Saxony. Russia
wanted Poland. Talleyrand objected, passed the warning
to Metternich and Castlereagh and signed a secret treaty
of alliance with them (January 3, 1815). The Czar and
Prussia yielded. Russia rested content with half of Poland, Prussia with half of Saxony. Prussia in compensation received the Rhineland. That was the unforgivable mistake of Talleyrand. It set up the Hohenzollerns,
a predatory dynasty, on the frontiers of France and assured that country of many bitter morrows.

The rest was easy. Germany became a federation under

the presidency of the Emperor of Austria. Norway was annexed to Sweden in order to reward Bernadotte for his treason. A Kingdom of the Low Countries was formed by combining Holland and Belgium and of it the Prince of Orange was made king. Mistress de facto of Italy, Austria brought the Po valley, Venice, and Milan again under her ferule in a Kingdom of Lombardy-Venetia. The Papal States went back to the Pope. Sardinia got Genoa. The Duchy of Parma was given to Marie Louise with the specification that the little King of Rome should not have the right of succeeding his mother on that throne. Murat was abandoned to the vengeance of the Bourbons.

The treaties of Vienna set out deliberately to throttle the Continent. In order to uphold them the Czar, the Emperor of Austria and the King of Prussia were soon to band together in a Holy Alliance that was at once mystical and diplomatic, absolutist and reactionary. In it all the peoples, and especially the peoples of Germany and Italy, were shortly to see an odious tool of oppression. It tried to establish peace within a framework which conformed to the wishes of the princes but took no account of events that had occurred or of the needs and feelings of subject populations. It was a peace of constraint replete with the germs of death. The revolutions of 1830 and 1848, which were to rock Europe and destroy the whole ancient order, derived directly from the conferences of 1815, which were conducted by men without souls who thought only of power and material interests. Talleyrand, Metternich, Castlereagh, Nesselrode, demonstrated at the Congress of Vienna that they were mediocre statesmen and infamous Europeans.

Labors at Vienna were approaching their close when the city was rocked by a piece of news that shook the conference to its foundations. Bonaparte—no one said Napoleon any more—Bonaparte had escaped from Elba and landed on the coast of southern France! The coalition that Talleyrand had thrown out of joint was immediately reformed. Talleyrand himself drew up the declaration of March 13th, 1815, whereby the Powers declared Napoleon an outlaw, "barred from civil and social intercourse and subject to public violence as a public enemy and a disturber of the peace of the world."

Talleyrand wrote those lines at the dictation of his grudges and his interests. Once more he was selling out his country, and for a very paltry price.

On touching shore on Elba Napoleon declared that he "was thinking of nothing but retirement." He was sincere. Still smarting from the hurts of a fall so great he really believed that he could settle down to the life of a petty Italian prince. He seemed relaxed and to have no regrets. He was almost happy.

Soon however his need for activity began to assert itself. It first found an outlet in organizing his laughable little state. He made plans for a flotilla of armed vessels, laid out roads, opened the iron mines, built salt factories. Eight hundred "grumblers" of the Old Guard had gone with him. He reinforced them with the three hundred soldiers who had formed the traditional garrison of the island and kept them in training by drills, reviews, trench digging. He had planned to write an autobiography during his moments of leisure and discussed with his officers in the most detached spirit the major episodes in his public career, especially those which had led directly to his fall.

He reverted no end of times to the campaign in Germany and to his refusal of peace at Prague.

"I was wrong," he said, "but put yourselves in my place: I had won no end of battles and very recently at Lützen and Bautzen. Those two victories had put me on my feet again in two days. I was counting on my soldiers and on myself. I determined to give the dice just one last throw. I lost, but those who blame me have never quaffed of the intoxicating elixir of Fortune."

The respectful silence which his auditors always maintained left him very much to his own thoughts and regrets. He would shake them off to plunge into reading. He enlarged his residence at Porto Ferraio and built a country place. He embellished his little capital, giving it new streets and an ever-flowing watering trough. He deepened the harbor basin and repaired its walls. He was on horseback at daybreak, riding over the island and inspecting works, in company with his Grand Marshal, Bertrand, and the brave and ever loyal Drouot. Sometimes he would take a sloop and sail around the coasts. Evenings he had formal parties as in the days of his power. He provided musical concerts or else performances of tragedies for audiences made up of his soldiers and families of quality among the islanders. Madame Mère and Pauline Borghese joined him to preside over his modest court till Marie Louise and his son should come, as he believed they would shortly be doing.

But as week followed on week this latter hope began to fade. Before very long Marie Louise was failing to answer his affectionate, insistent, imperative letters. She

went to take the waters at Aix. Instead of going on into
Italy, as he had begged her to do, she went back to
Vienna, in company with General Neipperg. Neipperg
was shortly to become her official paramour. Napoleon
did not dream that she would so soon prove unfaithful.
He did know that his wife was young and knew little
of the world. He thought that she was under constraint
from the House of Austria. He began to fear that his
son would grow up as a German prince.

Very soon, in spite of hasty retrenchments, he was in
financial difficulties. He had come away with 3,400,000
francs, the last remnant of the immense sums that he had
amassed during his days of prosperity and which he had
tossed into the public treasuries without counting them
when it was a question of resisting the invasion. His
public works, his army, his boats, his household, soon
ate up that little treasure. The 2,000,000 income that
had been guaranteed him by the Treaty of Fontainebleau had not so far been paid by the Bourbons and he
could guess that they never intended to honor that
pledge. As his personal funds gave out he was unable
to pay such soldiers as were left him. The suspension
of his allowance may have been a device to compel him
to dismiss his armed force, in other words to stand defenseless at a time when he had every reason to fear an
attempt on his life. Hot-headed Royalists in France were
talking openly of killing him, or else of deporting him
overseas to St. Helena in the South Atlantic or to Santa
Lucia in the Caribbean. The idea was unendurable to
him.

"I am a soldier," he said to Bertrand. "Let them murder me—I will bare my breast. I refuse to be deported."

PAULINE BORGHESE
From the Portrait by Gérard

Deportation would in fact have given the finishing
blow to his hazy but ever eager hopes. There he was,
so close to the shores of Italy and France! How could
he believe, at the age of forty-five, that his course had
really been run? He read the newspapers assiduously.
Through friends he had in France, especially Maret, he
knew of what was going on in Paris, and through Méneval, his secretary, who had stayed with Marie Louise,
the news from Vienna. He could not imagine it possible
that the Revolution, of which he now more than ever
believed his work to be the continuation, was to be stifled
by the Holy Alliance, that Europe was to be lulled to
sleep within the framework of "before '89."

So his eager ear caught the roar of the storm that was
thickening about the Bourbons. He saw the Restoration
commit all the mistakes that it should have avoided. It
antagonized the army by the prosecutions it started
against the former generals of the Empire. It humiliated
the wealthy middle classes through the insolent demeanor
of the new race of courtiers. It angered constitutional
liberals by dissolving the Chambers, and the business
world by carrying favors to English goods too far. The
former émigrés were forever harping on the question of
the old confiscations. The peasants therefore grew
alarmed lest their purchases of national lands be re-
voked. Taxation had been heavy under Napoleon, but
all his fiscal measures were kept in force in spite of
promises by the Bourbon government to reduce them.
A current of sullen anger began coursing through the
country. France had begun sincerely to miss the Emperor.

Napoleon had virtually decided to attempt a return

to France by the early days of 1815. His companions
were finding the time heavy on their hands. As he talked
with his soldiers they would say to him familiarly: "Sire,
when are we going home?" A report that the Congress
of Vienna was about to close encouraged him. Once they
had dispersed, the sovereigns would find it less easy to
combine against him. Through the intercession of
Pauline he had settled old scores with Murat. The King
of Naples had been rejected of the old Europe and had
now returned to him like a prodigal beseeching forgiveness. Maria Walewska came to Elba with little Alexander.
When she left she went by way of Naples and warned
Murat to be ready in case anything should happen.

Napoleon sat, one might say, with his plans ready
made when suddenly he received at Porto Ferraio a messenger who came from Maret. It was Fleury de Chabou-
lon. The information that Fleury gave as to the state of
public opinion in France settled matters in Napoleon's
mind.

He discussed his project with Madame Mère.

"I can't die here," he said. "France is in a turmoil.
The Bourbons have roused against themselves all interests, all convictions, that go back to the Revolution.
The army wants me. Every indication leads me to suppose that it will fly to me the moment it catches sight of
me. I may easily encounter some unforeseen pitfall along
my path. I may meet a general loyal to the Bourbons
who may be the man to stay the impulse of the troops.
In that case things will be over with me in a few hours.
But suppose it turns out that way! An end of that sort
seems to me far preferable to a prolonged residence on
this island with the future that awaits me here. So—I

am inclined to go ashore and try my luck once more. What do you think, mamma?"

The heroic mother of kings thought a moment. Her experience of all the extremes of good and evil fortune had had no slightest effect upon her. She answered simply:

"Go, my son—follow your destiny!"

Napoleon consulted Bertrand and Drouot. Bertrand approved. Drouot hesitated. Would not the Emperor's return tear the country wide open? Napoleon parried the objection. Everything had changed—he had changed himself! He did not intend to make any more conquests. He would be a liberal sovereign, bringing union and quiet to the French.

The English commissioner, Sir Neil Campbell, happened to be in Livorno on a pleasure trip. Taking advantage of Campbell's absence, Napoleon laid an embargo on all boats that had arrived at Elba. Then, on the 26th, he put his men—eleven hundred in all and four cannon—aboard his flotilla, a brig, the *Inconstant*, a schooner, the *Caroline,* and five light boats. He informed Murat of his intentions but ordered him to wait and see what happened in Paris.

After dark he boarded the *Inconstant*. It was a bright moonlight night. The wind was favorable at first but then suddenly fell. At dawn the flotilla was still drifting between Elba and Capraia in waters that were patrolled by the English and Bourbon fleets. Chautard and Taillade, the captains, took fright and were for returning to Porto Ferraio. Napoleon refused, again playing for sheer luck. Shortly after daybreak the breeze freshened and the boats sped northward. Just below Livorno

the *Inconstant* encountered the French brig-of-war
Zéphire, commanded by Captain Andrieux. It might
have been possible to board the vessel and seize her, but
that resort seemed too hazardous. The Emperor ordered
his grenadiers to take off their famous hair-hats and lie
prone on the deck.

Taillade took the megaphone and spoke the *Zéphire,*
sending a greeting to Andrieux. Napoleon listened to
the dialogue with beating heart:

"Where are you going?"

"To Livorno. And you?"

"Genoa."

"How is the great man?"

"Couldn't be better."

"Glad to hear it."

The *Zéphire* drew away and the *Inconstant* proceeded
on her way towards France.

The voyage lasted that day and the next. Most of the
time Napoleon passed on deck, field glass in hand.
Talking with his soldiers he spoke of their battles and
confided to them that he was going to Paris to deliver
France from bondage to the foreigner. In spite of the
hardness that had come to him from recent events, their
joy stirred him to warm feeling. Some of the men volunteered to make copies of the proclamations that he had
drawn up before starting, that the documents might be
distributed to the people and through the army. Their
eyes glistened as they read the lines in which, caught
between the alternatives of glory and death, he sounded
his last appeal:

"Soldiers: We have not been conquered. I have heard
your voice in my place of exile. Your general is given

back to you. Come and join him. Put on the tricolored cockade that you wore during the great days. Victory will join us in the charge. The eagle will fly with the national colors from belfry to belfry till it reaches the towers of Notre Dame. Then you will be able to boast of what you have done. You will be the liberators of your country."

To such of the soldiers as had not received the cross he gave it now. They spent the night of the 28th awake, intoxicated, drunk with happiness and with hope, asking for nothing better than to die for HIM. The Maures hills were on the horizon at dawn. At three o'clock in the afternoon the flotilla, with all boats flying the tricolor, anchored in the Gulf of Jouan. The men touched shore with cries which could not be repressed: "Long live the Emperor."

While the men ate their supper Napoleon sat down on the edge of an olive orchard to study his maps. He had sent a platoon of men to Antibes. Hearing no word from them—actually they had been arrested—he started out at the head of his grenadiers and in a brilliant moonlight marched upon Grasse by way of Cannes. He had not forgotten that the people in Provence were hostile: Toulon, Marseilles, the Rhone valley, were Royalist. He chose a route through the mountains. There, to be sure, the going would be slow and a few courageous opponents could halt him in any defile, but so far as he knew the inhabitants had remained patriotic. Cane in hand he marched along between steep ice-covered hillsides, the tails of his gray coat floating in the wintry mountain air. The few farmers who came running up waved at him in utter astonishment. He commanded halts on the outskirts of villages. The people brought wine for the soldiers and flowers for him. It was cold weather. Sometimes he would stumble or slip in the snow. He had abandoned his cannon at Grasse, in order to make better time. Four guns would be of no use, he reflected. His name had to suffice.

"Not a shot!" he ordered his soldiers. "Not one drop of blood!"

On the 3rd of March he was at Castellane, on the 4th at Digne, on the 5th at Gap. By then the mayors were welcoming him and he was sleeping in their houses. Already he had marched a hundred and twenty miles without encountering a trace of resistance. But he was now approaching Grenoble, which was in an uproar from excitement. General Marchand had decided to stop him there. He sent a battalion of the 5th Regiment to block the pass at Laffrey.

When Napoleon reached that point he stepped forward alone towards the men who stood trembling before him with crossed bayonet, blocking his advance.

"Soldiers of the Fifth," he said in a ringing voice. "Do you recognize me?"

A number of voices answered:

"Yes! Yes!"

He unbuttoned his vest and offered a naked breast.

"If there is one among you who wishes to kill his Emperor, he is free to do so. Here I am."

"Fire!" cried a young Royalist officer, Captain Randon, who was to be a marshal of the Second Empire.

But the soldiers dashed forward, their caps on the ends of their guns. "Long live the Emperor!" The cry was taken up. The men threw themselves upon him, kissing his hands, his coat, embracing his knees. Many of them sobbed aloud.

Napoleon was deathly pale. He brushed away a tear. Turning to Bertrand and Drouot he said:

"That tells the story! Ten days hence I shall be in the Tuileries."

Later on, at St. Helena, he was to say:

"Between Cannes and Grenoble I was an adventurer. At Grenoble I became a sovereign again."

That was true. On issuing from the gorge at Laffrey the man who, to use the magnificent phrase of Chateaubriand, "invaded France single-handed," cast before him along the roads as it were an aura of glory which no French heart could withstand. Catching fire at the distant sound of the "Marseillaise" that came up from somewhere towards the south and then spread through the town on the lips of a frenzied people, Grenoble rose against the Royalist governors and acclaimed the Emperor. Young, ardent, Colonel La Bédoyère, commanding the 7th Regiment of the Line, mustered his men in a public square, drew the regimental eagle from its hiding place and with drawn sword struck out along the Vizille road with the cry: "Let those who love me follow me." When he saw Napoleon's column he leapt from his horse and fell into the Emperor's arms.

The band was a veritable army when it arrived before Grenoble on the evening of that same day, the 7th of March. The whole population was on the ramparts. General Marchand, poor fellow, had had the gates closed, but stalwart workingmen and peasants knocked them down with battering rams of timber. Harried by cheering throngs Napoleon made his way with difficulty

through torch-lighted streets to the Inn of the Three
Dauphins, which was kept by one of his veterans. He
appeared at a window to answer the cheers of the throng.

Just then some artisans came up bringing great frag-
ments of wood:

"We are bringing you the gates since you were refused the keys."

The following morning Napoleon received the authorities and reviewed the troops. His platform was
simple, moderate. He promised peace with honor. The
time for conquests had passed. He wished quiet, quiet
for Europe and quiet for France.

His army now numbered 7000 men. He led them
out on the road to Lyons and started them off with eagles
unfurled and with tricolor cockades in their hats. He
himself stayed behind with the men he had brought
from Elba and did not depart till the day following,
the 9th. The night of the 9th he spent at Bourgoin.

When Louis XVIII learned of the landing on the Gulf
of Jouan he kept his head very well; but while Soult,
now Minister of War, and the courtiers at the Tuileries
were shrugging their shoulders, minimizing, or even
jesting, he was heard to say over and over again:

"It all depends on the first regiments. The business
has an ugly look."

All the same he did not lose heart. He sent his brother,
the Comte d'Artois, to Lyons to organize resistance with
Macdonald's help. The Duke of Angoulême was at
Bordeaux. He would hurry to Nîmes and cut off the
Usurper's line of retreat. Ney would march on Lyons
with the divisions in the Franche-Comté. The Council
of Ministers published an order that "every citizen should

hound Napoleon to death." If he were captured he was
to be shot. On being hastily convened the Chambers
outdid each other in adulation and boastfulness. The
Royalists pretended to thank God for this opportunity
to be rid of "the adventurer" for good and all. On calling at the Tuileries for his instructions Ney averred that
he would "bring him back a prisoner in an iron cage."
Meantime public opinion displayed a very ruffled surface. The Bonapartists were in a ferment. A number of
old revolutionaries began to intrigue. Fouché's first impulse was to flare up against Napoleon. Then he felt
inclined to aid him in case he should succeed. That the
Emperor was going to succeed Fouché more than half
believed.

The Comte d'Artois appeared at Lyons with the Duc
d'Orléans at his side. Vainly he showered smiles to right
and left. The crowds were either indifferent or hostile.
Macdonald staged a review of the troops on the forenoon of the 10th, ending with the traditional "Long
live the King!" Not a voice replied from the ranks. The
Comte d'Artois was worried. Macdonald found that the
king's representative was in the way and urged him to
return to Paris. The prince allowed himself to be easily
persuaded. Again the marshal tried to recall the soldiers
to their oaths of allegiance. One of them called out
to him.

"Oh, now, general—you would do much better to lead
us to our Emperor who is already near. He would welcome you with open arms."

Napoleon was in fact near. He was traveling in an
open carriage. He could make but slow progress through
towns or villages, so thick was the cheering press about

him. Everywhere he received ovations and official compliments from municipal governments. His triumph was slowly working up into a great and irresistible uprising of a nation.

At four o'clock on the afternoon of the 10th his advance guard appeared in the faubourg de la Guillotière in Lyons. Macdonald's troops began at once to fraternize with the Bonapartists. The marshal had erected barricades. They were thrown down. He could only take flight, at breakneck speed, accompanied by his aides. Napoleon entered Lyons amid a howling, almost brutal mob. Deathly pale, very much moved, he tried to force a smile. It was in truth a terrifying demonstration: "Death to the Bourbons! Down with the priests! Down with the nobles!" It was like a nightmare hanging over from the days of the Terror.

Establishing headquarters in the Archbishopric, he proceeded to resume his throne officially. He dissolved the Chambers by decree and called for an election by mass demonstration at a Champ de Mai, a Maypole holiday. The tricolor was restored as the national emblem. Émigrés were re-expelled and titles of nobility abolished. He was taking the line of an Emperor of the Revolution, a popular sovereign. He wrote to Marie Louise announcing his early return to Paris and ordering her to join him without delay, bringing their son.

He set out again on the 13th along the Burgundy road, and from bell-tower to bell-tower, as he had predicted, the eagle flew before him. Mâcon and Chalon-sur-Saône welcomed him madly.

Ney was at Lons-le-Saulnier, still resolved to halt his old leader. But his officers and soldiers were in a fer-

ment. The old flag was the only one in sight. Dijon
had just declared for the Emperor. The wildest rumors
were afloat. It was declared that Napoleon was coming
home with the consent of Europe. The marshal himself
was conscious of a wavering in his very recent Royalist
faith. It was in that state of mind that he received a
note from the Emperor summoning him to his side: "I
will embrace you," it read, "as I did that morning on
the Moskva." The old veteran could not resist that allusion to a common glory. "Can one dam the tide of the
sea with one's fingers?" he cried. He assembled his army
and standing in front of the men he declared in a ringing voice:

"Soldiers: The cause of the Bourbons is forever lost.
The Emperor Napoleon is our sovereign. His is the duty
henceforth of ruling our beloved country."

The men broke ranks and crowded around him, embracing him, smothering him. He ordered a march on
Autun to join Napoleon.

They met at Auxerre on the 8th. The Emperor
touched him with the flat of his sword and would not
allow him to speak. "No excuses!" he said. "Your excuse,
like mine, is in the course of events. They are stronger
than men. Let us say nothing of the past."

And he ordered him to march on Paris with his troops.

Louis XVIII left the Tuileries on the evening of the
day following. During the days preceding he had found
nothing but confusion and panic around him. Instead
of devising energetic remedies for the mistakes they had
committed, the ministers bickered and haggled. Soult
was removed from the Ministry of War and replaced
by Clarke. Proclamation after proclamation was glued

to the billboards. The King appeared before the Chambers displaying for the first time on his blue coat the cordon of the Legion of Honor. He made a noble and very adroit speech. But in the distance, as it were, the approaching footsteps of Napoleon could be heard. Ney's defection had upset things. The King was urged to flee. He refused. The ministers turned to Fouché for advice. He would not answer. An order for his arrest was issued. He was nowhere to be found. At that moment Napoleon was at Fontainebleau. Louis XVIII could not hold out forever against the panic in his court. Finally he made up his mind to repair into Flanders. At midnight on the 19th the legitimate monarchy was again riding by coach into exile.

The Emperor learned of the flight through Lavalette. He hurried on, eager to make Paris by the 20th, the birthday of the King of Rome. He arrived in the early evening by post chaise, escorted by a large group of officers. He found the Tuileries crowded with his former court officials in full dress—they had been waiting there for hours. He was dragged from his carriage, lifted upon their shoulders and carried to the entrance steps of the palace amid a din of shouts and cheers. He was set down, breathless, helpless, his hands folded in front of him, in his old office. The room was filled with men and women on their knees. They reached out their hands to touch him, reverently, as though he were a living god. The eagle had alighted at last on the towers of Notre Dame. The tricolor had sprouted at every Paris window.

CHAPTER XXXVI

The Hundred Days

THE FIRST MADNESS OVER, NAPOLEON PERCEIVED WITH his usual clear and realistic eye that "France had changed." It was going to be a superhuman task to set the country on its feet and put it in a state of defense against Europe. To assist him in that work he found only nervous, mistrustful aides about him, men beaten in advance. It was hard to make up a ministry. Fouché's influence had become very great during the days just past. Napoleon sensed the man's implacable hostility, but to "neutralize" him, as he said, he gave him back his portfolio of Police. Cambacérès became Minister of Justice, Caulaincourt of Foreign Affairs, Davout of War. Maret, Gaudin, Mollien, Decrès, resumed their former functions in the Secretariat of State, the departments of loans, treasury and navy respectively. Carnot finally accepted the Interior. "At such a moment," he said proudly, "no one has a right to refuse any assignment."

In his first pronouncements the Emperor manifested great unpretentiousness, in accord with the spirit of the moment. "There is no question of going back to the past," he declared, reassuring. "I know what must be avoided, what we must strive to achieve. I cherished grand dreams for France in a day gone by. I have given them up. I desire peace. I would never have brought myself to signing the Treaty of Paris. Now that it is signed I undertake to live up to it strictly. . . . But peace is not the only thing I want to restore to France. I want her also to have liberty. . . . Let me appease or else conquer the foreigner. After that I shall be satisfied to rule as a constitutional monarch. To save the cause of the Revolution, to safeguard our independence whether by diplomacy or by victory in the field, and then to prepare a constitutional throne for my son— those are the only glories to which I aspire."

Without losing a moment he plunged into work like a man swimming for dear life in the deep sea. Lobau would get the troops in Paris together and make sure of their trustworthiness. Exelmans would drive on Lille with 3000 cavalry, worry Louis XVIII and shoo him across the border. Clauzel would clean up the southwest and drive the Duchess of Angoulême away from Bordeaux, where she was showing an inclination to linger.

Imperial authority was re-established everywhere in the course of a few days. Even the Vendée submitted. Vitrolles was arrested at Toulouse. The Duc d'Angoulême was backed against the Rhone, forced to capitulate and put aboard ship at Cette. Masséna and Grouchy occupied Marseilles. Louis XVIII crossed the frontier and became an exile at Ghent.

So much for France. But Europe? Europe did not waver for an instant. Europe gave no sign of acquiescing in what had happened. At Vienna the Allies formed a new alliance against Napoleon on the very day when his escape became known. They foresaw that the Continent as a whole would soon be hurling a million men upon France—the Prussians, who were nursing the bitterest hate, proposed dismembering her outright. All the ambassadors in Paris proceeded to ask for their passports.

The Emperor did not seem disconcerted. He wrote to all the kings (April 4) protesting a sincere intention to abide by the Treaty of Paris and preserve peace. He tried to win Talleyrand back by working through one of the traitor's friends and accomplices, Montrond. He thought he could bring Vienna around on the basis of the family connection. Among the papers of Louis XVIII he found the treaty of January 3, which aligned France, Austria and England against Prussia and Russia. He thought that when the Czar saw that document his enthusiasm for the Bourbons would cool a little.

But he did not slacken preparations in the military field for all of those prospects. He called to the colors the soldiers who had been retired or furloughed by the Restoration. He called the class of 1815 and sent out an appeal to the National Guards. Eight army corps were thus scraped together and hurried in great part to the frontiers on the north and east. He reorganized his Guard, found horses for the cavalry and materials for the artillery. Hundreds of factories began working night and day to clothe and arm the troops. Heavy guns were brought from the coast defenses and set up in forts around Paris. They were to be manned by sailors from the fleet. Within weeks, Napoleon concluded, he could take the field with an army 400,000 strong. But he wondered whether he would not be doing better to strike at once with the forces already on hand. He could invade Belgium and take the coalition by surprise. He was later

to regret not having adopted that policy. At the moment
he decided that he should stand on his good right to
the end and not allow world opinion to assume that he
was returning as a conqueror.

One by one his hopes collapsed. Talleyrand refused
to see his envoy. Metternich declared that Austria would
never treat with "Bonaparte." The King of Rome was
taken from his mother and placed under close guard
against the chance of an abduction. Marie Louise was
now altogether under the sway of Neipperg. She basely
deserted the Emperor and appealed to "the protection
of the Powers" to save her from him. The faithful
Méneval was banished from Austria. When he got back
to Paris he did not tell the Emperor everything, but he
allowed him to guess a great deal. Napoleon did not bat
an eyelash though his inner distress was great. One of
his main thoughts in leaving Elba had been to recover
his wife and son. He now began to suspect that Europe
would never give them back to him.

Fourteen, sixteen hours a day of fiendish application
could not distract his mind from an ever besetting
anxiety. Close about him, in France itself, he could sense
the wavering of freshly replastered loyalties. The outspoken hatred of Europe had frightened money, trade,
manufacturing. His own party was divided. Some Bonapartists were for galvanizing the country with a military dictatorship. Others wanted the Empire to move in
a liberal direction. Napoleon himself was leaning towards
this latter policy and sincerely so. He was loath to reopen the floodgates of the Revolution. He repeatedly
declared that he did not want to be "the king of a
Jacquerie." He had promised that his second ascent to

the throne would inaugurate the reign of a constitutional monarch. He would keep his word.

Some days after his return to Paris he restored liberty of the press and made it thoroughgoing. On April 6th he asked Benjamin Constant to call on him at the Tuileries. Constant had been a long-standing enemy. As late as March 19th he had insulted the Emperor in the *Journal des Débats* and then gone into hiding. Napoleon now took him into his full confidence and asked him as a recognized liberal, as the brilliant standard bearer of the school of Siéyès, to draw up the outlines of a constitution. Constant worked a week on the plan and then submitted it. The Emperor discussed it with him, yielding on virtually every point: a representative system, broad-based suffrage, ministerial responsibility to the chambers, life tenure for judges, freedom of worship, guarantees of individual freedom. He did hold out against the opinion of his new counselor in one respect, and stubbornly. The new Empire had to be tied up in some way with the old. Constant felt that the constitution in its very title should quiet public alarms by emphasizing the break with the autocratic tradition.

"No, no!" the Emperor insisted. "That's trying to strip me of my past and make a different person of me, wipe away my glory and the glory of France, imply that everything about my first reign was bad. I shall not consent to that. I can readily yield to experience, and especially to the circumstances that now make a dictatorship such as I enjoyed impracticable. I shall not allow myself to be humiliated."

Constant had to give in. The imperial charter was

to be called an "Act Additional to the Constitutions of the Empire." A fundamental mistake!

By its title this constitution, which was a liberal constitution, the most liberal known to French history, was to be misconstrued by all parties. Royalists, republicans, liberals, all fell upon it tooth and nail. It was represented as a mere mask for despotism. For all of his promises Napoleon had not changed—he would always be a tyrant and nothing but a tyrant. Only a few scattered individuals without influence approved of it—Mme. de Staël, Sismondi.

Another basic question had still to be decided. Should the Chambers be convened or not? Napoleon was inclined to let things stand until after he had repelled the threatened invasion. But pressure was brought to bear upon him from all directions—Joseph, Benjamin Constant, even La Fayette, whom there were hopes of bringing around. At last Napoleon agreed, as a sop to mistrust. He called for an election, the Chamber of Representatives to begin its sessions towards the end of May.

The long list of concessions did not win the French business classes back to Napoleon. In their eyes the imperial régime was doomed from the moment of its reestablishment. The masses for their part were still with him. "Federations" began to form in western France and the movement gradually spread throughout the country. The "federations" were a sort of volunteer local militia. Napoleon thought he might be able to use them for home defense. He reviewed them in Paris.

Fouché still had his ear to the ground for trends in public feeling. He was convinced that a catastrophe was in the immediate offing. To forestall it he began maneuvering in some sort of an intrigue with Metternich whereby Napoleon would be replaced by his son, or at a hazard by the Duc d'Orléans. Napoleon got wind of the business and assailed Fouché with his old-time violence:

"You are a traitor, M. Fouché. I should hang you. All France would applaud."

The Duke of Ótranto replied with cold wit:

"I am not of Your Majesty's opinion."

Whereupon Fouché shifted operations to the court at Ghent and sent his man Gaillard to present his compliments and offer his services to Louis XVIII. Any step seemed proper to that accomplished rascal, provided it gave him a chance to stay in power.

A strong anti-war movement came to the fore in England, but Lord Castlereagh had given his word to the Allies. He rallied the Commons to the point of honor and they declared for the resumption of hostilities by a large majority.

The war broke out prematurely in Italy as a result of Murat's impetuousness. Over-riding the Emperor's orders he set out to make himself master of the peninsula the moment Napoleon was in Paris again. His troops invaded the Papal States, Pius withdrawing from Rome for the fourth time. Proclaiming himself King of Italy Murat advanced northward to the Po without meeting any important resistance. But a strong Austrian army was there thrown against him, under the command of Bianchi and Neipperg. Murat's Neapolitans gave evidence of unsteadiness in the face of the Austrian veterans. He drew back, but then finally turned on the enemy at Tolentino (May 3) and fought a battle with des-

perate heroism. Neipperg won and Murat's soldiers
disbanded. He got back to Naples with a mere handful.
With his kingdom wide open to the enemy and his capital blockaded by an English fleet, Murat boarded a brig
and made his way to southern France. Caroline, his wife,
had been opposed to his rash move from the beginning.
Left in charge of affairs she could only capitulate.

The disaster deprived Napoleon of a valuable auxiliary against Austria, but not the least unfortunate of
its effects was that Murat's coup gave the lie to the
Emperor's protestations of peaceful intentions. Napoleon
was enraged. He refused to allow Murat to come to
Paris and put him in bounds in the south as a mutineer.
One more blunder and a bad one! Murat was an
admirable cavalry officer. His help would have been
invaluable at the foot of St. John Hill.

The Austrians were now free to pour unimpeded over
the frontiers to the south and east. Blücher and Wellington were already in Belgium with 130,000 men. The
Russians were coming up from Poland and Bohemia.
The Germans were nearing the Rhine. Again a European tidal wave was making up to break over France.

Just when Napoleon should have been free to give
his every thought to such dangers he had to turn and
deal with matters of domestic politics. The "Act Additional" won approval in the plebiscite by a vote of
1,500,000 to 4000. But the vote, really, had not come
out. Three-quarters of those who had been entitled to
go to the polls had stayed at home. The Chamber of
Representatives had been elected largely under the influence of Fouché and Fouché's friends. Though it was
not hostile to the Emperor on the whole, it showed a

number of faces that boded ill for a near future: old Conventionists with a grudge, such as Cambon and Barère; liberals like La Fayette and Lanjuinais; henchmen of the Minister of Police, like Manuel and Jay. The Assembly was definitely contrary to the Bourbons. It was patriotic and fastidiously jealous of its prerogatives. Napoleon was to sense that at the very first session.

The famous *Champ de Mai,* or mass demonstration of the nation, which Napoleon had promised at Lyons to hold as a symbol of his new alliance with the country, had to be postponed, what with one thing and another, to the 1st of June. The Emperor appeared at the ceremonies in his coronation paraphernalia. Many thought he would have done better to wear the uniform of Austerlitz.

The official program was carried out in the parade ground in front of the Military School where Napoleon had studied as a cadet. There was a Mass and a *Te Deum,* then speeches by representatives of the electoral colleges. Finally the Emperor rose from a throne in his white satin breeches and, with sober face and a hand resting on the New Testament swore to uphold the constitutions of the Empire. The army and the crowds massed in the Champ de Mars applauded him wildly as he made the review. There were cries of "Long live the Empress! Long live the King of Rome! Let's go and get them!" The calls were taken up with gigantic echoes.

The distribution of the eagles came next—a truly grand moment, one of the grandest in the First Empire.

"Soldiers:" said Napoleon, "I entrust to you the eagle that goes with the colors of our native land. Do you

411

swear to die, if need be, to protect it from the enemies of the country and the throne?"

"We swear!" came the answer from fifty thousand throats.

"Soldiers of the National Guard: Do you swear never to suffer the enemy again to befoul the capital of our great nation?"

"We swear!"

"Soldiers of the Imperial Guard: Do you swear to outdo yourselves in the campaign that is about to open and to die rather than see the foreigner dictate to our country?"

"We swear!"

To that oath the Guard was soon to prove faithful.

It was sunset when the parade of the troops past the reviewing stand came to an end. Paris was stirred. The masses boiled with their old enthusiasms. But the politicians, self-seekers like Fouché, liberals like La Fayette, had listened to Napoleon's appeals unmoved. They heard a voice and a tone that were familiar to them from proclamations of old. A mood of antagonism, of resistance, deepened in them.

The Chambers opened on the 5th. Lucien had rallied to his brother in the hour of disaster and was now back in France with Madame Mère, Joseph, Jerome. Napoleon wanted to have him as president of the Chamber of Representatives. In that key position the man who had presided over the Five Hundred on the 18th of Brumaire might render very important services. The Chamber refused and elected Lanjuinais, a sometime senator who had stubbornly remained in opposition throughout the

Empire and had been one of the first to propose dethroning Napoleon in 1814.

The Emperor was angry and for a time seemed unwilling to sanction the nomination:

"They are trying to offend me by electing an enemy of mine! In return for all the concessions I have made their idea is to insult me and weaken me. Well, if that's the way things stand, I will resist. I will dissolve this Assembly."

The remark was treacherously passed around by Fouché and set the Chamber on edge. But Napoleon soon cooled down. On the advice of Carnot and Regnault de Saint-Jean d'Angély he invited Lanjuinais to the Élysée (where he had settled in the middle of April in order to lead a quieter life), and had a heart to heart talk with him.

"The past is nothing," he said. "I consider people only in their characters and their attitude at the moment. Are you my friend or my enemy?"

Lanjuinais was touched. He replied that he would support the Emperor as long as the latter acted as a constitutional sovereign.

"Then we shall get along all right," said Napoleon. "I ask nothing more of you than that."

And he confirmed Lanjuinais in the presidency of the Chamber.

The Chamber of Peers which Napoleon had nominated was by and large the old senate—a group of princes, marshals, generals, ministers, prelates, with a sprinkling of names from the old aristocracy. The Emperor could rely on the Peers no more securely than on the Representatives. The first debates that took place among them could have left him no doubts on the point.

On June 7th he held a joint imperial session of the two bodies. His address was manly, grave.

"Our enemies," he said, "are counting only on our inner dissensions. The army and I will do our part. It is for you, Peers and Representatives, to set the country an example of confidence, energy and patriotism. Like the senate of the great people of antiquity, you must resolve to die rather than survive any dishonor or degradation for France."

He was applauded but seemed indifferent to the ovation. He knew that those politicians would stand by him only if he came off victorious. Already his thoughts had drifted away from them to the soggy plains of Flanders where the massed enemy was awaiting him.

"If I win," he said to intimates, "we must force everybody to keep strictly to his own functions. That will give us time to get used to this new system of governing. If I lose, God knows what will become of you and of me. In any case, everything will be over within three or four weeks."

He received delegations form the two chambers on the 11th. They were more respectful than sincere in their good wishes. After that he signed a decree establishing a Council of Government, which was to rule during his absence. It was made up of the ministers and his brothers, with Joseph in the chair. Looking over the group he smiled bitterly and commented:

"I can see that you will certainly need a victory from me!"

On the evening of the 12th he dined with his family

at the Élysée. Mme. Bertrand was present. At one moment he whispered in her ear, half mirthful, half serious:

"Well, let's hope we are not going to be sorry soon that we ever left Elba!"

Dinner over he hurried from the room, leapt into a carriage and was driven off—towards Waterloo!

ThE HuNdred Days

at the Elysée. Mme. Bertrand was present. At one moment he whispered to her gravely and with half serious.

"Well, let's hope we are not going to be sorry soon that we ever left Elba!"

Dinner over he hurried back to the room, laid into a carriage and was driven off towards Waterloo.

CHAPTER XXXVII

Waterloo

Napoleon had worked a hundred days and a hundred nights, ransacking France from top to bottom to find soldiers and equip them. Nevertheless he found that he could send to Flanders not more than 125,000 full-fledged troops. The cavalry was in fine condition, well mounted, well organized. The artillery was not so good but it counted 350 pieces. The army was made up largely of veterans and was awaiting the Emperor's coming eagerly. The men had no slightest doubt that he would lead them to victory. "The troops," wrote General Foy, "are not just patriotic, not just enthusiastic. They are in a veritable rage for the Emperor and against the enemy."

Napoleon reached the frontier at Beaumont on the 14th. In taking the army in hand he too seemed suddenly to be freed of his worries and to be full of the old confidence and energy.

The two Allied generals had made the mistake of dividing their forces. Wellington, with a mixed army of 100,000—Englishmen, Hanoverians, Brunswickians, Hollanders, Belgians—had established headquarters in Brussels. Blücher with 120,000 Prussians lay deployed

416

along the Sambre and the Meuse from Liége to Charleroi. The Emperor noted their error in a flash and made his plan of operations accordingly. He would go back to the terrible game of hide-and-seek that had worked so well in the Campaign in France. But now he had far more strength at his disposal. He would drive between the enemy armies and attack them separately. With Blücher in flight on the Meuse and Wellington backed against the sea to the north, he would be in a very good situation. In fact, he could hope for almost anything. The Russians and Austrians were still far away. Before he would be called upon to deal with them he could count on very considerable reinforcements from the reserve depots and from the National Guard, to say nothing of the corps of Rapp, Lecourbe, and Suchet who were holding observation posts along the Rhine and in the Alps. Let the outcome in Belgium be favorable and Europe would again be obliged to sue for peace.

The French troops started for Charleroi on the night of the 14th-15th. Blücher was taken by surprise, for he had not been expecting a French offensive any more than Wellington had. The Prussians fell back on Fleurus and Ligny. In order to prevent a junction between them and the British, Napoleon ordered Ney to carry the position at Quatre Bras and so break the road between Namur and Brussels. Unfortunately Bourmont, a sometime Chouan who commanded one of Gérard's divisions, deserted to the enemy just then and made known the Emperor's plan. The "brave of the brave" hesitated to attack Quatre Bras, though it was defended only by a small force of red-coats. Napoleon did not rebuke the marshal but again ordered him to attack the next morning. As for himself, he had spent eighteen hours on horse-back and was further suffering from a distended bladder. He threw himself upon his camp bed and went to sleep.

Acting on Bourmont's information, Blücher concen-trated his army well out from Namur on the road to Brussels. Wellington had learned of the Emperor's ar-rival while attending a ball given by the Duchess of Richmond. He hurried reinforcements to Quatre Bras. Ney should have carried the position in the very early morning and then come down on Blücher's right flank. Again he hesitated.

Meantime Napoleon attacked the main Prussian army at Ligny. The day was muggy, the air thick with thun-derstorm. Nevertheless the troops went enthusiastically into battle and their spirits were running high. Napo-leon climbed up into a mill-tower to watch the troops deploy for the attack on Ligny and the three villages at Saint-Amand. He sent a new messenger to Ney urg-ing him to fall upon the enemy's rear. "The Prussian army is lost if you act vigorously. The fate of France is in your hands." Seeing no signs of Ney, he resolved to send in his Guard. The Guard attacked magnificently. It broke the Prussian lines and threw them back into a disorderly retreat. The confusion was so great that Blücher fell from his horse and was trodden underfoot. With evening coming on the Prussian second in com-mand, Gneisenau, took charge of the retirement. The Prussians had suffered heavy losses but their army had not been destroyed.

If Ney had obeyed Napoleon the indecisive victory at Ligny would have been turned into a triumph and the Prussians would have been eliminated from the cam-

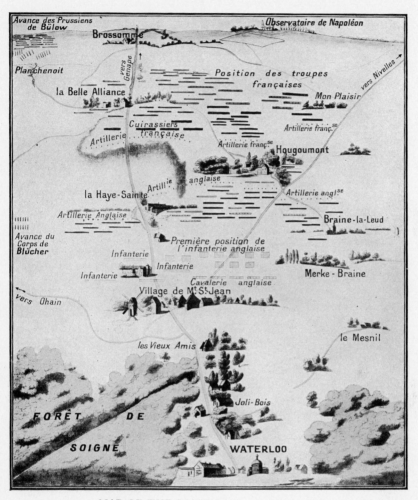

MAP OF THE BATTLE OF WATERLOO

paign. Why did the marshal fail to act? He was badly seconded, it is true, by Reille. But not till three o'clock in the afternoon did he make the drive on Quatre Bras. Perceiving the value of the position Wellington had again reinforced it. Ney was thrown back. He charged again and again with mad courage, but succeeded only in massacring his men. Taking no account of Napoleon's later orders, he even prevented Drouet d'Erlon from playing the part that Napoleon had assigned to him, in default of Ney, on the Prussian right. He ended by letting himself be forced back upon Frasnes where he hung on courageously under a storm of musket and artillery fire. Realizing his mistakes at last he cried, despairingly:

"I wish I could get every one of those cannonballs in the belly!"

At night the firing died down, with the French and English in their positions. The useless butchery had cost 10,000 lives.

On the whole, however, the French victory at Ligny had one important result. It definitely separated Blücher from Wellington. Believing that the Prussians had been disposed of for several days, Napoleon went ahead with his plan and now attacked the English.

He detached thirty thousand men under Grouchy to follow Blücher and hold him, if he gave signs of coming to life again. Grouchy was a fine cavalry officer but a worthless general. Napoleon sent Ney to advance towards Brussels. He himself should have hurried more, but he wasted two hours inspecting the battlefield of Ligny, caring for the wounded and distributing rewards. He figured that the troops had been fighting for two days and needed a little rest. Not till eleven o'clock did he advance on Quatre Bras, which the English slowly evacuated.

Still again Ney failed to execute the maneuver that Napoleon had ordered. Rebuking him bitterly, the Emperor took charge of the advance guard himself and led the pursuit of the English. The storm broke at last. A torrential rain turned the fields into swamps and the roads into quagmires. The men broke ranks under the deluge and advanced pell-mell. Nevertheless the Emperor managed to pepper the English rear guard with cavalry charges and a steady fire of solid shot tore huge gaps in it. Wellington hastened his retreat and did not halt till he reached the slopes of Mont Saint-Jean, a broad high hill overlooking the whole region. He took up a strong position there.

In company with Grand Marshal Bertrand and a page Napoleon reconnoitered Wellington's position on foot, indifferent to the missiles that fell about him and spattered him with mud. As the sun went down the English began to light their fires. Soon, as Napoleon was later to say, "the horizon looked like one vast conflagration," curtained behind by the dark forest of Soignes. Wellington fixed his headquarters on the edge of the wood in the little village of Waterloo.

Satisfied with his inspection the Emperor went back to "Cobblestone Farm," where he had quartered his staff. Fearing that the Prussians might be marching by way of Wavre to lend a hand to Wellington, Napoleon despatched a new order to Grouchy to scatter them at all costs. He was so much afraid that the English would decamp during the night that he got up at two o'clock and made another reconnaissance. Then he came back and dried his clothes at a great fire.

At dawn the rain ceased, a fresh breeze rose and the sun came out. The Emperor gathered his generals at breakfast and outlined his plan. The army being massed at the foot of St. John Hill, the château of Hougoumont would be carried on the French left, the Haye-Sainte farm in the center and the Haye and Papelotte farms on the right. The main attack would then be on the enemy's left. Wellington would so be pushed back upon the forest of Soignes where the rout would be complete.

"The enemy outnumbers us by more than a quarter," he said. "Nevertheless the situation is nine to one in our favor."

Soult alone was nervous and did not hide the fact. Napoleon broke him off harshly:

"You think Wellington is a great general because he whipped you once. I tell you that Wellington is a bad general and that the English army is a bad army."

"I hope so," whispered Soult.

The Emperor left his treasure and his baggage at Cobblestone Farm and set out for the Belle Alliance farm across the road to Genappes. He ordered the troops to move into their battle positions, and he reviewed them as they passed.

The men had had a terrible night. The rain had prevented them even from cooking supper. Nevertheless they cheered the Emperor wildly. He sat very erect on his horse, mastering his pain and his fatigue. Infantrymen, chasseurs, lancers, dragoons, hussards, the Old Guard, the Young Guard, marched past him with drums rolling and trumpets sounding, while the new flags that had been distributed at the *Champ de Mai* dipped in salute. All the bands were playing the Imperial song—*Veillons au salut de l'Empire*. A thunder of enthusiasm filled the air.

"If my orders are well executed," said Napoleon, "we shall sleep in Brussels tonight."

The plan might have succeeded, especially if it had been carried out without delay. But heeding the ruinous advice of Drouot, who had been greatly influencing him since Elba, Napoleon decided to wait for several hours to allow the ground to dry somewhat and to give Grouchy time to get into the battle.

Grouchy had lost half of the 17th looking for the Prussians. He found them at last marching on Wavre. Napoleon's last message never reached him. Instead of rushing to Waterloo he rested at Gembloux, while Blücher, having rallied his army, was sending Bülow's corps, one of his best, to St. John Hill to support the English. Napoleon's delay, Grouchy's incompetence, the rapid maneuvering of the Prussians—those details together make up the decisive elements in the battle that was to take its name from Waterloo.

Napoleon, exhausted, slept from ten to eleven o'clock on his camp bed. Then he got up and went to the Rossomme farm, situated on a grass-covered knoll. With his maps spread out before him on a rickety table he finally gave the signal for the attack. A hundred and twenty cannon opened on the English, who at once replied.

Reille's corps began the attack upon the woods and château at Hougoumont. The position was well defended and it held. The struggle was fierce and costly—

indecisive. Suddenly Napoleon perceived through his glass a dark spot to the right of the English left. Was it Grouchy that early? Probably the Prussians rather! A prisoner soon removed his doubts. It was Bülow's corps hastening to reinforce the British left. The situation looked serious. Napoleon sent Lobau to hold off the new adversary and hurried a courier to Grouchy telling him to come on at all speed.

It was half past one when the Emperor hurled Ney at the Haye-Sainte farm. After a number of bitter attacks the marshal succeeded in winning the orchard. Meantime Drouet d'Erlon crossed the Ohain road and began to scale the left and center slopes of St. John Hill. But the troops of Picton and Pack were cached in the tall wheat. Suddenly they rose and gave the French a volley at point blank range. The French fell back in disorder pursued by the gray-coated Scots of Ponsonby. Napoleon saved the situation by a charge of Milhaud's cuirassiers, who broke the rush of the Scotchmen. Losses were equal and nothing had been gained.

It was getting late and Bülow's Prussians were now stiffening the English wing. Grouchy had still not been heard from. The Emperor ordered new assaults on the Haye-Sainte farm and on the château of Hougoumont. Ney this time carried the former, but Reille and Jerome failed at the château, which was desperately defended by Macdonnell's Guards.

Drunk with his success Ney thought himself able to sweep the whole hill clear. Supported by Milhaud's cuirassiers, he first overwhelmed the British artillery, then several squares of infantry, finally the British cavalry, for a supreme effort but with disastrous losses. That gave him the edge of the hill-top. Napoleon was watching from his knoll. Ney, he thought, had gone in too soon and too seriously.

"He's ahead of time by an hour!" he exclaimed.

And Soult added:

"That man is always the same. He is going to spoil everything as he did at Jena, as he did at Eylau."

All the same, Kellermann's three thousand horse were thrown in to support him. Taking their lead Ney dashed up the hill. Wellington had drawn up five divisions to meet the attack. The French overcame them in a magnificent onslaught. The powerful cavalry of the Guard went in to their support without orders and so the third English line was reached.

But that line did not give way. It could be broken only with infantry. Ney called for some, meantime pulling his exhausted squadron together. Beside himself, virtually mad, he galloped up to Drouet d'Erlon and shouted into his ear a prophetic jest:

"Keep it up, old man! If we don't die here, we'll die anyway before the squads of the émigrés."

While plugging away at the enemy front, which Wellington was continually repairing and reinforcing, Napoleon had to deal with another and growing danger. Bülow had almost reached Plancenoit in the French rear, and he was being followed by other Prussian forces. Ney kept begging for infantry. The Emperor shrugged his shoulders.

"Infantry!" he said. "And where does he expect me to get infantry? See what I have on my hands, and what I have left!"

All he had left, in fact, was the 13,000 infantry of the

Guard. Ney would have to hold on with his own strength. The Prussians had to be thrown back first.

The other Prussian troops that Napoleon had seen were Blücher's. Blücher joined Bülow and decided to carry Plancenoit. The Young Guard fought gallantly but the village was taken. The Old Guard however came to the rescue and the Prussians had to retire. That relieved Napoleon's mind in that direction.

It was getting late and there was now no hope that Grouchy would arrive in time. Napoleon decided to finish with the English. He sent in the Old Guard to smash the center on St. John Hill.

The crisis of the battle had come. Informed by a traitor of the French intentions Wellington shortened and thickened his line and ordered his soldiers to die where they stood:

"Die to the last man—to give the Prussians time to come up!"

It was almost eight o'clock. The Old Guard advanced in echelon formation, marching slowly. The English met them with a withering fire. The hair-caps did not waver for a time. They drew together as comrades fell. Their cry of "Long live the Emperor" was so mighty that it drowned out the roar of the cannon. But soon, in the face of superior numbers and under a rain of grape from the flanks, they seemed to hesitate and then they began to fall back.

Napoleon was at the foot of the hill on the Haye-Sainte farm with the six battalions he still had left. He was about to dash with them to the Guard's support when he was taken from the rear, enveloped, overwhelmed, by a mass of charging Prussian cavalry. Zuythen

had come up from the very point at which Grouchy
should have appeared. The faltering of the Guard, the
appearance of a new enemy mass on the field, started a
panic in the French army.

"We are betrayed!" the soldiers shouted. "Each man
for himself!"

Ney retreated from the hill-top with the remnants of
his cavalry. Wellington now took the offensive, coming
down with all his forces upon the French line that was
outflanked on either side. The rout began, accelerated
by the unremitting fire of the English and Prussian
infantry.

The Emperor took in the disaster at a glance. Vainly
he tried to rally the fugitives. Calm, stern, in the rain
of hurtling cannonballs, he gathered the remains of the
Guard into squares. Night was falling.

The Guard stood like a shoal of rock flung out against
a storm. Past that bulwark of men who had sworn to
die the whole army rushed like a loosened flood, pouring down the Charleroi road. The English advanced in
pursuit. Assailed from all directions, crushed, expiring,
the Old Guard refused to surrender. Cambronne, the
commander, hearing the summons, made (or did not
make) his historic and heroic reply: "The Old Guard
dies but does not surrender." The enemy then turned
all its artillery upon that one point. Now one last square
was left. It shrank smaller and smaller. Finally only a
hundred and fifty men still survived. They had no car-
tridges left. They therefore charged with the bayonet
until the very last of them had fallen.

The oath of the Champ de Mai had been observed to
the uttermost.

THE DEATH OF THE OLD GUARD AT WATERLOO
By Raffet

Ney was the last to come down from the top of the hill. Vainly he shouted into the dark at the shadows that were rushing past him:

"Come, boys, come and see how a marshal of France dies."

That too was in vain. Five horses had been killed under him. Finally, despairing, he walked away from the field on foot.

Napoleon was left with what remained of the First Regiment of Grenadiers, who gathered like a defending screen about him. He too hoped for the mercy of a bullet or a cannonball. It did not come. His men dragged him out of the furnace.

"Sire," someone said, "the enemy is happy enough already!"

He let himself be led away. He rode with his horse at a walk, a torrent of thoughts coursing through his brain. From time to time he would address a word to Soult or to Jerome, who had stuck to him, not waiting to hear their answer. He reached Genappes at eleven that evening and rode on to Quatre Bras. At Charleroi he entrusted the command of the army to Jerome and sent Grouchy, who had still not been heard from, an order to fall back upon Namur. He himself continued on to Paris, making only one short stop at Laon. He arrived at eight o'clock on the morning of the 21st.

The race to Paris was a mistake. Having lost the battle the Emperor should have stopped on the frontier, rallied his forces and reinforced them with Grouchy's army. That would have given him at least freedom of movement and decision. But he was blinded by his distrust of Paris and rushed head down into the hornet's nest which Fouché, Lanjuinais and La Fayette began preparing for him on first reports of a defeat. He was figuring—the last illusion among a thousand—that he could rouse the Chambers by an appeal to their patriotism and again gather the nation around him to repel the invader. They all were to desert him. He was aware of that the moment, staggering, sick, overpowered by fatigue and disappointment, he climbed the steps of the Élysée on that bitter morning of June 21st.

Davout and Lucien insisted that he should at once dissolve the Chamber. Napoleon rejected that counsel, intending to abide resolutely by his oath to the constitution. France should say whether she wanted no more of him. He would not try a coup d'état. The question of abdication came up that very forenoon at the first meeting of the Council of State. It was put forward by one of his own friends, Regnault de Saint-Jean d'Angély, who had been worked upon by Fouché. The Emperor at first was staggered. Finally he mastered himself:

"The presence of the enemy on French soil," he said, "will, I trust, bring the Representatives to a sense of their duty. . . . I do not fear them. If I were to say the word they would all be knocked on the head. . . . When I landed at Cannes I could have understood their rebuffing me. Now I am bound to the nation. To sacrifice myself is to hold out its hands for chains."

But parrying a blow that it felt might be coming, the Chamber proceeded to declare itself in permanent session and voted that "any attempt to dissolve it would be a crime of high treason." Napoleon hesitated. Beyond the walls of the Élysée he could hear the mobs acclaiming him. However, as he was to say that afternoon to

Benjamin Constant, he would have none of a civil war. He had "not come back from the island of Elba to see Paris drowned in blood." In the Chamber a strong majority, which had been organized by Fouché and was taking directions from him, demanded an abdication without a moment's delay. The Peers remained inert. Everybody around Napoleon, with the exception of Lucien, urged that move upon him as a way to avoid deposition. Finally he gave in. At another meeting of the Council held on the morning of the 22nd he dictated a "Statement to the French people":

"In opening war to support our national independence I counted on unanimity of all efforts and wills. . . . Circumstances now seem to me to have changed. I offer myself in sacrifice to the hatred of the enemies of France. May they prove sincere in their declaration that they aim at my person only. . . . Do you unite one and all for the public safety that you may remain an independent nation. . . . My political life has run its course. I proclaim my son Emperor of the French, under the title of Napoleon II."

With the abdication now in hand the Chambers proceeded to nominate a Governing Commission of five members, Carnot, Fouché, Grenier, Caulaincourt and Quinette. Fouché was presiding officer. He could not prevent Napoleon II from being proclaimed Emperor; but since he had control of the situation in Paris he could negotiate with the English for the capitulation of the capital and the return of the Bourbons.

Invited by Fouché to leave the Élysée, where he was in the way, Napoleon took refuge at Malmaison. That was on June 25th. He spent four gloomy days in the château which had once belonged to Josephine and was filled to its every corner with memories of too happy days. He was waiting for passports to America which Fouché had promised. He counted on ending his days in the United States as a simple citizen.

He was roused from his despondency by a sudden shock on hearing that the Prussians had reached Le Bourget. Grouchy and Vandamme had arrived in Paris with the remnants of Waterloo. Napoleon sent an offer to the Commission to place himself at the head of those forces in order to give Blücher another beating. He promised that, after vindicating French honor in that way and enabling France to get better terms of peace, he would take ship for America as had been planned. Fouché rejected the proposal with a sneer. Napoleon thereupon bade good-by to his mother, Hortense, Joseph and other intimates who had stood by him, and set out for Rochefort on the Atlantic seaboard.

On arriving there on July 3rd he learned that the safe-conduct to America had been refused him and that a British fleet was blockading the coast. Sensing that Fouché was intending to hand him over to the Royalists, from whom he could expect nothing better than the fate of the Duc d'Enghien, he resolved, on the advice of those about him, to appeal for hospitality to England. In spite of his long struggle with that country, he felt no bitterness against the English. He thought of them as a magnanimous people. He knew that they had treated Paoli generously in the old days, and more recently Lucien too. He also thought himself personally popular with the opposition Whigs in England.

Louis XVIII re-entered Paris on July 8th, "in the

THE ABDICATION OF NAPOLEON
From the Painting by Bouchot

baggage-wagons of the foreigner," as the phrase went. The King's agents were already trying to arrest Napoleon when he slipped away to the Isle of Aix, in the gulf off Rochefort. That was to be his last refuge in France. There he dictated to his aide de camp, General Gourgaud, a letter of five lines of which he held a tentative draft in his hands. It was addressed to the Prince Regent of England:

"Your Royal Highness: In view of the factions that divide my country and of the enmity of the greatest powers in Europe, I have brought my political career to a close and I am going, like Themistocles, to seat myself on the hearth of the British people. I place myself under the protection of English law and request that protection of Your Royal Highness, as of the most powerful, the most trustworthy, and the most generous of my enemies. Île d'Aix, July 13, 1815. Napoleon."

The next day he was taken aboard the *Bellerophon* by Captain Maitland, who at once made all sail for England.

Lord Liverpool and his principal associates, Castlereagh and Bathurst, hated Napoleon, as did the majority of the English. They could not forget that he had twice threatened England with invasion. England had no defenses and no standing army. Had the preparations that Napoleon made at Boulogne ever attained their goal England would have been conquered without much difficulty. They could not forget either that if the French had won at Waterloo, England, with her money and her courage gone, would have had to eat very humble pie.

The English cabinet therefore resolved to put Napoleon out of the way of doing harm for good and all. He would come back from America, they thought, just as he had come back from Elba. He would not come back from a rock lost in the South Atlantic three thousand miles from England and which the English navy could easily watch.

No real betrayal of hospitality or trust can be alleged against the English. Napoleon had placed himself in their hands without guarantees of any sort. All the same, history has been inclined to pass an unfavorable judgment on the conduct of those British statesmen towards the greatest figure of their age. Greater generosity, even at a risk, might have seemed more worthy of British chivalry.

A minority of Englishmen were of that opinion even then. When the *Bellerophon* came to anchor off Plymouth the sea was soon covered with boats of all kinds, which ventured out into a dangerously choppy sea that those aboard—now the merely curious, now outspoken admirers of "Boney"—might have a glimpse of the great Captive. Whenever his now somewhat paunchy figure was spied on the deck, there was a loud cheering and a wild fluttering of handkerchiefs. There were even Englishmen who questioned the legality of Napoleon's deportation and thought of invoking *habeas corpus* in his behalf.

The movement in Napoleon's favor was strong enough to alarm the British cabinet and hasten its decision. On the 7th of August the *Northumberland,* a larger, faster and safer ship than the *Bellerophon,* commanded by Admiral Cockburn, picked up the Emperor off Start Point and headed out into the Atlantic with a stormy wind abeam and in a rough sea.[1]

[1] [During the War of 1812 Admiral Cockburn had been in command of the English fleet in Chesapeake Bay which had attacked Baltimore and burned Washington.]

CHAPTER XXXVIII

St. Helena

THE VOYAGE LASTED SEVENTY DAYS, NAPOLEON DEBARK-
ing at Jamestown on the evening of October 17th. If
some defense can be found for deporting Napoleon to
that somber rock, which juts from the ocean floor like
a marine citadel, hardly any excuse can be found for the
basic principles of British policy towards him as a captive.

After all, Napoleon had been anointed Emperor by
a pope and for a whole decade that title had been attached to his name in hundreds of international papers
in Europe. The English had never "recognized" the Empire, however, and refused to admit that Napoleon was
anything else than "General Bonaparte." The whole
drama of the captivity lies in just that. It was a deliberate, gratuitous and obstinate insult; and, sensitive to
an attitude that implicitly marked him as a mere con-
vict, Napoleon reacted and insisted at all times on being
the Emperor in everything and for everybody.

The situation at St. Helena was complicated by many
human factors. Sir Hudson Lowe, Napoleon's jailer, was
not the deliberate tormentor he is often accused of being. He was merely a conscientious dullard—a "stupid
man," to use Wellington's expression, vain, suspicious,

433

nervous, who had been chosen for the very reason that he was dull and could be relied upon to execute the orders that he received from London to the last letter. Mistrustful, always overdoing his job, Lowe was not satisfied with a prison wall of sea three thousand miles wide. He further required 600 guns, seven warships and three thousand sentinels. Fearful even then that Napoleon would slip on a pair of gull's wings some night and soar away, Lowe set up such an odious system of espionage and took such offensive measures of surveillance that Napoleon finally shut himself up inside the wretched quarters that Bathurst had provided for him at Longwood and for four years remained incommunicado to anyone not of his immediate entourage.

With him were the Grand Marshal Bertrand, a faithful, taciturn soldier, married to an obscure relative of Josephine; Count de Las Cases, a literary adventurer who saw a great story in Napoleon's reminiscences and conversation and went to St. Helena to get it; General Montholon and his wife, attractive and far-sighted schemers, who hoped to repair social and financial disasters in Europe with a patriotic record and a good slice of the fortune that Napoleon was supposed to have laid away; General Gourgaud, a young idealist, quick-tempered and morbidly jealous; finally, O'Meara, a physician supplied by the English to act as a spy and who spied also on them. The mutual rivalries of these people, their saddening conflicts of interest, embittered virtually every moment of the Captive's last years and intensified the petty irritations inflicted on him by his English jailers.

Napoleon had lived in the handsomest palaces in

Europe, surrounded by every luxury and comfort. At St. Helena he found himself in six small rooms in a rundown country farmhouse, furnished with second hand articles which had been gathered together haphazard from a community that had never been rich. He killed the hours of six interminable years lying on his back on a worn-out sofa that had been made a little respectable by a covering of chintz. The little bedroom in which he hid to escape being seen by English watchmen is of all rooms in the world the one that seems most to breathe an atmosphere of greatness and tragedy. That Napoleon suffered terribly in it there can be no doubt. Suffering sweats from the very walls of Longwood, which, even today, are too damp to hold the glue on the faded green wall-paper that covers them.

It was a suffering born not so much of physical discomfort—Napoleon was used to the hardships of military life—as of the absurd suspicions of his jailers, of the bickerings and squabbles of his attendants, of the ceaseless combat of a prodigiously active genius with empty days and an insignificant audience, of ill-health, at last, the dull pain of an enlarged liver, the knife thrust of a pyloric cancer—and all with the certainty that he would have to die on that rock and indeed had better die soon if he wanted to have one Frenchman left near him to close his eyes.

The last two years were painful indeed. One by one his companions dropped away: Las Cases, Gourgaud, O'Meara, Mme. de Montholon, departed in succession. The Bertrands were in semi-disgrace as a result of intrigues by Montholon. That left the Emperor alone with the latter and a few faithful domestics. Montholon himself was planning to depart. The Bertrands were asking for permission to go to Europe on a trip from which they would never have returned. The Emperor did his best to hold them, by appeals now to their vanity, now to their loyalty, now to their interests—"It would not be long now—and then he would make them rich." Few great men have had an end so anguished; for there came a time when it seemed indeed as though death were the only way out for him.

Napoleon died prematurely at the age of fifty-two. Was his end hastened by the treatment accorded him in his imprisonment? The question has been furiously debated. Dispassionate history concludes today that Napoleon could not have contracted at St. Helena the liver complaint which his autopsy established. He had shown liver symptoms as early as 1810 and acutely during the Campaign in France and during the Hundred Days. Liver trouble was moreover hereditary in his family on his mother's side. Most of his brothers and sisters suffered from it. It seems also to be established that, because of the malaria and other swamp fevers that were endemic on the island, St. Helena was not a good environment for a person afflicted with such a disease.

Napoleon, however, did not die of chronic hepatitis—he died of a stomach ulcer, probably cancerous, a malady of which his father had died before him and of which two of his sisters, Pauline and Caroline, were also to die. To such a disease he would have succumbed at the Tuileries just as certainly as he did in the rundown farmhouse at Longwood.

That his physical ills were aggravated by the conditions thrust upon him is certain. The stupid and

uncalled-for restrictions that were laid upon his freedom forced him into a complete lack of exercise and
into a mental state far worse than any which the depression incident to his misfortunes could have accounted
for. Incompetent medical attendance must also have
done its share. None of his doctors—neither O'Meara,
nor Antommarchi, nor Arnott—diagnosed his malady
successfully, though he himself divined it, leaving instructions that his body be opened to determine the
cause of his death that his son might be forewarned
against an unfortunate heredity.

The last important act in Napoleon's life was his testament. Taking to his bed for the last time on April 10,
1821, he gathered all his failing strength together to work
the document out. He dictated the first draft to Montholon, then recopied it in his own hand, taking special
pains that his handwriting should be more legible.

The testament is in many respects a political document—it was his last communiqué and the most stirring
of all he ever wrote. He thinks of his old soldiers, of
France, of everybody who had helped him or shown him
devotion. He digs deep down into his memory to make
sure that he has forgotten no one—companions of his
youth, comrades at Toulon and in Egypt, friends of the
Consulate, generals and ministers of the Empire. This
slow and methodical exploration of all the course of a
great life, making sure that he pays every debt of gratitude, shows Napoleon at one of his best moments.

He foresees that his son will some day replace the
Bourbons—a prophecy that was to come true not in the
King of Rome but in the son of Hortense—and leaves
him political counsel. He pretends to know nothing of

the infidelity of Marie Louise and leaves her gifts and exhortations. The money that he thought he had left after all his testamentary disbursements he divided between his companions in captivity, his testament bearing traces of the animosities of the last moments, in that he sacrifices the deserving but unattractive Bertrand to the engaging intriguer, Montholon.

Napoleon's will could not be directly executed. His donations far overreached his actual fortune, and so far as they related to monies owing him from the French government they were never honored by the Bourbons. This lack of chivalry on the part of Louis XVIII and his two successors was always a sore spot with the Bonapartists, and one of the first acts of the Second Empire was to execute the will in full, paying the donations to the descendants of Napoleon's legatees.

Napoleon died in the drawing-room at Longwood just after sunset on May 5, 1821. Some days earlier, on the 27th, he had received the last sacraments at the hands of Father Vignali—a sincere reversion to the religion of his childhood, but also a thought for the future of his son whom he wished to free of any embarrassment from Catholic opposition.

Lowe carried his pettifogging irritations to the very mound over the grave in the Vale of the Geranium. He spied on the preparations for the burial, edited and revised the autopsy report, refused to allow Napoleon's viscera to be taken to Europe according to the will, and insisted that the inscription on the tombstone should be "Napoleon Bonaparte" and not "Napoleon" (the stone was left without any inscription at all). That the British would not allow his body to be returned to Europe Napoleon had himself foreseen, and he chose the site of the grave himself.

He lay there twenty years, visited only by the great white birds that fly across the ocean to St. Helena with each turn in the seasons. He lay there twenty years, in the crater of an extinct volcano, so deep that it hears no sound of the surrounding sea, so narrow that only a stretch of blue sky is visible from the grassy floor. He lay there, forgotten by his people and paid with ingratitude by the many whom he had enriched and covered with glory.

His body lay there—for only his body was inert. The madness that laid hold on France at the time of the hero's return from Elba expressed a sentiment that was to lurk long and potent in the depths of the French heart. Napoleon's wars had cost the country dearly in treasure and in lives, but those who did not live by bread alone ever had an instinctive feeling that somehow he had embodied the human being's aspiration to an heroic life that is above selfish interests, that, at any rate, he had loved France, wanted her great and made her great, and that, as he said to his marshals at Fontainebleau, it is better to die in trying to do great things than to live safely among vulgar or commonplace things. On this feeling Napoleon's legend was born and grew, and the legend in turn kept the feeling alive and intensified it. For fifty years it was to be an important force in French life.

The treaty that was forced upon France after Waterloo was the most humiliating in all French history: territorial penalties—Savoy, Nice, the Sarre, Bouillon, Marienburg, Landau; a money indemnity of 700 millions—three billion dollars today; occupation of departments on the north and east by Allied forces for five years. Louis XVIII had come back to the throne most ingloriously, and after the shooting of Ney and La Bédoyère had in a measure avenged the death of the Duc d'Enghien, his régime settled down into a riot of humdrum materialism that was badly disguised by a fatuous pretense of returning to before '89. A reaction set in and not only in France. In Europe also the popular masses that Napoleon's invasions had awakened to national self-consciousness could not be forever reconciled to the colorless out-of-date despotisms that the Metternichs and the Talleyrands pressed down upon the Continent in 1815.

In Vienna, shut up in a gilded cage, lived the Eaglet, the son of the hero who impersonated and embodied a noble something that had been stamped on and crushed by superior force at Waterloo. This boy and the grave in the Vale of the Geranium were the targets of all hopeful eyes during the banal '20's that followed on the era of glory. At many a moment during that decade, had the Aiglon appeared on the bridge at Strasburg all France would have risen around him and carried him on high, for a second return from Elba, to the Tuileries. But Metternich held his captive close, as close as Lowe had held the great Captive at St. Helena.

By 1830 the Napoleonic myth was so powerful that it caught the eye of the political speculators and, when the cry went up in France for the King of Rome, the Duc d'Orléans put himself at the head of it, and, like a stock broker garbed in the blue coat of Marengo, overthrew the legitimate Bourbons and established the July Monarchy.

Louis Philippe ruled as the bastard heir of Napoleon and he needed a tangible symbol of that legacy. So in March, 1840, Thiers, the historian of the Empire, now a minister, had no difficulty in persuading the King to ask England for Napoleon's body. Lord Palmerston consented. The Prince de Joinville, therefore, a handsome, dignified, haughty sailor, was sent to St. Helena in the frigate *Belle Poule* to arrange for the homecoming of the lifelong foe of the whole race of the Bourbons.

Joinville found the Emperor sleeping, his body fully preserved, in his grassy tomb, watched over by three weeping-willows and an English veteran. The coffin reached Paris on December 15th. Lying on a golden shield which was held up by figures of Napoleon's Victories, it was carried to the nave of the Invalides.

But Louis Philippe quite missed the mark in his calculations. The myth of glory had survived the death of the King of Rome, and it was conscious of its legitimate tradition. The demonstrations inspired by the Return of the Ashes redounded not to the advantage of the July Monarchy but to the Napoleonic line itself. The Second Empire corresponded to an impulse in French life that had, as it were of historical necessity, to work itself out.

The opportunity came in the disturbances of '48-'49. When the Second Republic fell, Louis Napoleon, son of Hortense, came forward as the heir, even more than as the nephew, of the great Napoleon. As Napoleon III he was to tear up the treaties of 1815 and restore France to a leading place in Europe. Mistakes in policy finally led him to the disastrous war of 1870. Seventy-three years intervene between the appearance of Napoleon at Toulon and the surrender of Louis Napoleon at Sedan. The eagle had flown over Europe for three-quarters of a century, and the course of its flight marks the establishment and the florescence of the civilization that was born of the French Revolution.

INDEX

449